RESOURCE-BASED INDUSTRIALIZATION: SOWING THE OIL IN EIGHT DEVELOPING COUNTRIES

RESOURCE-BASED INDUSTRIALIZATION: SOWING THE OIL IN EIGHT DEVELOPING COUNTRIES

R. M. Auty

CLARENDON PRESS · OXFORD
1990

Oxford University Press, Walton Street, Oxford OX2 6DP
Oxford New York Toronto
Delhi Bombay Calcutta Madras Karachi
Petaling Jaya Singapore Hong Kong Tokyo
Nairobi Dar es Salaam Cape Town
Melbourne Auckland
and associated companies in
Berlin Ibadan

Oxford is a trade mark of Oxford University Press

Published in the United States
by Oxford University Press, New York

British Library Cataloguing in Publication Data
Auty, R. M. (Richard M.)
Resource-based industrialization: sowing the oil
in eight developing countries
1. Developing countries. Petroleum industries.
Development
I. Title
338.2'7282'091724
ISBN 0–19–823299–3

Library of Congress Cataloging in Publication Data
Data available

Typset by Cambrian Typesetters, Frimley, Surrey
Printed in Great Britain by
Bookcraft Ltd.
Midsomer Norton, Avon

CONTENTS

ACKNOWLEDGEMENTS

I am grateful to the many officials in all eight countries who freely gave of their time during data collection 1984–6. The data collection was funded by the Nuffield Foundation and the ESRC. The Harvard Institute for International Development provided a stimulating environment for writing up the study 1986–7. Alan Gelb opened up new economic horizons and provided much encouragement throughout the research.

FIGURES

TABLES

ABBREVIATIONS

b.	billion (thousand million)
bcmd	billion cubic metres per day
bl.	barrel
bpd	barrels per day
cfd	cubic feet per day
cif	carriage, insurance, freight
C–S	Chenery–Syrquin (norms)
DCF	discounted cash flow
DRI	direct-reduced iron
ERR	economic rate of return
FOB	free on board
GDP	gross domestic product
GDRP	gross domestic regional product
HBI	hot briquetted iron
ICOR	incremental capital–output ratio
IMF	International Monetary Fund
IRR	internal rate of return
ISI	import substitution industry
LDPE	low density polyethylene
LLDPE	linear low density polyethylene
LNG	liquefied natural gas
mbpd	million barrels per day
mbtu	thousand British thermal units
mcf	thousand cubic feet
mh	man-hour
mill	one-thousandth of a dollar
MIOC	middle-income oil-importing country
mty	thousand tonnes per year
MNC	multinational corporation
MNRC	multinational resource corporation
NIC	newly industrializing country
OPEC	Organization of Petroleum Exporting Countries
RBI	resource-based industrialization
RRC	revenue retention coefficient
SOC	infrastructure
SOE	state-owned enterprise
tpa	tonnes per annum

PART 1
Introduction

1

Country Size and Efficiency Constraints on Resource-Based Industrialization

THE IMPORTANCE OF RESOURCE-BASED INDUSTRIALIZATION

The oil shocks of 1973–4 and 1979 each transferred the equivalent of 2 per cent of global GDP to the oil-exporting countries. The resulting windfalls provided unprecedented opportunities for the oil-exporting countries to accelerate economic growth, promote healthy structural change, and speed spatial decentralization. Resource-based industrialization (RBI), which is the further processing of natural resources such as minerals into metals and timber into wood products, played a central role in such efforts.

After infrastructure, RBI was the most important vehicle for domestic investment of the oil windfalls in a sample of six high-absorbing oil-exporting countries analysed by Gelb (1988). RBI absorbed more than $40 billion (excluding large linked infrastructure investment) through the two oil booms in the eight oil-exporting countries examined in the present study. Such investment was large in relation to the domestic economy (the equivalent of 15 per cent of non-oil output, on average). It was also large in relation to global markets. For example, Saudi Arabia alone brought the equivalent of 3 per cent of global ethylene capacity into production in the mid-1980s.

The high expectations for RBI were largely unfulfilled, raising important questions about the causes of its failure; its wisdom as a development strategy; and the consequences for both the oil-exporting countries and key sectors of global manufacturing industry. Specific issues concern: the extent to which RBI is constrained by country size; the political limits on effective industrial development; the merits of state enterprises versus multinational resource corporations (MNRCs); the links between RBI and other tradeables subsectors; and regional policy in developing countries. There are also general lessons concerning the efficacy of large capital transfers; the creation of competitive advantage; managing resource booms; the role of natural resources in industrial development; and the international location of economic activity. Finally, the study sheds light on the debate between those who argue that the post-1960s change in the international economy is merely the result of an unusual cyclical downswing (Bruno 1984, Lawrence 1984) and those who claim that major structural change may be under way (Krugman 1979, Beenstock 1983).

CONSTRAINTS ON RBI

Earlier research on RBI in four small Caribbean mineral economies (Auty 1984*a*) generated five hypotheses which provide the framework of the present study:

1 mineral resources vary systematically in their capacity to trigger RBI growth;
2 small countries capture less of RBI's economic stimulus than do large countries and risk stronger negative backwash effects;
3 RBI performance is highly sensitive to the efficiency of macro-economic policy in individual countries;
4 RBI performance is also strongly affected by the product strategy and organizational structure of firms used to launch RBI;
5 pressure to pursue the dynamic scale economies makes RBI a risky industrial strategy for most developing countries: overambitious RBI strategies may actually retard economic growth, healthy structural change, and spatial decentralization.

These hypotheses are explored in the context of four pairs of oil-exporting countries. Each pair comprises a large and small country in a major cultural region. The four pairs comprise: Venezuela and Trinidad and Tobago; Nigeria and Cameroon; Saudi Arabia and Bahrain; and Indonesia and Malaysia. At the extremes, countries with large populations and extensive geographical areas (Indonesia and Nigeria) can be compared with micro states while the relatively efficient Asian political regimes may be contrasted with less effective ones in Africa and Latin America. In addition, the sample countries allow cross-comparison between low-absorbing capital-surplus countries (Saudi Arabia and Bahrain) and the capital-deficit high-absorbers which Gelb (1988) focused on; between middle-income oil-exporters (Venezuela and Trinidad and Tobago) and lower-income oil-exporters; and between pioneers of RBI (Bahrain and Venezuela) and late-starters (Cameroon and Malaysia).

The specific questions addressed in successive chapters are:

- What is the potential economic stimulus from the downstream processing of bauxite, iron ore, oil, and gas?
- How does country size affect the potential RBI stimulus?
- To what extent did the RBI projects meet expectations and what was the role of external factors in accounting for the divergence between expected and observed results?
- How effectively did the low-absorbing and high-absorbing countries deploy their windfalls for RBI and how did the resource endowment and the type of political regime moderate the outcome?
- What forms of organizational structure and product strategy characterized the successful RBI launch enterprises?
- How did individual RBI sectors differ in their realization of the potential RBI economic stimulus?
- What was the contribution of RBI to accelerated economic growth and structural change?
- To what extent did RBI contribute to the spatial decentralization of economic activity?
- Can a model of RBI be constructed and what are its policy implications for both existing RBI projects and future RBI investment?

PRESENTATION OF THE STUDY

The presentation is structured in five sections. The Introduction outlines the objectives of the study and, in Chapter 2, sets them in the context of three important strands in the development literature: export base, commodity booms, and RBI. The export base literature reveals the importance of staple flexibility, which RBI lacks, for successful export-led growth. The commodity boom literature indicates that booms tend to trigger patterns of consumption and investment which are difficult to reverse, and that RBI may amplify this effect. The RBI literature is equivocal about RBI's merits as an industrial strategy and reticent about implementation constraints such as country size and macro- and micro-efficiency.

Part 2 measures the potential direct and indirect economic stimulus from RBI for each of the four natural resources; measures how country size affects the economic stimulus; describes the expected RBI performance; and explains the role of external factors (market fluctuations and interest rate swings) in accounting for the disappointing RBI outcome.

Specifically, Chapter 3 uses cost estimation to assess, under controlled assumptions, the potential direct economic stimulus (measured in terms of added value, net foreign exchange earnings, and direct employment) and the indirect stimulus (the backward and forward linked industries plus the final demand spending). It shows that the potential economic stimulus from hydrocarbons (and especially gas) is higher than that from hard minerals, especially bauxite.

Chapter 4 examines the extent to which the larger of the eight oil-exporting countries overcame scale barriers to RBI entry. It notes that the oil windfalls effectively swept away investment and technological barriers. This was not so for market barriers, however. Even the largest countries in the sample often embraced insufficient domestic demand to capture forward linkage benefits for the home economy. In Chapter 5, the RBI feasibility projections are shown to have been over optimistic: actual prices were half the levels expected and anticipated resource rents on energy inputs failed to materialize. The RBI feasibility studies underestimated the compounding effect of depressed demand (through lower prices, reduced capacity utilization, and mounting debts) and overestimated the importance of cheap resource inputs.

Under such difficult conditions, the resilience of the RBI projects, the subject of Part 3, was severely tested. The efficiency with which the low-absorbing and high-absorbing countries deployed their oil windfall is examined in Chapters 6 and 7, respectively. The term 'low-absorber' is a misnomer since Saudi Arabia absorbed the bulk of its very large oil windfall domestically. Moreover, it did so with remarkable technical (if not economic) efficiency, in contrast to the apparently better placed high-absorbers. Political regime proved critical: the long-serving pater-nalistic autocracies of Arabia, like their Indonesian counterpart, proved most effective at insulating planners from immediate political pressures for over rapid windfall absorption. Chapter 8 demonstrates that micro-efficiency closely reflects macro-efficiency. In particular, Saudi Arabia's highly autonomous joint-ventures, in which MNRCs held 50 per cent of the equity, proved the most effective RBI launch enterprises and complemented the country's solid macro-economic achievements. Chapter 9 examines investment efficiency. It shows that the RBI incremental capital–output ratios (ICORs) ranged upwards from five; that petrochemicals (especially fertilizer and LNG) outperformed metals; and that large, wholly state-owned steel plants encountered the most implemention and operating difficulties.

Part 4 examines the impact of RBI on economic growth, structural change, and geographical decentralization. Although growth in the non-oil economy did accelerate through the two oil booms in Arabia and Cameroon and held steady in several other countries, it declined significantly in Venezuela and Nigeria. Chapter 10 shows that healthy industrial diversification was not achieved. Effective adjustment to the mid-1980s' oil price downswing therefore depended much on the resilience of the agricultural sector as well as on accumulated overseas reserves and timely and bold macro-economic adjustment. Chapter 11 examines spatial diversification: it shows that RBI was a poor vehicle for triggering regional growth, the more so where RBI plants were unclustered, far from (large) markets, and very recently established.

In the final part, Chapter 12 outlines a simple model of RBI and notes the policy implications. The model is rooted in scale economies and the relatively high cost of constructing RBI plants in developing countries. The capital-intensive RBI plants have high fixed costs and are remote from major markets so that they must rely heavily on resource rents to offset these competitive disadvantages. In the absence of such resource rents, new developing country RBI projects are marginal until their capital has been amortized, typically a decade after start-up. Thereafter, technical improvements and an expanded cash flow permit investment in potentially cost-reducing brownfield expansion, vertical integration, and the capture of agglomeration economies. The economic stimulus from RBI in developing countries is typically initially muted, distinctly lagged, and volatile.

These unfavourable characteristics of RBI were accentuated by the heightened uncertainty of the post-1960 international economy. They make RBI a high-risk strategy and an unsuitable base for most developing countries' industrialization. Policy makers must be wary of the magnitude of both the potential development benefits and backwash effects likely to be associated with the downstream processing of key natural resources. Country size proves less a constraint on RBI than macro- and micro-efficiency. The conclusions from the study are summarized in Chapter 13.

2

Harnessing Mineral Enclaves: Export Base, Mineral Boom, and RBI Literature

The oil windfalls triggered by the 1973–4 and 1979 oil shocks presented oil-exporting countries with the opportunity to reduce the enclave nature of mineral production. Export base theory, with its emphasis on the linkage configuration of export staples, can account for the historically disappointing performance of primary exports in the tropics as generators of diversified, mature economic regions. It also explains why the post-war global socio-economic changes that were conducive to improved linkage prospects were more effective in the case of tropical crops than tropical minerals. Export base theory suggests that staple flexibility is an important characteristic of successful export-led growth which capital-intensive activities like mining, with high barriers to entry (and exit), lack.

The literature on commodity booms confirms the general pre-shock failure of the developing mineral economies to realize the promise implicit in their eased foreign exchange and fiscal constraints, relative to non-mineral countries. It shows: that the upswing of the boom tends to promote patterns of investment and consumption which are resistant to necessary downswing corrections; that undesirable structural change may occur which is difficult to reverse; and that imprudent windfall absorption may overwhelm even an economy with a large non-oil tradeables sector. The ability to execute risk-minimizing policies appears to be closely and systematically linked to political regime.

The literature on RBI tends to be equivocal about the strategy's benefits; lacks systematic cross-country and cross-sector appraisal; and downplays the inherent tendency of RBI to take the form of an overambitious 'big push'. It also says little about variations in RBI implementation capacity among developing countries and the risks of RBI degenerating into a sink for economic resources. Such issues are crucial to the debate within development economies concerning the need to create competitive advantage. The major effort by the oil-exporting

countries to establish RBI provides ample empirical evidence to form a
theory from which policy implications can be derived.

THE LIMITED ECONOMIC STIMULUS FROM
TROPICAL NATURAL RESOURCES

Differing tropical and temperate regional growth

The demand for primary products by the industrial cores of the North
Atlantic triggered the emergence of prosperous diversified regions in the
temperate periphery based on primary product exports (for example, in
the Midwest, the Pacific North-west, Upper Canada, the Pampas, the
Witwatersrand, and South-east Australia). However, it was decidedly
less effective in the tropics. This was despite a promising start in the late
nineteenth century in some tropical regions (Lewis 1978). There, with
the faltering of world trade after 1913, the export of primary products
was associated with regions which, far from diversifying their economic
structure, frequently became locked into a staple trap (a state akin to
dependent development) and often displayed the characteristics of
externally orientated enclaves (Singer 1950). This tendency led Singer,
Myrdal, Prebisch, and others to advocate in the 1950s a strategy of
protected import substitution industry (ISI) for tropical regional growth
(Thoburn 1977).

After two decades of relative neglect, interest in the growth potential
of the natural resource base has been rekindled (Roemer 1979). This
reflects four trends: the potential unlocked by the new green revolution
in agriculture (Mellor 1976); the spectacular initial success of OPEC
(Hallwood and Sinclair 1980); expectations of global shortages of
natural resources (Meadows *et al.* 1972); and disappointment with the
industrial panacea, which ironically created enclaves of an urban
character (Owen 1968, Gould 1970, Mabogunje 1972, Odell 1978,
Lipton 1977). Moreover, by the 1980s the growth of protectionism cast
doubt on the continued feasibility of an 'outward-orientated' growth
strategy (Balassa 1982) based on competitive manufactured exports—an
alternative to both ISI and RBI (Streeten 1981, Cline 1982, Fishlow
1984). RBI still appeared a promising avenue for tropical regional
growth during a period of shrinking overall opportunities (Adelman
1984). This was so, even though the unexpectedly deep recession of the
early 1980s aborted an expected commodity boom, especially in fuel
and non-fuel minerals. It is therefore important to understand why
temperate primary product exports were more successful in achieving

diversified regional growth than tropical ones, and whether the constraints on the latter area have eased.

Two sets of explanations have been advanced for the historically poor performance of tropical primary exports. One set stresses local factors linked via technological and enterprise characteristics to the nature of the staple (Baldwin 1956, Hirschman 1977); the other emphasizes the role of external factors and, particularly, the political character of the core–periphery link (Myint 1964, Girvan 1971, Furtado 1976, Lewis 1978). A fuller explanation is possible if the local and external factors are fused in an explanation of staple flexibility. Successful regions need to capture the stimulus from productive (backward and forward), fiscal (taxes), and final demand (spending by factors of production) linkages for the domestic economy and—if necessary—to diversify by replacing the staple.

Enterprise types and the spatial configuration of their linkages provide the key to understanding why primary product exports lead to sustained diversified regional growth in some regions and to the stagnation of the staple trap in others (Figure 2.1). Plantations, yeoman farms, and mines furnish the basis for an enterprise classification, with the presence or absence of foreign ownership a secondary factor affecting flexibility of response and linkage stimulus. The key elements in the spatial structure are the settlement pattern and associated transportation network. The tighter the degree of spatial integration and the more extensive the area integrated, then:

- the greater the region's probability of encompassing sufficient diversity of resources to circumvent the staple trap via staple substitution,
- the higher the region's chances of embracing sufficient aggregate demand to permit local industrialization,
- the better the region's prospects for evolving a diversified and self-sustaining economy.

Production function flexibility

Baldwin (1956) identified the production function of the staple as the critical variable and developed his argument through a comparison of nineteenth-century yeoman farming and plantation regions. It will become clear that the production function of mining shares many characteristics with Baldwin's plantation.

The tropical staple dictated large-scale production which required a high initial investment in processing facilities but thereafter afforded limited scope for incremental modification of the historically rigid

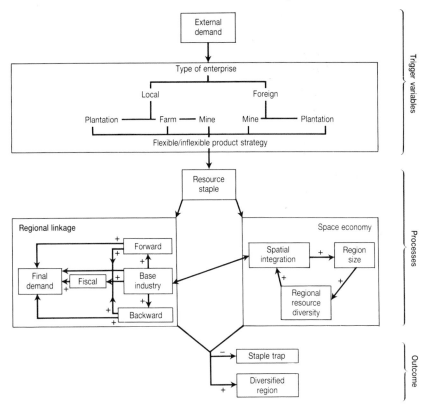

FIG. 2.1. Trigger variables, linkage, and the space economy

labour-intensive production methods. The resulting skewed income distribution of the small wealthy élite and large semi-subsistent workforce, yielded inadequate final demand linkage to encourage local manufacture of consumer goods while the self-contained plantation dampened fiscal linkage by usurping many government functions to itself and finding little need for taxation to promote general social welfare. The skewed pattern of income distribution concentrated capital in the hands of families that were for the most part orientated to extra-regional cultural centres and disinterested in investing locally to promote backward and forward linkage.

In contrast, the temperate staple had low barriers to entry and a small minimum viable size of production unit (the yeoman farm). Such a system yielded steady increases in productivity in response to increments in capital, permitting incomes to advance and providing an expanding source of tax revenues (fiscal linkage). The resulting unskewed income distribution encouraged the expenditure of tax revenues on local infrastructure while the manufactured goods demanded by the local populace were easily produced and sold locally, creating employment for entrepreneurs and workers drawn from the yeoman farms. In addition, local capital was available to invest in local factories to supply the manufactured inputs required to produce the staple (backward linkage) and process it prior to export (forward linkage).

Implicit in Baldwin's model of growth in the temperate region is the emergence of a hierarchy of central places to facilitate the local exchange of goods and services (Berry 1967, Johnson 1970) and to connect the emerging region to distant export markets (Vance 1970, Gilmour 1972). The expanding geographical size and per capita income of the emerging region constantly pushes aggregate demand above the thresholds required for the local provision of a widening range of manufactured goods and services, some of which become competitive in distant markets. The region's geographical growth increases the diversity of the natural resource base, creating new opportunities for primary product export and manufacture. In short, the spatial structure associated with the yeoman farm widens local economic opportunities and reduces the risk of being locked into a staple trap.

In contrast, local opportunities for diversification in the plantation (or mining) regions were stifled by their spatial structure, which was one of small fragmented markets (the largely self-contained plantation with low per capita incomes or mines with a small labour force), served by a dendritic transportation network to syphon out exports but not to facilitate local specialization and exchange (Gould 1963, Johnson 1970, Plattner 1975). Although such regions might grow and create new resource-based export opportunities, they were much more likely to fall into the staple trap than the temperate region of yeoman farms. This was not just a consequence of the rigid production function noted by Baldwin, nor of the fragmented spatial structure: it was due to the inflexibility arising from the difficulty of substituting the staple in plantations and mines.

The mineral enclave

Historically, the rapid diffusion of foreign-owned and capital-intensive technology in tropical mining had a debilitating effect on locally owned firms: employment was sharply reduced and wages at first remained low despite the adoption of western technology. Tropical mines therefore shared key elements of spatial structure and linkage with plantations. Often located in remote areas, tropical mines provided the archetypal enclave economy orientated to the distant industrial cores for capital, intermediate inputs, downstream processing, and markets.

Although high wages might have been paid, as the mid-twentieth-century emergence of a labour aristocracy in response to unionization of tropical mining shows, this was historically seldom the case. Moreover, since neither the colonial administrations nor local oligarchies applied political pressure to boost retention of resource rents, all four categories of linkage tended to be stunted and the rate of leakage abroad of the economic stimulus was very high. For example, in the early years of the Zambian copper industry less than one-quarter of the export value accrued to the mining region since most of the revenue flowed out to service the capital held overseas (Kessel 1977). Similar high levels of leakage occurred in the Malaysian tin industry as late as the 1930s (Thoburn 1973) and for much the same reason: a capital-intensive production function, foreign ownership, and weak local pressure groups.

Dependency theorists, notably those in the Caribbean, argued from the mid-1960s that foreign-owned plantations and mines continued to minimize the local economic stimulus from primary products exports (Girvan 1971, Beckford 1972). They asserted that, as the first stages of vertically integrated production chains, tropical plantations and mines formed the essential base of large-scale businesses, yet only a small part of the total added value accrued to tropical regions. Moreover, since the final high added value stages of the production chain tended to locate in the advanced economies, alternative locations for the first stage (be it mine or plantation) could easily be substituted if necessary, leaving the initial base of the chain to stagnate or decline. Worse, where an MNRC operated the monoproduct mine or plantation, such regions faced competition for investment from elsewhere in the corporate system. Consequently, MNRCs could apply earnings to build up competing loci of production in direct competition with the funding region (Chinitz 1961).

In the rapidly evolving post-war era, mines remained much closer to the stereotype of economic enclaves than plantations (Graham and Floering 1984). Their large capital requirements, as well as technical and marketing needs, usually favoured direct foreign investment. Such investment generated sizeable capital outflows and was associated with modest productive linkages and limited final demand linkage from spending by the small labour aristocracy. Fiscal linkage therefore appeared to hold most potential for stimulating the local economy (Auty 1983a). It is against this background of historically stunted linkages that developing countries sought more actively from the 1960s to enhance the domestic economic stimulus from mineral resources through the formation of producer country cartels and the pursuit of RBI (Radetzki 1977).

BOOM EFFECTS AND ABSORPTION CONSTRAINTS

Fiscal linkage provided the main stimulus from mining in many developing mineral economies during the post-war period. This spawned two important fields of research, namely, the capture of resource rent (Emmerson 1980), Francis 1981, Mikesell 1986), and the nature of Dutch disease effects (Corden 1982, Corden and Neary 1982). For the oil-exporting countries, the actual capture of resource rents presented few problems and is not considered further here. Indeed, so successful were the oil-exporting countries during the 1974–8 and 1979–81 oil booms that they created formidable problems of windfall absorption. Their disappointing overall performance (Gelb 1988) was consistent with the pre-shock experience of the mineral economies as a whole (Nankani 1979). This section reviews the literature on Dutch disease and windfall deployment and develops a framework for analysing how macro-economic efficiency constrains RBI.

Commodity booms and Dutch disease

The mineral economies are defined as those developing countries which, over a specified period of time, generate more than 10 per cent of their GDP and more than 40 per cent of their export earnings from the mineral sector (Nankani 1979). They have advantages over less favourably endowed developing countries arising from the opportunity presented by their mineral exports to alleviate fiscal and foreign exchange constraints and to pursue an additional route to industrialization through the downstream processing of the mineral resource. Despite these potential advantages, the mineral economies have not always outperformed other groups of developing countries and the achievements of individual mineral economies have been erratic (Roemer 1985).

The theoretical impact of the booming sector on the rest of the economy has been traced by Corden (1982, Corden and Neary 1982) with the aid of a three-sector model. The three sectors are: the boom sector; the lagging sector (non-boom tradeables, usually agriculture and manufacturing); and the non-tradeables sector. In the short run, capital is assumed fixed while labour is mobile between sectors: over the medium to long term, all factors save land are mobile. Two effects are noted: spending effects and resource movement effects. Spending effects from the boom, evident from the outset, cause the price of non-tradeables to rise relative to both the boom and lagging sectors as well as to imports, so that real currency appreciation occurs. Such a price shift attracts labour from the lagging sector into the non-tradeables sector, so that output in the lagging sector declines. High export prices also increase the marginal product of labour in the boom sector so that the lagging sector experiences a second source of labour loss. The lagging sector, therefore, risks contraction through the shift of resources into the boom sector and non-tradeables sectors. The net consequences for the non-tradeables sector are uncertain in Corden's model since the muting caused by the resource movement effect is offset by the boost from the spending effect.

In the long run, with all factors of production mobile save land, industrial output could rise if it is more capital-intensive than non-tradeables; it could fall if it is not; and the prices of non-tradeables could decline if output in that sector expanded particularly rapidly. The latter outcome would result in currency depreciation in place of the initial real appreciation triggered by the spending effects.

The utility of Corden's model, already weakened by its inability to determine long-term effects, declines further when it is applied specifically to developing countries. Several modifications are required in order to adapt it to the oil-exporting developing countries (Roemer 1985). First, the extraordinary capital-intensity of the boom sector and its traditional orientation to external capital may make the resource movement effects negligible. Second, with high levels of unemployment, both the spending and resource movement effects could be dampened. However, labour market imperfections, notably the existence of labour aristocracies in the modernizing sector, make such an outcome unlikely. Third, large intersectoral variations in capital-intensity within developing countries compound the uncertainties of the direction of change noted by Corden. Finally, the assumed sharp division between tradeables and non-tradeables may well have limited application in developing countries, since high levels of protection effectively render many tradeable goods into non-tradeables, including agricultural products as well as manufactured ones.

The high level of distortions in developing country economies makes a catalogue of observed boom effects more insightful than attempts at the formulation of a theory to account for Dutch disease effects. Lewis (1982) notes that constraints on Corden's spending effect increase the probability that the newly generated capital will be poorly allocated. Managerial resources in the public sector are overtaxed so that discrimination occurs in favour of large capital-intensive projects; many projects are likely to be poorly conceived; and fiscal discipline is corroded. In addition, inflationary ripple effects from expatriate management and the labour aristocracy in the boom sector may adversely impact both the lagging and non-tradeable sectors, despite the relatively small fraction of the total labour force which they represent (Singer 1962, Brewster 1972).

More ominously, booms increase the scope for governments to accommodate rent-seeking behaviour. Gelb, Knight, and Sabot (1986) suggest that even under non-boom conditions, the cumulative accommodation of rent-seeking demands may severely depress the overall productivity of capital within an economy in little more than a decade. The associated crowding out of private investment compounds the deleterious effects. The rapid creation of large public sector resource sinks is possible under boom conditions: and especially so if the boom proves more transitory than expected, as in the case of the second oil boom. Under such circumstances, commodity booms may encourage unsustainable fiscal expenditures, accentuate capital misallocation, and impede the necessary adjustments which the abrupt onset of the downswing requires, with serious consequences for long-term economic growth.

Prudent absorption policy

While the windfall absorption policy choices are easily outlined, it is more difficult to generalize about their relative merits. This is partly because the outcome depends heavily on country-specific characteristics; partly because some important options have a long-term payback; and partly because a key variable, the duration of the boom, has exhibited a strong tendency to be erroneously predicted (Gelb 1988).

The large petroleum reserves of the capital surplus oil-exporting countries meant that the oil shocks presented them with the option of using the huge oil windfall to increase overseas investment sharply and draw on the rents to boost domestic consumption (Stauffer 1985). However, this implied continued reliance on imported goods and skills, a prospect which even Saudi Arabia with its massive oil reserves rejected. In pursuing diversification of the non-oil economy, the capital surplus countries were more amply cushioned from downswing shocks through the medium term by their greater ability to accumulate sizeable reserves; to make liberal use of imported goods and skills; and to accommodate political pressure groups without compromising the efficiency objectives of key state enterprises.

Gelb (1988) has shown that oil windfall deployment proved difficult for countries with low per capita oil reserves. Assuming efficient investment capacity and a finite boom of uncertain duration, he suggests that a prudent absorption strategy might comprise the following. First, the windfall should be sterilized by accumulation of external savings and the creation of specific development accounts to distinguish transient windfall expenditures from routine expenditures. Consumption increases might be a laudable use of the windfall provided they take the form of direct transfers to carefully targeted needy groups, but this proves difficult to execute. All too often, consumption is boosted through anti-inflation measures such as domestic price controls and exchange-rate appreciation which increase domestic purchasing power over domestic and imported items respectively. Such policies run the risk of depressing incentives for domestic producers (thereby exacerbating Dutch disease effects) and creating unsustainable expenditure patterns which hamper post-boom economic adjustment.

Domestic absorption through investment requires careful project synchronization to ensure that such spending does not overtax domestic absorptive capacity. Infrastructural expansion provides an obvious outlet and one which can ease potential domestic bottlenecks. However, as Gelb (1988) notes, it has a long payoff and may do little to stimulate directly productive activity through the short and medium term. Moreover, overrapid infrastructure spending can significantly reduce the efficiency of investment, as bottlenecks inflate prices relative to pre-boom levels. Directly productive investments such as RBI share such problems: while, in addition, poor sectoral policy and maladroit implementation can severely reduce viability. Although liberal access to foreign goods and factors of production can smooth the adjustment to boom conditions, such policies are more easily pursued by capital-surplus countries than those with large population/resource ratios.

The quality of macro-economic management is a key determinant of RBI performance. Pinto (1987) has identified a commitment to free currency convertability and to balanced budgets as key elements of successful macro-economic policy under uncertain boom conditions. Timely exchange-rate adjustments help to sustain the non-boom tradeables sector and reduce the risk that negative spillover from absorption will undermine the non-oil economy. The requirement of balanced budgets also imposes a useful discipline by requiring sharp adjustments to resource shortfalls in the absence of which burgeoning consumption becomes increasingly difficult to reverse. Postponement of the inevitable downward adjustment only increases the hardship which must be endured.

Basing his findings on an examination of sub-Saharan Africa, Wheeler (1984) has concluded that mineral economies experience greater difficulty in adjusting to commodity downswings than the non-mineral primary product exporting economies. Commitments made during economic booms are particularly difficult to reduce in less favourable circumstances, and political pressures initially favour maintaining consumption expenditures and investment at the expense of the imported intermediate inputs required by existing enterprises. The amplified volatility of mineral export earnings during the 1970s compounded this flaw. However, there are systematic and sizeable differences between countries in their capacity to execute a prudent absorption strategy, to which attention is now directed.

Political regime and absorptive efficiency

In a study of the integration of Newly Industrializing Countries into the international economy, Haggard (1986) has developed a framework for cross-country comparison of the political constraints on economic policy which avoids the limitations of the case study without becoming enmeshed in vaguely defined theories. There is little consensus among such theories, according to a recent review of the political constraints on reform (Grindle 1986).

Haggard conceives the political constraints as working on three levels: the international level, the country level, and the government level. Briefly, the international system has most impact through external shocks which are often of critical importance in demanding/creating the conditions for policy change. At the national level, Haggard accords social groups less ability to translate their goals into concrete policy demands than other observers such as Lipton (1977). Rather, social groups are envisaged as imposing broad constraints on the actions of governing élites either indirectly—by determining country size/income— or more immediately by affecting the critical balances between the propensity for consumption and saving and between rural and urban interests. In a recent cross-country comparison of Latin American and East Asian responses to the oil shocks, Sachs (1985) identified the fraction of population in urban centres as the key determinant of policy.

At the third, governmental, level an active role is ascribed to government élites who determine the extent to which pressures for short-term goals prevail over long-term developmental objectives. A link is assumed between political systems and the capacity of government élites to arbitrate effectively between conflicting social demands. The thorny notion of political strength and weakness is of central importance and Shafer (1983) provides a useful conceptualization. In the context of an assessment of the costs and benefits to a mineral economy host government arising from the nationalization of multinational resource corporations Shafer argues tht successful countries retain institutions which insulate key economic enterprises from corrosive external and internal political pressures. His model, in which weak governments effectively trade long-term economic benefits for political support, focuses on the key issue implicit in Haggard's approach to the effectiveness of policy reform.

It is easier to postulate such regime/performance relationships than it is to operationalize them. There appear to be two basic conditions for successful windfall deployment: first, the regime must be able to formulate a long-term development policy geared to broad national interests: and, second, the bureaucracy must be capable of executing such a policy, i.e. the administration must be competent. The eight oil-exporting regimes studied here appear to have had more success in surmounting the former obstacle than the latter.

HARNESSING MINERAL ENCLAVES THROUGH RBI

Individual country or staple case studies have provided the principal vehicle for examining RBI in the past (Wall 1980, Thoburn 1973, Kessel 1977, Auty 1983a) but sufficient data are now available to undertake a more systematic evaluation of RBI using a cross-country comparison.

The projected costs and benefits of RBI, by staple

The literature on RBI is by no means unequivocal about the net benefits of an RBI strategy (Radetzki 1977, Roemer 1979). The prospective direct benefits include: higher net foreign exchange earnings; increased government revenues, both through taxation of the higher added value and capture of additional resource rents (notably through transfer cost savings due to weight loss during processing); and expanded high-productivity employment. In addition, from the 1960s developing countries secured increased access to loan capital, often in the form of suppliers credits, so that RBI could attract cheap capital inflows. Such inflows could be used to expand national control of commanding industrial sectors.

The potential costs of the strategy are less obvious, but include:

overstretched managerial and implementation capacity; projection of the problems of the mineral economy (cyclical markets, inflexible investment, and Dutch disease effects) into the industrialization drive (Auty 1984*a*); and the creation of sizeable rent-seeking opportunities in the public sector.

Of particular significance for the oil-exporting countries considered here is the displacement effect of RBI exports on crude oil exports, noted by Stauffer (1975). In comparing the netback for gas-based industries with that from gas used in support of crude oil exports (through re-injection and replacement of oil as refinery fuel), Stauffer calculated the latter yielded the higher return. This was because the very high cost of transforming gas into transportable exports consumed a sizeable fraction of the rent per unit of heat value compared with easily transportable crude oil. Consequently, if industrial countries imported intermediates instead of making them themselves, their demand for energy would decline. The export of gas-based industrial goods thereby effectively substitutes low-rent exports for high-rent crude exports. However, Stauffer qualified his argument by noting that the displace-ment effect would have little impact on those countries with small, rapidly depleting oil reserves such as the high-absorbing oil-exporters. Moreover, the (unquantified) long-term benefits from industrialization might justify a strategy of RBI even for countries with large future oil-producing potential, such as Saudi Arabia and Kuwait. This conclusion is echoed by Turner and Bedare (1979).

RBI's less tangible indirect benefits (such as industrial diversification) were frequently stressed. This was because RBI's highly capital-intensive nature created a tension for all but the capital surplus oil-exporters between the promotion of RBI and the expansion of more employment-intensive activities. The indirect benefits cited, in addition to economic diversification, include: spatial decentralization; technology transfer; and employment from linked industries, most notably via improved prospects for expanding the more labour-intensive downstream pro-cessing (Chapman 1982). The productive linkages generated by heavy resource-based industries relative to other categories of manufacturing appear to be high in developing countries. An index of linkages developed by Yotopoulis and Nugent (1973) shows that resource-based industries were above the median value with basic metals the highest, some 15 per cent above the median value.

The developing country feasibility studies paid far less attention to the viability of such potential downstream industries than to RBI. The viability of the downstream industries has been disputed (Balassa 1977).

More specifically, pressure to capture the dynamic scale economies (via brownfield capacity expansion, vertical integration, and agglomeration economies) tended to give RBI the character of a 'big push' strategy. The resulting strain on implementation capacity was neglected by the feasibility studies.

The 'big push' and the country size constraint

Although there appears to be little clear link between country size and overall economic performance (Perkins and Syrquin 1987), the 'big push' character of the RBI sector confers strong potential advantages on larger countries. Size (defined in terms of area, population, and aggregate GDP) appears likely to be positively correlated with higher *domestic* added value and net positive externalities. There are at least four important reasons for this: two relate to the capture of productive linkages and two to implementation capacity.

First, the domestic market in large countries is capable of absorbing a significant fraction of new plant production while the future growth of domestic consumption provides a 'shadow' market as a fallback for investors should expected export markets fail to materialize. The aluminium industry provides a clear example: the attractions of Brazil as a location for integrated smelting in the late 1970s were reinforced by its large 'shadow' market. Second, a large economy with an extensive geographical area has better prospects for securing the complementary resources domestically and of furnishing the minimum viable size of input-supplying plant required to capture potential linkage effects.

Implementation efficiency should be greater in larger countries. First, large corporations reduce implementation risk but are often perceived to threaten the economic and political independence of large countries less than they do small ones. Small countries have understandably been particularly sensitive to MNC dominance. This has generated political pressure for state intervention in just those (small) countries most likely to require the package of skills that a carefully negotiated agreement with an MNC can provide. Second, the economic impact of the typically large-scale resource processing plant is likely to be smaller relative to total GDP in a large economy: the unfavourable side-effects of cyclical export earnings, fluctuating revenues, and inflationary ripples to the lagging tradeables sector are more likely to be muffled. The corollary is that small economies are particularly susceptible to the risk that entry into downstream resource processing will prove overambitious and retard the necessary diversification into more labour-intensive competitive manufacturing and agricultural activity (Auty 1984*a*).

Small countries are likely to experience high rates of revenue leakage (as will regions with isolated or small clusters of RBI plants in large countries (Auty 1983*a*)). This is consistent with Richardson and Richardson (1975), who suggest that as tools for regional policy, growth poles should be either small and close to existing concentrations (effectively reducing congestion) or large and remote. The latter echoes the 'big push' character of RBI: even large countries can only capture scale benefits by sharply increasing their commitment to RBI—with all the risk which that entails. In a study of industrialization of Argentina and Brazil, Teitel and Thoumi (1986) note that the early stages were characterized by agro-industry and food preservation; there followed the engineering of increasingly sophisticated consumer products. RBI such as steel and petrochemicals emerged strongly in the most recent stage when the economies of both Brazil and Argentina were significantly larger than those of the eight oil-exporting countries examined here. In their recent analysis of structural change, Chenery, Robinson, and Syrquin (1986) also point to RBI emerging relatively late in the industrial transition.

Even the largest of the eight sample oil-exporting countries was not big enough to safely make RBI the cornerstone of its development strategy. If GDP is taken as the dominant criterion of country size with population and area more flexibly applied, then the large country may be defined first in terms of GDP which, in 1982 US dollars, is likely to be in excess of $50 billion. The population of such a country may be expected to exceed 20 million while the land area is likely to be in excess of 400,000 sq. km. The GDP of the small country, by comparison, will generally be less than $10 billion; the population below 10 million; and the land area less than 100,000 sq. km. (Auty 1983*d*). Although the larger countries among the eight oil-exporters had populations, areas, and (to a lesser degree) GDP well in excess of the above definition, only China, India, and Brazil among the developing countries as a whole appear large in relation to RBI requirements.

Yet arguments for caution in pursuing RBI (Barnett and Meunier 1985) are criticized by developing country nationalists and others who justify initial poor RBI performance by the long-term gains from the creation of competitive advantage. They cite Japan and South Korea as examples (Krugman 1988). However, RBI requires the commitment of large sums of capital over long periods of time which makes demands on macro-economic policy and enterprise management which even South Korea was hard-pressed to achieve (World Bank 1986*a*).

Micro-efficiency constraints on RBI implementation

The prominent role assigned to state enterprises in the execution of RBI carried the very real risk that any inefficiencies displayed at the macro-economic level would be compounded at the micro level. Many studies of the functioning of state enterprises in the developing countries were triggered by the severe recession of the early 1980s (Jones 1982, Shirley 1983, Radetzki 1985) and they reveal that the performance of state enterprises in developing countries has been disappointing, though not universally so (World Bank 1983*a*, Trebat 1983, Nellis 1986).

Shafer (1983) suggests that developing country governments failed to appreciate the extent to which MNC ownership can insulate economic enterprises from the debilitating effects of predatory domestic political pressures as well as from external financial and market difficulties. Radetzki (1985) has suggested that poor performance by state enterprises may be attributed to a learning experience so that over a period of ten to fifteen years the performance of state enterprises rises close to levels attained by private firms. However, his work is based on three case studies, only one of which displays the improving trend and that resulted from the establishment of a stronger and more efficient political regime. Radetzki's thesis receives little support in the literature. An analysis of the performance of state enterprises in the Commonwealth Caribbean (Auty 1986*c*) strongly supports Shafer concerning the link between weak political regimes and the corrosion of state enterprise efficiency. The particularly lacklustre performance of state enterprises in sub-Saharan Africa (Nellis 1986) is also consistent with this intepretation (Auty 1988*a*).

Some qualification of the direct link between regime strength, macro-economic efficiency, and the performance of state enterprises is required, however, since efficient state enterprises can coexist with inefficient ones within the same country (Trebat 1983). A sophisticated explanation of such divergent performance which is based on managerial coalitions has been developed by Escobar (1982) in a comparison of state enterprises in Brazil and Venezuela. Basically, state enterprises are viewed as evolving coalitions of efficiency-orientated engineers and politically sensitive commissars so that the balance between the two groups—which can change in response to specific policy issues—determines enterprise performance. The managerial coalition indicates that state enterprises may differ in their capacity to resist political corrosion depending on factors such as leadership and the leverage arising from the role played by the particular enterprise in the economy. Managerial autonomy is the critical factor and the structure of the individual enterprise is considered by some observers (Ayub and Hegstad 1986) to be the key determinant of autonomy.

A second determinant of state enterprise resilience which is particularly important to state firms engaged in RBI, is the product strategy (Vernon 1983*a*). Those firms which pursued a product strategy that focused on the entire production chain from resource to market were better equipped to cope with the price downturn than those which neglected downstream links. In the context of corporate structure and product strategy joint-venture partnerships with MNRCs proved an important means whereby state enterprises would enhance their autonomy and improve market access. Consequently, the attitude of governments towards joint-ventures with MNRCs is a critical determinant of state enterprise performance.

These two elements, organizational structure and product strategy were employed by Rumelt (1974) in an analysis of the performance of large enterprises in the US economy. Briefly, the product strategy emerged as the critical characteristic and especially the degree of dependence on a single product and the extent to which diversification, when it occurred, was into products which were related to the basic product line. Organizational structure tended to be subservient to product strategy in Rumelt's classification. For Rumelt the key to organizational structure was the manner in which field units were integrated into the corporate system.

Organizational structure may be more significant for developing countries, especially in as much as it determines state enterprise autonomy. Of particular interest for state firms spawned by the large public sector bureaucracies, a divisional structure postponed the diseconomies associated with administering large organizations by passing day-to-day decisions to those on the ground. This left the head office to monitor returns from the divisions with an eye to long-term strategy. The divisions thus compete with each other for the allocation of investment since this will go to existing or new product lines promising the highest rate of return beyond the short term. While the divisional structure is triggered by the pressures of administering a large business, it has been noted by Chandler (1962) that—once established— the multidivisional structure institutionalizes a strategy of product diversification (Auty 1981).

SUMMARY

The growth stimulus from tropical primary products has been particularly disappointing, especially in mining. Historically, the capital-intensity of mining created economic enclaves which transferred their economic stimulus out of the mining region and often out of the domestic economy. Even after post-war developing-country gains in political and economic power, tropical mining's productive linkages tended to be stunted, rendering taxation the most significant form of linkage.

Ironically, the successful capture of resource rents during the oil booms raised new problems of public sector management. Overrapid windfall absorption appears difficult for most political regimes to resist; is likely to confer ephemeral favours on limited sections of the population; and requires timely but difficult macro-economic adjustments during downswings. Although RBI was a popular use of the windfalls, the literature is equivocal about RBI's merits and reticent about implementation constraints such as country size and macro- and micro-efficiency.

The dynamic scale economies (arising from brownfield capacity expansion, vertical integration, and agglomeration economies) give RBI the character of a 'big push' which may cause RBI to dominate national development and severely overstrain domestic implementation capacity. RBI peformance is likely to be highly sensitive to macro-economic efficiency and strongly influenced by the organizational structure and product strategy of the RBI firms. Part 2 examines the oil-exporters' expectations from RBI in depth under controlled assumptions of country size and macro- and micro-efficiency levels.

Potential and Actual RBI Resource Rent

3

The Potential Stimulus from Resource Processing in the Base Case:

A Large Efficient Developing Country

THE NEED FOR A BASE CASE

The performance of RBI projects implemented by the oil-exporting countries through the 1974–8 and 1979–81 oil booms was adversely affected by both external shocks and domestic implementation problems. Consequently, in order to compute the potential economic stimulus from RBI it is necessary to model RBI performance with the impact of external shocks and individual country idiosyncrasies removed. This can be achieved by estimating costs for a 'base case' defined as a large (Brazil-sized) developing country with an efficient government and effective factor markets.

The potential economic stimulus from RBI may be conveniently subdivided into the direct and indirect (linked) effects. The direct gain from downstream investment is measured in terms of value added calculated from cost estimates. Employment creation and domestic revenue retention provide additional indices. The potential indirect effects (based on productive and final demand linkages) are measured via employment multipliers. The employment multipliers are drawn from secondary sources since their calculation from primary data lies beyond the means of the present study.

Measures of the direct economic stimulus are made for each of the basic resource production stages (extraction, refining, and smelting) in the four resource processing chains (based on oil, gas, iron ore, and bauxite) under carefully controlled assumptions. Four principle sets of assumptions define the base case. Three concern the internal (domestic) environment and one the external environment. The three key internal assumptions are:

- a large country,
- an efficient government capable of ensuring sound project implementation with negligible backwash effects,
- commercially oriented enterprises operating in flexible factor markets.

The key external assumption is:

● stable long-term prices at levels which yield a normal profit to an efficient greenfield (i.e. new vintage of plant) producer.

The principal assumptions are further elaborated.

The three internal assumptions

An efficiently executed RBI strategy should complement healthy diversification of the non-resource tradeables sector. RBI in developing countries is too risky to substitute for such diversification. Moreover, a poorly executed RBI strategy can undermine economic diversification. To be effective an RBI strategy must be small enough in relation to the total economy so that it does not dominate diversification efforts and discourage growth of the non-resource tradeables sector. Yet the RBI strategy also needs to be large enough to embrace several RBI projects so that reliance on any one is not total.

As noted in Chapter 2, large developing countries have better prospects than small countries for the successful implementation of such an RBI strategy. Recapping briefly, large countries have more RBI options to choose from; they can capture a larger fraction of the potential linkages; they have greater capacity for effective project implementation; and they possess greater scope for muting negative spillover effects.

Effective macro-economic management can greatly reduce the risk associated with RBI. Fundamental elements of such macro-economic policy include: the maintenance of stable, effective price signals and a commitment to fiscal balance (Pinto 1987). More specifically, the minimization of price distortions and the retention of a competitive exchange rate for non-resource tradeables facilitate the evaluation, construction, and operation of RBI projects. The pursuit of a realistic exchange rate proved especially crucial during the 1974–8 and 1979–81 oil booms and was a major factor distinguishing between successful and unsuccessful RBI strategies.

Fiscal policy has a key role to play in price stability. It requires the government to tax away windfall gains and sterilize them until they can be absorbed domestically via effective investments and carefully targeted consumption subsidies. Simultaneously, the tax base needs to be broadened to reduce dependence on the resource sector. Such enhanced fiscal prudence contributes towards domestic price stability and, by smoothing resource boom and downswing cycles, assists sustained economic growth. RBI projects are especially vulnerable to capital cost inflation during construction. They also require high capacity utilization, which means access to a predictable domestic demand or, via a competitive exchange rate, to export markets.

The two assumptions of large country size and effective macro-economic policy create conditions conducive to effective project implementation. Other base case assumptions about the RBI firm ensure commercial orientation. First, state enterprises are assumed to secure a minority MNRC equity partner which has a sufficient share of the equity (and total capital) to maintain a strong incentive to push for the primacy of commercial criteria over socio-political ones. The MNRC partner can fill any deficiencies in domestic skills, whether in marketing, finance, technology, or management and thereby minimize inefficiencies caused by domestic gaps in such skills. The resulting joint-venture is more market-sensitive than wholly state-owned firms.

The base case assumptions yield an efficient, autonomous, and commercially orientated enterprise. The developing country government has a majority equity stake in the RBI projects while remaining unencumbered by the need to oversee the RBI firms' day-to-day operations. The government is thereby freed to concentrate on sound macro-economic management and must look elsewhere for sources of patronage for rent-seeking constituencies.

The external assumptions

These three principal internal assumptions (concerning country size, macro-efficiency, and micro-efficiency) are consistent with the construction of plants which are within budget and operate according to commercial criteria. The remaining set of assumptions concerns external conditions and yields stable long-term prices at levels permitting competitive operation by efficient greenfield producers. This implies a normal return on capital and the absence of resource rents. Actual mid-1980s prices were lower than the base case assumptions for two principal reasons. First, international markets for capital-intensive RBI like steel, aluminium, and petrochemicals became increasingly rigid during the 1970s. This reflected the interplay of many factors which, under the heightened uncertainty of the post-1960s global economy, combined to reduce producer homogeneity (Auty 1987a). Abrupt and unstable changes in producer competitiveness occurred with the proliferation of new entrants, the increased volatility of energy prices and exchange rates and the unpredicted onset of changes in long-term demand trends. Firms resisted closure since it was by no means clear which ones were at the margin.

The resulting glutted markets meant that actual mid-1980s prices were set by the cash costs of established amortized producers. Plants constructed before the mid-1970s global inflation incurred low capital costs relative to the RBI plants constructed during the two oil booms. The plants of older vintage were fully amortized, or close to it, as the oil-exporting countries' greenfield plants came on stream. All else being equal, and in the absence of inflation accounting, established amortized producers held a considerable cost advantage over new entrants. Their cash costs set prices below those assumed in the base case (the replacement costs of efficient greenfield producers). This price divergence is one of many ways in which the actual conditions experienced by RBI in the eight oil-exporting countries differed considerably from the base case assumptions.

MEASUREMENT OF RBI'S ECONOMIC STIMULUS

The direct economic stimulus

Cost estimation (Auty 1975, Auty 1983a) is used to measure the direct economic stimulus from RBI under the base case for the extraction, refining, and smelting stages in each of the four resource chains.

Value added is the key measure of the direct stimulus, with the ICOR providing the leading efficiency index. Following Hashimoto (1983), other measures of the direct economic stimulus are the capacity to generate extra capital resources (measured by the ratio of foreign to domestic investment); the net foreign exchange earnings (measured in terms of revenue minus overseas payments and summarized in the revenue retention coefficient after Brodsky and Sampson (1980)); and the employment generated. To facilitate comparison between production stages and natural resource chains, all indices (except the ICOR) are standardized by calculating them on a per tonne basis and then expressing them as a ratio to the total investment cost per tonne.

The indirect economic stimulus

Linkage analysis is used to conceptualize the indirect economic stimulus. Four categories of linkage are commonly recognized (Hirschman 1977); two are production linkages (backward and forward linkage) and the others are fiscal linkage (taxation) and consumption (final demand) linkage. Thoburn (1973) has made the most comprehensive effort at measuring linkages in a developing country with reference to tin, palm oil, and rubber production in Malaysia. Thoburn defines three preconditions as necessary for the investment generated by new resource processing to be counted as linkage. First, it must be socially profitable;

second, it must not displace other domestic investment; and third, it must be unlikely to emerge in the absence of the triggering activity. In practice, problems of definition and measurement make the use of linkages a highly subjective exercise in which these criteria function as guidelines rather than as rigorous conditions.

Linkages are therefore used here to describe rather than to quantify the indirect economic stimulus from different production stages. The employment multiplier provides a concise measure of the indirect economic stimulus associated with new economic activity (Mandeville and Jensen 1979). Although the calculation of such multipliers from primary data sources lies beyond the scope of the present study, employment multipliers are widely used in the literature. They furnish a broad order-of-magnitude index of the indirect economic impact.

However, some caveats are required concerning the use of employment multipliers to measure the indirect economic stimulus. The apparent precision of the employment multiplier is suspect in the absence of universal criteria for its calculation: hence its use as a broad order-of-magnitude index. Moreover, where the employment multiplier has been calculated for specific projects, it must be suitably qualified to allow for differences in employment-intensity related to variations between countries related to income level and market imperfections.

The production linkages in the extraction stage are dominated by forward linkages since the entire resource-market chain is effectively forward linkage from resource extraction. However, for other production stages, productive linkages comprise both the backward linkages (other than the resource input) triggered by the RBI project and the forward linkages which its presence renders feasible (Auty 1983*a*). Final demand linkage (local spending by factors of production) is often subsumed with production linkages in the calculation of project multipliers, but it can be identified when subcategories of the employment multiplier are recorded.

Fiscal linkage can figure in either the direct or indirect effects, depending on the efficiency with which government captures rents and—if the government is successful in this goal—on where it chooses to reinject the revenues. Fiscal linkage is potentially an important element of the economic stimulus with resource rents prospectively the key component. Resource rent is zero in the base case since, by definition, prices are set to give a normal return to workers and owners of capital. However, in reality, governments preside over considerable leakage of such linkage—not only to capital and labour—but also to input suppliers and consumers. The net social gain coefficient can provide a measure of the efficiency with which governments capture potential rents (Pearson and Cownie 1974).

The economic stimulus (direct and indirect) from the extraction of unprocessed resources is first calculated before that from resource processing. This provides a template against which to evaluate the gains from shifting into processing. Thereafter, the analysis proceeds in four steps. First, the direct stimulus from hydrocarbon processing is estimated. The rents from oil are potentially higher than those from gas. Second, the direct stimulus from metals processing is calculated. The sector's relatively modest downstream linkage options are contrasted with those of hydrocarbons processing and explained. Third, the employment multiplier is used to measure the prospective indirect benefits. Lastly, the potential stimulus from downstream resource processing is summarized.

THE ECONOMIC STIMULUS FROM THE
RESOURCE EXTRACTION STAGE

Key Estimation Assumptions

The standardized assumptions used throughout the base case cost estimations are illustrated in Table 3.1 with reference to bauxite mining. The debt/equity ratio assumed in the two base case mining ventures (and in all the downstream projects) is 50 : 50, a level considered prudent in light of the actual experience during the two oil shocks (Wilson 1985). This is because such a ratio optimizes the trade-off between the advantage of potentially low-cost debt financing and the flexibility which equity financing possesses to ride out price downswings. However, in the case of hydrocrabon extraction, 100 per cent equity financing is assumed, reflecting the higher risks associated with this type of investment.

The cautious gearing of the base case yields a high incentive to make market-sensitive investment and operating decisions. This is because of the high absolute equity which both the domestic and foreign joint-venture partners must commit. The base case assumes 30 per cent equity participation by an MNRC and the remainder by an autonomous, commercially orientated, domestic enterprise. The figure of 30 per cent foreign equity appears to lie above the minimum required for the MNRC partners to retain sufficient incentive to push for efficiency criteria. Industry sources consider that an equity share of 25 per cent represents a critical minimum threshold. Under most commercial law

TABLE 3.1. *Cost estimation: the example of bauxite mining*

Input	$/tonne	% Domestic	$ Domestic
Fuel			
Drying	0.35	100	0.35
Lubricants	0.20	100	0.20
Materials and services	3.50	80	2.80
Labour: 0.83 mh/t at $4/mh	3.30	90	3.00
TOTAL OPERATING COST	7.35	86	6.35
Depreciation at 5%/principal	5.75	70	4.03
Interest on loan (10-yr ave)	2.30	50	1.15
Equity return 13% (85 pre-tax)	7.48	81	6.08
Cash cost (no interest)	13.10	79	10.38
Cash cost (with interest)	15.40	75	11.53
Replacement cost	22.88	77	17.59

Key assumptions: (1) Greenfield mine of 3 million tonnes/yr capacity costing $345 million ($115/tonne). (2) Financed: 50% loan (half suppliers' credits and half local loan, both with 8% interest and repayable in ten annual instalments); 50% equity (35% local and 15% foreign).

Economic Stimulus
1 Foreign investment = $138 million = $46/tonne.
2 Net foreign exchange = $17.59/tonne capacity.
3 Value added = $18.73/tonne; domestic added value = $14.24/tonne.
4 ICOR = 6.1; GDP/$ invested = $0.16.
5 Revenue retention coefficient = 0.77
6 Direct employment = 1,250 workers = $276,000/job.

Sources: Adelman (1986a and 1986b); Bina (1985); Brown *et al.* (1983); Hashimoto (1983); Franz *et al.* (1985).

the 25 per cent ratio corresponds to the minimum needed to secure a veto over major decisions such as the sanctioning of new investment.

Where MNRCs hold less than 25 per cent of the equity of RBI projects they are inclined to look to margins on the supply of equipment (both during and after plant construction) to compensate for poor returns on the basic equity. Given the typical debt/equity ratio (70 per cent and upwards) employed in many RBI projects, a 10 per cent MNRC equity stake corresponded to less than 4 per cent of the total capital invested in the project. For example, a $1 billion project would require a $150 million equity commitment from an MNRC under the base case assumptions compared with $30 million with only 10 per cent equity and a 70 : 30 debt : equity ratio.

The actual investment figures employed in the base case are drawn from industry sources, a simple task in the case of the two mining projects, but much more difficult for hydrocarbons. This in part reflects

TABLE 3.2. *Comparative stimulus from resource extraction*

Resource	I/O ($)	R/O ($)	NFE/I	VA/I	DVA/I	RRC	ICOR
Bauxite	115	22.9	0.18	0.19	0.14	0.77	6.2
Iron ore	100	23.5	0.18	0.18	0.15	0.78	5.4
Oil	60	22.1	0.26	0.36	0.26	0.71	2.8
Gas	92	20.3	0.16	0.21	0.15	0.71	4.7

Symbols: I = Investment; O = Output; R = Revenue; NFE = Net Foreign Exchange; VA = Value Added; DVA = Domestic Value Added; RRC = Revenue Retention Coefficient; ICOR = Incremental Value Added Ratio.

Sources: As Table 3.1.

the greater uncertainty and variability in the quality of hydrocarbon deposits, even in an established production province. It is also due to the greater arbitrariness and secrecy in assigning exploration and development costs to individual fields. Adelman (1986*a*) attempted to assess oil production costs in order to determine the real scarcity value of the resource. Although the detailed data Adelman employed refer to 1978, subsequent reserve depletion and price inflation make the $3,000/bl. discovery and development figure employed in Table 3.2 (which summarizes the direct stimulus from resource extraction), if anything, somewhat on the high side for major OPEC producers in the mid-1980s. Data supplied by PDVSA, the Venezuelan state oil corporation, and the Nigerian National Petroleum Corporation support the view that Adelman's procedure for estimating mid-1980s costs (Adelman 1986*b*) errs on the high side.

The total oil production cost of $22/tonne (or just over $3bl.) in Table 3.2 is close to the transfer charge reported for the Saudi Arabian state oil corporation, Aramco, to its new export refineries. It is slightly higher than the bloated operating costs recorded by Aramco for all its operations in 1985 (Financial Times 1986*a*). In effect, the figure of $22/tonne represents padded production costs (reflecting free spending during a boom) in a low cost oil province. It is therefore at the lower end of the range for the eight sample countries under study. Hence, in the mid-1980s the total production costs of a long-established Nigerian producer were just over $18/tonne while those of Cameroon, the newest entrant producing from offshore fields, were just over three times that figure. Similarly, gas costs reflect operations at the more competitive end of the spectrum. However, it should be noted that lower gas costs may be justified where production of gas occurs as a by-product of oil extraction or where credits accrue from the sale of associated natural gas liquids.

The remaining key cost components are labour and materials. The assumed cost of labour, which includes fringe benefits and embraces management as well as semi-skilled manual workers, is $4/hour or $8,000/year. This is towards the lower end of the range employed in a recent World Bank study of the aluminium industry (Brown *et al.* 1983). The rates used in that study are actual rates which reflect varying degrees of union success in capturing rents, so that a figure towards the lower end of the range is appropriate for the base case. Although devaluations intended to correct for declining oil prices had caused actual mid-1980s remuneration rates in some countries (notably Nigeria and Indonesia) to fall slightly below the assumed base case level, rates in most countries remained higher—often considerably so.

The magnitude and instability of change in some cost parameters in the mid-1980s could substantially alter the competitiveness of RBI projects and their economic stimulus. For example, the Venezuelan metals projects operated for some months in 1986 with an exchange rate for exports one-fifth that of three years earlier and an exchange rate for imported inputs half that level.

In calculating domestic revenue retention for labour and material costs, some 10 per cent of labour costs are assumed to leak abroad as payments to foreign management while one-fifth of spares are assumed to be imported. These figures are relatively low for the sophisticated equipment in use. However, according to industry estimates, they reflect levels which are appropriate for the large efficient country assumed in the base case. The cost of natural resource inputs along the production chain reflect base case estimates of the extraction stage or, further downstream, the costs of the refining stage.

The direct economic stimulus

The four extraction operations (bauxite and iron ore mining; oil and gas production) are compared in Table 3.2. This shows that, with prices set at the replacement cost for an efficient greenfield producer, oil extraction requires the least investment/tonne, generates the highest foreign exchange and domestic added value per dollar of investment, and yields the most favourable ICOR of the four resources. Bauxite records the weakest overall performance, though one which is not far below that of iron ore and gas.

Capital charges dominate extraction costs for all four resources, overwhelmingly so in the case of hydrocarbons. Labour comprises less than 15 per cent of bauxite mining costs and less than 5 per cent of iron ore and hydrocarbon production costs. The capital-intensive production function is reflected in low employment/unit of investment, especially in hydrocarbons extraction (Table 3.2). Although actual conditions may vary according to specific resource characteristics, worldscale bauxite and iron ore mines generate direct employment at around $300,000 to 800,000 per job, respectively, while hydrocarbons generate employment at $5–10 million per job. Direct employment at a worldscale iron ore mine would be of the order of 1200 compared with one-third to two-thirds that level at a large oil or gas field.

With prices set at actual 1984 levels there is no potential rent component for iron ore production under the base case whereas bauxite mining generates a rent equivalent to one-fifth of production costs. In contrast, oil and gas extraction record prospective rents equivalent to seven to nine times the production cost. The inclusion of mid-1980s' freight charges has a negligible effect on oil, since the cost of shipment in large bulk tankers was around 3 per cent of the price. In the case of ore exports, however, the inclusion of freight rates around $8/tonne eliminates the rent on bauxite and imposes a negative rent equivalent to one-third of the replacement cost on the greenfield iron ore mine.

Downstream ore processing offers the prospect of securing resource rent especially where, as in the case of bauxite, such processing entails a significant weight loss. Gas occupies a position intermediate between oil and metal ores since, unless the reserves are in close proximity to a large market (as in the case of Canada and Mexico *vis-à-vis* the United States) the costs of transforming the gas into a transportable state such as LNG, methanol, or urea eliminates a substantial fraction of the potential rent. For example, estimates made for Trinidad and Tobago in the early 1980s suggest that shipment of gas as LNG, ammonia, and methanol would earn netbacks (from which the cost of gas extraction must be deducted to yield a rent component) of $85, $36, and $32/tonne respectively (Auty and Gelb 1986). Even the more favourable LNG option entails giving up more than 50 per cent of the potential generous rent in order to get the gas to market.

The indirect economic stimulus

In mineral extraction, linkages other than fiscal linkage tend to be modest since mining frequently occurs in a remote location under distinct enclave conditions. By definition, mineral extraction for export generates little forward linkage so that the productive linkages are dominated by backward links. The manufactured inputs employed, such as machinery and chemicals, are mostly produced in specialized plants serving numerous consumers. They tend to be imported into the mining region from major domestic industrial centres in the large country base case (and from abroad in the case of small countries). Since the base case assumption precludes resource rents, the emergence of communication and township infrastructure is the major linkage generated by mineral extraction. Estimated employment multipliers are correspondingly low, ranging between 1 and 2. For example, the employment multiplier for a remote 3 million tonne greenfield bauxite mine in Latin America was estimated at 1.5. The $300 million mine is expected to spawn a permanent settlement of only 4,000 people (Alusuisse 1980).

Not surprisingly, before the 1973–4 oil shock when rents were much lower and foreign investment dominated ownership and capital flows, the domestic economic stimulus from wasting mineral assets could be criticized as disappointingly small (Thoburn 1973). More radical critiques viewed the mines as the foundation of wealth accumulation in the industrialized countries for which developing country resource suppliers were inadequately rewarded (Girvan 1971). Girvan calculated that half the added value from Jamaican bauxite leaked out on imported inputs and foreign capital servicing during the early 1960s. Since the value added in bauxite mining was 4 per cent of total added value along the entire production chain, domestic revenue retention was only 2 per cent of the total potential added value. Studies such as this underpinned the developing country drive into downstream resource processing during the 1970s.

THE DIRECT ECONOMIC STIMULUS FROM DOWNSTREAM PROCESSING

Before comparing RBI's potential economic stimulus for the different resources, some general features of resource processing should be noted. Investment in RBI is accompanied by large stepped falls in the scale of worldscale production units (Table 3.3) going, first, from extraction to intermediates and, second, from intermediates to fabrication. Average plant size declines relative to markets, indicating easier entry and greater flexibility in adjusting capacity to demand compared with the upstream stages. Value added per tonne and the employment intensity of production also tend to rise going downstream. However, the increase in labour intensity per tonne of output which accompanies the shift from the intermediate to the fabrication stage is often only modest and, as

TABLE 3.3. *Scale, employment, and value added, by production stage*

Resource/Stage	Worldscale (mmty)	Employment (mh/t)	Value added ($/tonne)
Bauxite/Aluminium			
Bauxite mining	3.00	3.46	76.2
Alumina refining	0.80	3.42	275.9
Aluminium smelting	0.20	12.00	473.0[a]
Fabrication (foil)	0.05	4.50	447.0
Iron Ore/Steel			
Iron ore mining	10.00	0.30	22.1
DRI	0.55	0.20	21.7
Steel	0.70	2.00	56.2[b]
Fabrication (ships)	0.50	13.00	200.0
Oil Extraction/Refining			
Oil extraction	37.52	0.01	21.68
Oil refining	12.45	0.13	14.05
Gas Extraction/Processing			
Gas extraction	24.90	0.03	31.70
Ethylene cracking	0.50	3.74	316.06
LLDPE	0.20	5.20	126.10[c]
Plastics (foil)	0.007	5.33	118.90

Notes: Conversions are expressed per tonne of final product, involving the following weight-loss ratios:

[a] 4.18 tonnes bauxite and 1.9 tonnes alumina/tonne aluminium.

[b] 1.20 tonnes ore and 0.8 tonnes DRI/tonne of steel.

[c] 1.56 tonnes gas and 1.05 tonnes ethylene/tonne LLDPE.

Sources: See Tables 3.1 and 3.4.

aluminium shows, not automatic. There is little evidence to support claims of a sharp increase in employment-intensity beyond the intermediate stage.

A comparison of Table 3.2 and 3.4 shows that investment/unit of capacity rises significantly moving downstream, especially for aluminium and plastics. Of particular significance is the fact that RBI provided access to large inflows of cheap capital if the prudent gearing assumed in the base case was abandoned. Table 3.4 also shows that net foreign exchange earnings per dollar invested rise sharply from the extraction stage, specially for the later intermediate processes, and that domestic revenue retention also rises, though relatively modestly.

In contrast, value added per dollar invested declines moving from extraction to downstream processing and the ICOR declines significantly. Under the base case assumptions, the ICORs for the resource

TABLE 3.4. *Comparative stimulus from RBI*

Process	I/O ($)	R/O ($)	NFE/I	VA/I	DVA/I	RRC	ICOR
First Stage							
Alumina refining	1000	217.1	0.167	0.150	0.112	0.77	6.65
DRI	173	72.7	0.331	0.157	0.116	0.79	6.37
Oil refining	91	18.5	0.138	0.156	0.114	0.68	6.45
Ethylene cracking	1200	274.2	0.179	0.169	0.145	0.78	5.92
Ammonia	410	87.3	0.165	0.157	0.116	0.78	6.38
Second Stage							
Aluminium smelting	2000	1255.5	0.370	0.158	0.118	0.88	6.33
Steel rod	357	190.0	0.426	0.157	0.118	0.80	6.35
LLDPE	750	441.4	0.525	0.162	0.122	0.89	6.18
Urea	208	97.9	0.408	0.139	0.094	0.87	7.19

Symbols: See Table 3.2.

Sources: Anthony Bird Associates (1983); Auty (1983a); Auty (1983d): Banque Indosuez (1985); Barnett and Schorsch (1983); Brown *et al.* (1983); Hashimoto (1983); Sheldrick (1985); UN (1984); UNIDO (1981).

processing stages are uniformly poor, at around seven. This reflects the base case assumptions of low capital return on capital-intensive projects and a small (non-rent-seeking) wage component. It underlines the importance of risk premiums and resource rents in rendering RBI investment attractive. Yet the capture of such benefits was by no means guaranteed and failure held wider and more serious implications for the oil-exporting countries.

The global targeting of RBI by the oil-exporting countries required sustained rapid growth in demand (or capacity reductions by OECD countries if demand slowed) in order to capture resource rents. In this context, the displacement effect of relatively low-rent RBI on high-rent crude exports noted by Stauffer (1975) is important. The large-scale expansion of RBI by the oil-exporting countries carried the double risk that excess capacity would not only prevent capture of resource rents at the RBI stage, but also erode the very high resource rents on crude oil exports.

Hydrocarbon Processing

None of the downstream hydrocarbon processing options modelled matches gas and oil extraction in terms of the value added per dollar of investment and the incremental capital output ratio (compare Tables 3.2

and 3.4). These characteristics aside, oil refining has more in common with the extraction stage: its investment per tonne is modest and its aggregate capital requirements are high for a worldscale unit of some production complexity ($1.1 billion). Oil refining also opened fewer routes to further downstream processing because forward linkage was constrained by the high opportunity costs of oil which arose from the steep 1973 and 1979 rises in oil prices. Consequently, although oil has numerous potential downstream options, refining was the only one pursued to a significant degree by the oil-exporting countries. Since the products of the oil refineries were principally directed towards final consumption, the refinery's capacity to open up a lengthy chain of forward linkage was correspondingly stunted.

In contrast, natural gas was considered to have low opportunity costs and to provide a wide range of second- and third-stage processing options, many of which in turn fed additional intermediate as well as final manufacturing activities. The aggregate capital requirements of the gas-based hydrocarbon processing plants modelled are more modest than those of a worldscale oil refinery. Ethylene requires around $600 million and the three other plants around one-third that level. The combination of a wide range of downstream petrochemical options, smaller plant sizes, and gas-fired metals plants in both aluminium and steel, contributes to the remarkable flexibility of gas for RBI. However, it should be noted that the relatively high costs of transporting gas to markets, compared with transporting crude oil, yielded inherently lower netbacks—and therefore potential rents—per unit of heat value compared with oil (Stauffer 1975).

Ore processing

The hard minerals open fewer downstream processing options than gas, especially bauxite. Moreover, many of the metal fabricating operations are capital-intensive: plant scale may be relatively large (compared with plastics plants for example), employment modest, and value added limited. Table 3.3 shows that the steep increases in value added going from mining to refining and smelting need not continue into the fabrication stage.

The recent emergence of the direct-reduced iron ore/electric arc furnace has increased the options for steel production in developing countries (Miller 1976). Previously, the combined scale and capital requirements for the integrated steel process posed a formidable barrier to entry (the capital investment per tonne of capacity for DRI steel is half that of the integrated process). However, DRI/steel links are restricted because final demand accounts for a significant fraction of production. More than half the demand for steel in developing countries is for round steel used by the construction industry (Barnett and Meunier 1985). Yet steel fabrication does tend to open more options and to be more labour-intensive than aluminium working. However, such gains are offset by the more modest employment-intensity and value added from steel intermediates compared with both aluminium and plastics (Tables 3.2 and 3.4).

THE INDIRECT ECONOMIC STIMULUS

The enigmatic size of the indirect effects
The low employment-intensity, value added, and ICORs of downstream resource processing under the base case assumptions underscore the importance of resource rents in RBI's direct economic stimulus. Not surprisingly, the advocates of RBI frequently buttressed their case with reference to the benefits from RBI's indirect economic stimulus. For example, Indian planners argued that although a $1.5 billion olefins complex would generate only 3,000 permanent direct jobs ($500,000 per job), the complex would reduce domestic materials prices sufficiently to stimulate an additional $300 million investment and a further 43,000 jobs ($7,000 per job) in further processing.

For metals, Girvan (1971) calculated that more than one-third the added value from the bauxite processing chain accrued downstream from ingot smelting with employment per tonne of capacity seven times that of the more capital-intensive smelting stage. His claim is not supported by data on the production functions of different aluminium fabrication operations which tend to be more capital-intensive than smelting (Debell and Richardson 1974) nor by an analysis of linkages from aluminium smelters in the Pacific Northwest region of the United States (Auty 1983*a*). Nor do petrochemicals appear any different: in a sceptical review of numerous claims for high indirect multipliers, Chapman (1982) noted the persistent failure of large petrochemical projects to trigger the indirect stimulus anticipated.

The persistent gap between claims for the indirect RBI economic stimulus and actual achievements is partly explained by underestimation of the capital-intensity of most downstream processes, both in metals and petrochemicals. It partly reflects neglect in most (small) developing countries of the degree to which market access constrains the capture of such linkages. The large size of the RBI intermediate plants relative to domestic demand, even in the large base case country, requires tapering sales to export markets when capacity is expanded. Yet transfer costs, tariff barriers and the need for close customer access reduce competitiveness in such markets, especially in metals production. Consequently, export competitiveness declines with progress along the production chain as advantages associated with proximity to large OECD domestic markets become more important. This can be clearly seen in the case of ethylene-based products where a sizeable competitive advantage at the ethylene stage is almost eliminated by the LLDPE stage (Banque Indosuez 1985). In metals, even OECD aluminium smelters located in sizeable regional markets attract little forward linkage (Auty 1983*a*).

However, generalization for all developing countries requires caution since rising per capita income appears to mute the employment multiplier: the higher the income the lower the multiplier. In the poorer developing countries a sizeable informal sector may amplify the employment multiplier. A large informal sector in a protected market may successfully tap resource rents. India's large protected domestic market and cheap informal labour might well, therefore, generate a sizeable indirect economic stimulus from its ethylene complex, though perhaps lower than the ratio of 15 (noted above) claimed by that country's planners. However, the base case assumptions preclude resource rents, labour aristocracies, and informal sectors since they are manifestations of market imperfections.

Employment multipliers for isolated RBI plants

Advocates of RBI have deployed its contribution to regional growth as an argument in its favour. In the large base case country, the more remote the plant the smaller will be its regional (as opposed to domestic) economic stimulus. The isolated plant may be expected to share with the resource extraction stages the need for specialized chemicals and equipment inputs which are most effectively supplied from large plants serving numerous customers at major market locations. Moreover, compared with their counterparts in industrial country locations, isolated RBI plants are likely to internalize many maintenance services while plant design may specifically incorporate service-reducing features to minimize the risks of equipment failure in remote locations.

In the absence of significant weight loss in processing (a feature only of bauxite among the resources considered here) local forward linkages are also likely to be few. Final demand linkage is also minimal because of low aggregate employment and minimal local spending. Consequently, the isolated RBI plant is likely to retain the enclave characteristics of the extraction stage—though less so in the large base case economy than in a smaller one.

A recent study of the aluminium industry in Queensland attempted to quantify the local and statewide employment multipliers from an alumina refinery and aluminium smelting. The extension downstream from bauxite mining was assumed to merely add value to unprocessed exports without triggering other new activity. Hence, backward linkages which might arise from expanded mining and power generation were omitted. The resulting local employment multiplier was 2.0 and 1.9 for the refinery and smelter, respectively; while the statewide multipliers were 4.2 and 3.3, respectively (Mandeville and Jensen 1979). The energy-intensive nature of aluminium smelting demands the provision of 350 MW of power for a worldscale unit, a size sufficient to trigger hydro or thermal power plants close to minimum viable size and to boost the employment multiplier by 25 per cent.

An estimate of the steel employment multiplier has recently been made for an isolated DRI/steel plant in northern Mexico. The revenue flows from such a plant are 25 per cent each for materials and energy inputs; 20 per cent for wages; and 30 per cent to capital (industry sources). The DRI/steel plant generates 500 direct jobs within it, split evenly between operations and maintenance. A further 2,500 are engaged in backward linkage activities supplying refractories, scrap, and contract services while forward linkage (steel transformation) generates 1,500 jobs. Final demand linkages were estimated to trigger an additional 3,000 jobs through the provision of food and services. The resulting employment multipliers of the steel plant are 8.0 via productive linkages with a further 65 per cent boost from the final demand triggered by the production chain. Consequently, each initial steel job creates fourteen other jobs—a relatively high ratio at the upper bound of the employment multiplier effect which reflects the operation of market imperfections.

Indirect effects of the 'big push'
The large base case country can choose between dispersing the RBI plants and clustering them at one or more locations to capture agglomeration economies. It can also pick between domestic and export orientation. These options arise because the domestic market under the base case can absorb the output of one olefins complex, two worldscale aluminium plants (and one alumina refinery), at least one integrated steel unit, and several DRI/steel, ammonia, and fertilizer plants.

Employment multipliers were estimated for two RBI agglomerations in the eight oil-exporting countries: Ciudad Guayana in Venezuela and Al Jubail in Saudi Arabia. The two RBI complexes differ from each other in terms of their product orientation, per caput income, degree of remoteness, and timing. The Ciudad Guayana complex is the more established of the two: it was commenced in a remote region in the late 1950s based on metals (steel and aluminium). In contrast, the Al Jubail growth pole was begun in the mid-1970s (by which time Saudi per capita income was considerably above that of Venezuela), close to the large Aramco oilfields and based largely on petrochemicals. The lower income, greater distance from other centres and older vintage of the Guayana complex results in higher multipliers than those for the Saudi one.

Employment multipliers were estimated for both complexes: in the mid-1960s by the Harvard/MIT Joint Centre for Ciudad Guayana and in the mid-1970s by Colin Buchanan Associates for Al Jubail. Table 3.5 shows the changing employment structure projected in the mid-1960s as a result of the expansion of RBI in the Guayana resource frontier region of Venezuela (Friedmann 1966, Rodwin 1969). By 1980 total employment was expected to reach 100,000 with just over one-quarter of those jobs in RBI. The ratio of RBI to light manufacturing was estimated as 0.54; while the ratio of RBI to total employment was estimated at 3.85. These figures are relatively low and they are not too different for those for the individual plants noted earlier. They also proved to be underestimates (Corporación Venezolana de Guayana 1984), largely because of successful rent-seeking behaviour.

The Al Jubail estimates assumed that the ratio of workers in secondary industry to RBI would be around 2 compared with 2.6 for the ratio of service to industrial workers and 6.2 for the ratio of RBI to total workers. A ratio of 2.7 was used for the total population to the total workforce. On these calculations the projected 8,500 workers in RBI were expected to trigger a further 53,000 jobs and provide the economic base for a community of 170,000 people. In 1976 Buchanan made even more favourable growth assumptions, raising the RBI/population ratio from 20 to 30. The new figures projected that 11,000 RBI jobs would create a community of 320,000 population within a twenty-five-year period. Wage levels at Al Jubail were more than four times those of the base case (and twice those of Venezuela) and no informal sector existed. Unlike Ciudad Guayana, Al Jubail's multiplier initially fell well short of that expected. The muted multiplier for Al Jubail is a recurring feature of the most recent RBI projects which is explored at length in Chapter 11.

TABLE 3.5. *Projected employment trends, Guayana 1965–1980*

Subsector	1965	1980	1980 ratio
Heavy manufacturing	5,350	26,000	1.00
Primary:			
Mining	2,530	6,900	0.27
Energy	170	900	0.04
Agriculture	1,500	5,500	0.21
TOTAL	4,200	13,300	0.51
Light manufacturing	1,700	14,000	0.54
Construction	3,170	7,600	0.29
Trade	2,010	10,000	0.38
Housing and infrastructure[a]	4,990	29,100	1.12
TOTAL EMPLOYMENT	73,000	100,000	3.85

[a] Subdivided 1980:

Finance, Insurance, Real Estate	1,300
Communications	400
Passenger Transport	3,750
Freight	1,450
Government	3,900
Educational Services	3,700
Medical Services	2,000
Sewage, Water and Sanitation	1,100
Business Services	1,200
Recreation Services	1,000
Domestic Services	5,000
Other Services	4,300

Source: Blanco and Ganz (1969: 73, 76, 85).

The employment multiplier is an elusive figure: for RBI, ratios range from 4 to 10, with the higher levels associated with large RBI complexes and the presence of a sizeable informal sector. A figure towards the lower end of the range is more in tune with the base case assumptions: higher levels appear likely to be associated with the presence of significant resource rents, underlining yet again the importance of that factor for RBI.

CONCLUSION

The potential economic stimulus from RBI must be estimated under controlled assumptions. The resulting 'base case' is defined as a large developing country with an efficient government and flexible factor markets in which appropriately scaled RBI projects can be effectively implemented with negligible backwash effects. Efficiently implemented RBI projects can attract foreign capital, raise output, boost net foreign exchange, and increase government revenues while diversifying the economy both structurally and spatially. Downstream processing of iron ore triggers more investment options than bauxite, but the processing of hydrocarbons, notably gas, yields more options still.

However, RBI generates relatively high ICORs at product prices which yield a normal profit so that its attraction rests heavily on resource rents and indirect (final and productive linkage) effects. Unfortunately, resource rents (which have historically been higher for oil than gas and for hydrocarbons than for metals) may not be enhanced by resource processing. Moreover, since RBI exports may displace high-rent crude resource exports, RBI production may actually diminish total resource rents.

The indirect economic stimulus from RBI, while potentially large under highly specific circumstances (agglomerated projects yielding sizeable rents in countries with large informal sectors) is more modest in the base case. As a result of the operation of all three key RBI characteristics (high ICORs, the displacement effect, and the muted indirect stimulus) the initial economic impact from RBI investments may be disappointing. In particular, the capture of resource rents was crucial to achieving a good RBI performance. Before examining this aspect further, attention now turns to a fuller exploration of the impact of country size on the base case RBI economic stimulus.

4

The Country Size Constraint on RBI

Only China, India, and Brazil among the developing countries are of a size comparable to the base case. Table 4.1 compares the eight oil-exporting countries with Brazil in terms of GDP, population, and area, the three most commonly used country size indicators (Perkins and Syrquin, 1987). It shows that none of the eight countries matches Brazil in overall size, even though they were selected as pairs of large and small countries in four global cultural regions. However, Indonesia and Nigeria do rank as large or medium on all three country size criteria. Bahrain and Trinidad and Tobago clearly rank as tiny on all three criteria. The remaining four countries occupy intermediate positions. If the three size criteria are not accorded equal weight and greater importance is assigned to economic output over population and to population over area, then Nigeria and Indonesia emerge as medium-large countries; Saudi Arabia and Venezuela as mid-sized; Malaysia and Cameroon as medium-small; and Bahrain and Trinidad and Tobago as tiny.

It will be recalled that the hypotheses concerning the constraints which smaller countries face in the capture of the potential economic stimulus from RBI state that the smaller the country:

- the narrower the choice of RBI projects (and the greater the reliance on individual projects and the lower the capacity of the economy to absorb potential negative spillover effects);
- the lower the domestic revenue retention (and the more stunted the economic linkages);
- the greater the dependence on export markets (and the greater the vulnerability to cyclical swings);
- the greater the dependence on MNRCs (and the higher the resulting political tensions over external economic dominance).

The following analysis of the country size constraint is structured around a discussion of the barriers to entry into RBI (Bain 1954). The three key barriers are technology, investment, and markets and each is examined in turn. The chapter concludes with an estimate of how the

TABLE 4.1. *Country size and domestic indices*

	(1) Area (m.km²)	(2) Population (m.)	(3) GDP (1981 $b.)	(4) Steel (m. tonnes)	(5) Aluminium (m. tonnes)	(6) Liquid fuel (m. tonnes)
Brazil	8.512	132.6	187.1	10.58	0.373	51.8
Saudi Arabia	2.150	11.1	109.4	6.60	n/a	n/a
Indonesia	1.919	158.9	80.6	3.43	0.044	21.2
Nigeria	0.924	96.5	73.5	3.75	n/a	8.1
Venezuela	0.912	16.8	47.5	3.25	0.063	17.2
Malaysia	0.333	15.3	29.3	2.65	n/a	7.2
Cameroon	0.475	9.9	7.8	0.15	0.021	0.5
Trinidad and Tobago	0.005	1.2	8.6	0.06	n/a	3.4
Bahrain	0.001	0.3	5.2	n/a	n/a	n/a

Sources: (1)–(3) World Bank (1986b); (4) International Iron and Steel Institute (1984); (5) Aluminium Association (1983); (6) World Bank (1983b).

potential economic stimulus shrinks with declining country size. Three qualifications of the hypothesized country size constraints emerge from the discussion. First, while none of the countries is as large as the base case, the oil windfalls permitted even the tiniest country to contemplate executing the largest projects—provided it accepted that the domestic economic stimulus would be signficantly lower than in larger countries and that greater dependence on MNRCs would be required to cushion the higher risks. Second, the pursuit of external and internal economies of scale encouraged premature RBI entry and overexpansion. This could trigger a Hirschmanian chain of unbalanced growth which might impart a 'big push' character to the RBI strategy. Third, such scale pressures introduced an X-efficiency factor into RBI strategy design and execution whereby larger countries traded their potential advantages for over-ambitious and less careful implementation. The corollary is that smaller countries, more mindful of risk, pursued more prudent policies and minimized their potential scale penalty.

TECHNOLOGICAL BARRIERS TO ENTRY

The RBI projects contemplated during the two oil booms involved investments ranging from around $175 million to upwards of $3 billion. The fact that Trinidad and Tobago came close to completing agreement with Tenneco/Midcon for the construction of a $3 billion LNG plant suggests that with appropriate institutional arrangements (and resource endowment) technology transfer did not present an insuperable barrier for even a tiny country wishing to proceed with a very large and complex project. However, some technologies were easier to transfer than others, so that both the risk of failure and the degree of external dependence varied, as a comparison of the RBI options shows.

Metals production: shifting technological barriers to entry
Whereas technological change in the steel industry worked to reduce the scale barrier to entry for developing countries, trends in the global aluminium industry moved in the opposite direction. Large integrated plants dominated steel production until the rapid diffusion of mini-mills commenced in the 1960s. Recent data suggest that the minimum viable size for a blast furnace is 1.5 million tonnes. Since at least two such units are required to service a series of steel furnaces, the blast furnace sets the minimum viable size for integrated steel at 3 million tonnes. Even then, additional cost savings arise from the operation of three blast furnaces and, therefore from a shift up to 5 million tonnes (Barnett and Schorsch

1983). In contrast, greenfield DRI/steel units can be competitive at around 500,000 tonnes, greenfield scrap-based mini-mills have a minimum viable size around 200,000 tonnes, and secondhand scrap-based plants can be viable at less than 150,000 tonnes. However, since scrap-based plants do not further resource-processing, it is the DRI/steel process which is of more immediate interest here.

DRI/steel production was pioneered by HYSL in Mexico and Midrex in West Germany and its small scale and relative technical simplicity caused it to diffuse rapidly through the developing countries, notably in Latin America. The initial competitive advantage of DRI/steel lay in round products, used largely in the construction industry. These products typically account for half the demand in developing countries compared with one-third in the industrial countries. However, mini-mills and DRI/steel units have profited more from technological change than integrated plants so that they have begun to undercut the latter on an expanding range of products (Barnett and Crandall 1986).

Integrated steel plants are much more capital-intensive than DRI/steel: their capital costs per tonne of capacity are twice those of a DRI/steel unit. The integrated steel plant's large size presents a significant investment hurdle to most developing countries. The finishing facilities of an integrated plant add to scale and cost hurdles and impose greater technological demands. The rolling of flat products in which the integrated plants excel sets a minimum viable size of 1 million tonnes on cold rolling and 4 million tonnes on hot coil. To achieve adequate production runs on such equipment requires sizeable demand for specific flat-rolled products. Yet highly fragmented product markets pose an additional obstacle to integrated steel production in the developing countries noted below.

The rolling process in integrated steel calls for higher quality steel billet and tighter process control than in the case of rolled products because of the more rigorous specifications of end users. Apart from some NICs (Newly Industrializing Countries) such as South Korea and Brazil, industry experts consider the technical capacity of developing countries inadequate for successful entry into integrated steel production.

Although DRI/steel plants cannot supply the full range of products demanded in developing countries, the minimum viable size of 750,000 tonnes poses a smaller initial barrier to entry than the 4 million tonnes of integrated steel. DRI/steel expansion can occur in increments of 500,000 tonnes compared with 1.5 million tonnes for integrated steel plants.

The finishing of DRI/steel is less demanding than that of an integrated plant, in terms of both scale economies and technical requirements. The minimum viable size of plate mills is around 750,000 tonnes while for both rod and bar mills it is 500,000 tonnes and for seamless tube it is 250,000 tonnes. The cost savings in DRI/steel which arise from moving from 60 to 90 per cent capacity utilization are greater than those arising from a shift in installed capacity from 500,000 to 750,000 tonnes. DRI/steel can therefore capture most of the scale benefits from milling by operating two mills (to increase market flexibility) with 750,000 tonnes combined capacity.

Unlike steel, the aluminium industry experienced rising scale barriers. Whereas aluminium smelters of 50,000 tonnes were considered to be of minimum viable size in the 1960s, cost-reducing pressures had pushed this figure to around 200,000 tonnes by the 1980s, with more modest cost savings expected by adding a further 100,000 tonnes of capacity. The initial capital cost ($1 billion in a remote developing country site compared with two-thirds that figure if infrastructure is already established) is a substantial barrier to entry.

Finishing boosts aluminium's added value and improves marketing prospects. However, although aluminium ingot can bear freight costs more readily than steel (because the price ratios of aluminium ingot to flat and round steel products are three and five to one, respectively) aluminium finishing adds significantly to the initial investment and skill requirements. This is because plants of optimal size are large, ranging upwards from 25,000 tonnes for aluminium siding to 50,000 tonnes for packaging foil, 100,000 tonnes for auto sheet, and 200,000 tonnes for can sheet (Debell and Richardson 1974). The provision of power (350 MW for a worldscale smelter) further raises the initial investment and can double it if hydroelectric power is utilized. Full vertical integration (discussed below with reference to markets) further adds to the investment barrier.

Yet other factors worked to assist new developing country entrants into aluminium. Even the largest aluminium MNRCs sought joint-venture partners for expansion because rising capital costs sharply increased investment risk. Joint-ventures reduced such risk for MNRCs and provided access to an experienced technological and marketing partner for new state enterprises. In addition, the overexpansion of alumina capacity in the early 1970s glutted the market and removed what had historically been a critical technological barrier to entry.

Nevertheless, whereas entry into DRI/steel production appeared not to dictate procurement of an experienced technology partner, entry into aluminium production did. This factor had important implications since the steel sector generated proportionately more new RBI investments—and more failures—than any other RBI subsector in the eight oil-exporting countries.

Petrochemicals: large projects dictate technological partners

As with metals, petrochemical projects which were relatively small like fertilizer, methanol, and simple oil refineries presented few obstacles to successful technology transfer to developing countries. Larger projects such as complex oil refineries, olefins, and LNG dictated experienced MNRC partners. The Indonesian state-owned fertilizer corporation, PT Pusri became a model for RBI project implementation in developing countries. Pusri's success lay in the care taken with the initial fertilizer project in choosing technical assistance for plant design and construction as well as staff training. Although this boosted start-up costs compared with a more self-reliant strategy, such costs were quickly recouped through the smoothness of the start-up and the financial benefits flowing from rapid attainment of full capacity. More critically, the high operating performance established from the outset set standards which were viewed as both attainable and the minimum tolerable in subsequent projects. By the early 1980s PT Pusri was entirely locally staffed, operated its own consultancy business and ran an offshoot consultancy firm as a joint-venture with the MNRC equipment supplier.

The larger projects required experienced MNRC equity partners, not simply to guarantee the technical efficiency of the plants, but also—as with aluminium—to pool the investment risk and ensure market access. For example, in the early 1980s a 1 billion cfd (cubic feet per day) LNG plant called for a capital investment of more than $3 billion, excluding gas exploration, extraction, and pipeline investment. The liquefaction plant comprised one-third of the investment, the LNG tanker fleet a half, and the import terminal the remainder (Anderson and Daniels 1981). Successful financing of such a project was contingent on securing equity participation from the host government, the gas suppliers, and the gas purchasers (Office of Technology Assessment 1980). Nevertheless, with such a financial package, an LNG plant was a feasible option even for a country as tiny as Trinidad and Tobago (Auty and Gelb 1986).

Summarizing, the technology of the smaller RBI plants could be successfully transferred by wholly state-owned enterprises provided care was taken to involve experienced firms in training personnel and executing the initial project. For larger projects technological barriers could be overcome through joint-ventures with experienced MNRC equity partners and even the smallest of countries could contemplate the implementation of large, complex plants. However, significant MNRC equity participation in large projects in small countries would encounter political objections. This was especially so if capital outflows (perhaps due to legitimate investment incentives) appeared to occur at the expense of government rents. Yet, LNG aside, large RBI projects were undertaken with little or no MNRC equity participation. For example, aluminium projects were proposed and implemented with as little as 10 per cent MNRC equity participation. However, such arrangements failed to ensure an MNRC commitment to effective plant operation. They neglected risks in marketing and investment, to which attention now turns.

INVESTMENT BARRIERS TO ENTRY

RBI project investment characteristics

Four important characteristics of RBI investment area:

- sizeable internal economies of scale,
- increases in those scale economies moving upstream,
- economies of vertical integration,
- agglomeration economies.

Table 4.2 summarizes the relationship between scale and unit investment costs for representative RBI projects under the assumption that adequate basic infrastructure already exists. First, it demonstrates that there are significant scale economies for all products. The final column in Table 4.2 shows the total investment requirements for worldscale units, i.e. plants of a size considered the minimum required to assure international competitiveness. The capital costs of RBI plants during the second oil boom ranged upwards from around $175 million for methanol and fertilizer plants through $250–350 million for simple oil refineries and ethylene plants to multibillion dollar integrated steel plants and LNG systems. Yet even these high figures still understate the total investment cost for reasons discussed later.

A second important characteristic of most, though not all, RBI projects is the tendency for the scale of production to increase going upstream along the processing chain from the fabricated product to the mineral extraction stage. For example, a worldscale cold rolling mill has a capacity of 1 million tonnes compared with 4 million tonnes for an integrated steel plant and 10 million tonnes for a worldscale iron ore mine. Or, in the case of bauxite processing, the vertical chain runs from a 50,000 tonne foil plant to a 200,000 tonne smelter, a 1 million tonne

TABLE 4.2. *Scale and capital cost for selected RBI projects 1979–81 oil boom*

Project	Scale and capital cost					Worldscale ($b.)
Methanol[a]						
Capacity (1,000 tpy)	180	365	730	910		0.175
Capital Cost ($1981/t)	360	290	240	240		
Ammonia[b]						
Capacity (1,000 tpy)	300	590				0.186
Capital Cost ($1980/t)	315	275				
Ethylene[b]						
Capacity (1,000 tpy)	110	225	500	680		0.328
Capital Cost ($1980/t)	1000	800	655	610		
Refinery (Hydroskim)[c]						
Capacity (1,000 bpd)	25	60	120	240		0.367
Capital Cost ($1981/bl.)	3200	2300	1780	1530		
Refinery (Hydrocracker Unit)[c]						
Capacity (1,000 bpd)	5	10	30			0.240
Capital Cost ($1981/bl.)	11000	10000	8000			
LNG Project (10000 km haul)[d]						
Capacity (mcfd)	250	500	1000	2000		1.716
Capital Cost ($1982/cfd)	7.6	6.4	4.7	4.3		
Steel Mini-mill[e]						
Capacity (m tonnes)	0.10	0.25	0.50	1.00	1.50	0.275
Capital Cost ($1981/t)	550	400	300	275	275	
Steel Integrated Unit[e]						
Capacity (m. tonnes)	0.50	1.00	2.00	3.00	6.00	3.15
Capital Cost ($1981/t)	2000	1500	1200	1050	800	
Aluminium Smelter[f]						
Capacity (m. tonnes)	0.10	0.20	0.30			0.70
Capital Cost ($1980/t)	4080	3480	3300			

Note: A worked example of scale and capital cost figures for methanol. As capacity rises from 180,000 tpy to 365,000 tpy the cost per tonne of capacity falls from $360 to $290 (indicating the presence of scale economies). Scale economies are exhausted at 730,000 tonnes, since an increase to 910,000 tonnes does not lead to any change in the cost which remains steady at $240 per tonne.

Sources:
[a] Rischard (1982)
[b] UNIDO (1981)
[c] Wijetilleke and Ody (1984)
[d] Dinapoli (1984)
[e] Barnett and Schorsch (1983)
[f] Brown et al. (1983)

alumina refinery, and a 3 million tonne worldscale bauxite mine. One important consequence of this is that the second (refining) stage in resource processing is often the most demanding in terms of capital investment and represents a 'hump' which must be surmounted to link resource extraction to the less risky projects further downstream.

Vertical integration is a third characteristic of RBI which has been particularly important in boosting barriers to entry in aluminium, olefins, and LNG. The large fixed RBI investments need to run close to full capacity for profitable operation so that a competitive and secure supply of raw materials as well as access to market outlets have been important objectives. New entrants in aluminium, olefins, and LNG have traditionally sought full vertical integration in the face of market imperfections which created uncertainty over the competitive pricing of key inputs as well as market access. Despite the rapid post-war expansion of global markets for RBI products market imperfections have persisted so that vertical integration remains advantageous (Auty 1983c, Vernon 1983a).

The advantages of the larger country in securing a vertically integrated raw material supply are well illustrated by contrasting the alumina sourcing options open to Venezuela with those of Bahrain or Trinidad and Tobago. Yet domestic sourcing signficantly inflates the investment barrier, by $1 billion for a worldscale alumina refinery and $350 million for a bauxite mine. In the absence of an adequate domestic market, full vertical integration calls for overseas investment which has proved politically difficult to justify even for firms in low-absorbing countries with 'surplus' capital resources. Although reliance on joint-ventures with MNRCs can provide market access such a partnership may prove especially unpalatable to small countries fearful of domination by MNRCs. Smaller oil-exporting countries are therefore disadvantaged not only by the scale of investment such large integrated projects demand but also by the loss of productive linkages and the risk of MNRC dominance.

Finally, RBI exhibits agglomeration economies, both in terms of the infrastructure requirements of the larger projects and also for the linked supplying and processing activities. RBI projects frequently require large infrastructure investments for transportation and utilities which typically comprise upwards of 30 per cent of total capital requirements. Such infrastructure is itself subject to internal economies of scale. It is an important factor pushing up the minimum viable size of directly productive activities like bauxite mines and smelters (Brown *et al.* 1983).

The combination of internal and external economies of scale exerts constant pressure for further RBI expansion. Efforts to rectify imbalances between complementary investments can trigger a Hirschmanian chain of unbalanced growth (Hirschman 1958) which, especially in the case of larger countries with wider options, holds the potential to compound mistakes as well as successes. In the extreme, such pressures confer a 'big push' character to the strategy of RBI (Rosenstein-Rodan 1943).

In summary, there are significant economies of scale in all RBI projects. They pose especially large initial barriers to entry in the cases of aluminium, complex oil refineries, olefins, and LNG. Moreover, the economies of scale tend to increase going upstream from fabrication to resource extraction so that RBI investment represents a 'hump' between resource extraction and the smaller less risky downstream investments. Vertical integration further boosts the individual plant investment barrier to entry in the cases of aluminium, olefins, and LNG. The agglomeration economies add further expansionary pressure. The net effect may trigger sizeable investments to rectify imbalances along the production chain and thereby transform an RBI strategy into a 'big push'.

Understated investment costs

Before making any comparisons between the scale of investment and the potential investment capacity of the eight oil-exporting countries it should be noted that the figures in Table 4.2 understate the actual costs likely to be encountered. There are four main reasons for this and they reinforce the scale-related pressures for expansion noted above. First, RBI requires appropriate infrastructure and the sizeable investments required tend to bear down most heavily on the initial projects of an RBI strategy and/or projects in isolated locations. Second, construction costs are likely to be higher in most developing countries than those assumed in the base case. This is because the specialized capital equipment must be shipped longer distances than in industrialized countries while gaps in skills require significant numbers of highly paid expatriate workers. UNIDO (1981) estimated for the early 1980s that, if construction costs in the US Gulf equalled 1.0 then similar plants in Latin America would have a ratio of 1.2; the Middle East of 1.6; and Indonesia 2.1. These ratios, calculated at the peak of the second oil boom, subsequently declined.

A third factor which pushes up investment costs arises through the 'enhancement' of domestic RBI benefits by the installation of additional processing facilities designed to improve market flexibility. This can significantly boost total investment even for those smaller projects where pressures for vertical integration are otherwise weak. For example, the addition of a urea plant to process all or part of the ammonia production may boost the basic ammonia plant investment by a half or two-thirds. Or again, the addition of hydrocrackers to reduce the high proportion of fuel oil to total products in hydroskimming refineries (and thereby more nearly match the domestic product profile in developing countries) can substantially add to construction costs (Table 4.2). Examples from metals include the addition of briquette plants (and even electric arc furnaces) to widen the market for specialized DRI projects and the installation of a second product mill downstream from the steel furnaces. Efforts to capture the indirect benefits from the domestic fabrication of RBI products like steel and LLDPE add further to RBI 'enhancement'.

A fourth factor boosting total investment costs arises from the attraction of brownfield expansion. Even where worldwide plants are established from the outset, there remain scale benefits to be derived, albeit often modest ones. They arise when further expansion of production lines permit the fuller use of maintenance or infrastructure facilities. In addition, pecuniary economies of scale can be secured through the spread of marketing and other overhead costs over an expanding volume of production. Such brownfield expansion typically provides additional capacity at 75 or even 50 per-cent of the investment cost of greenfield capacity. An extreme example of this process arose in the mid-1980s in Guayana (Venezuela) when the region's low opportunity costs for engineering and construction manpower was used to justify additional large investment in hydro-based RBI.

Having noted why the investment figures in Table 4.2 tend to understate actual capital outlays, attention now turns to an evaluation of individual country investment capacity.

Country size and RBI investment capacity

Some simple assumptions about the total rate of domestic investment and its broad sectoral allocation are required before specifically addressing the issue of the country size constraint on RBI investment. Data are drawn from the short second (1979–81) oil boom in order to minimize problems arising out of the very high inflation rates in the international capital goods industry in the 1970s. During the second boom aggregate investment in the eight oil-exporting countries was around one-quarter of their GDP. Assuming first that the manufacturing sector accounted for one-fifth of GDP (a figure erring on the high side since actual shares ranged from around 6 per cent in West Africa and Arabia to 25 per cent in Malaysia) and second that investment in it exhibited an ICOR of three, then to achieve a not atypical 10 per cent annual growth rate in manufacturing output would require the investment of 6.5 per cent of GDP, or about one-quarter of the total investment resources.

If just over one-third of this (i.e. 2.5 per cent of GDP) is assumed the maximum assignable to RBI without crowding out investment in other intermediate and consumer goods, then the actual resources available to each country for RBI investment are shown in column 3 of Table 4.3. Compared with the $4.5 billion annual RBI investment available for a large country like Brazil, the annual investment resources for medium-large, mid-sized, and small countries would be, respectively, $1.9 billion, $1 billion, and $200 million. Finally, if for simplicity of exposition it is assumed that project outlays are made in three equal annual instalments, then the medium-large countries could implement a mix of large and small RBI projects, but small countries would be constrained by risk-minimizing considerations to two of the smallest projects.

The oil windfalls opened up much greater possibilities, especially if—as many observers thought in 1980—the high oil revenues were sustained over a considerable time period rather than evaporating in a brief once-for-all boom. Column 4 of Table 4.3 shows the size of the additional capital resources available if RBI investment was allocated one-third of the windfall (a not atypical figure). The effect is to quadruple the total resources available for RBI (Table 4.3, column 5). This excludes the matching investment inflow from MNRC equity and foreign bank lending which 'prudent' financing permitted, let alone the additional capital available if suppliers' credits were used to boost the loan component of finance to 70 per cent, a common outcome in practice. Medium-large countries could now entertain the simultaneous implementation of several large projects while even the smallest countries could proceed with one large project alongside several smaller ones.

Summarizing, if the revenues from the oil windfall are excluded then the largest projects were clearly beyond the reach of small countries unless they were prepared to concede most of the equity/ownership to MNRCs. The oil windfall transformed this situation by allowing even the smallest countries to entertain the prospect of implementing very large projects as, indeed, tiny Trinidad and Tobago did (Auty and Gelb 1986).

TABLE 4.3. *Potential country investment capacity, 1979–1981 oil boom ($b)*

Country	(1) Total investment at 25% of GDP	(2) Manufacturing's share of total investment	(3) Intermediates' share of total investment	(4) Intermediates' share of oil windfall	(5) Total investment in intermediates
Brazil	47.0	11.3	4.7	—	4.7
Indonesia	20.0	4.8	2.0	5.2	7.2
Saudi Arabia	27.0	6.5	2.7	21.7	24.4
Nigeria	18.0	4.3	1.8	6.6	8.4
Venezuela	12.0	2.9	1.2	1.7	2.9
Malaysia	7.0	1.7	0.7	n/a	n/a
Cameroon	2.0	0.5	0.2	n/a	n/a
Trinidad and Tobago	2.0	0.5	0.2	0.6	0.8
Bahrain	1.0	0.2	0.1	n/a	n/a

Sources: Gelb (1986*a*), World Bank (1986*b*)

TABLE 4.4. *Worldscale plant's share of global/national market, second oil boom 1979–1981*

Product	(1) Worldscale plant size (m. tonnes)	(2) Share of global market (%)	(3) Share of Brazil market (%)
Ammonia	0.590	0.5	65.2
Methanol	0.730	7.0	384.2
DRI/steel	0.500	0.1	4.7
Aluminium smelter	0.200	1.3	53.4
Ethylene cracker	0.500	1.4	41.7
Integrated steel	4.000	0.6	38.2
LNG	7.300	16.6	n/a

Sources: Sheldrick (1985a); Rischard (1982); Hough (1984); International Iron and Steel Institute (1984); USITC (1983).

MARKET BARRIERS TO ENTRY

Along with technology and scale of investment, the market provided a third potential barrier to RBI entry. As originally envisaged by its proponents in the 1970s RBI was intended to substitute/complement exports of unprocessed resources by/with processed exports (Radetzki 1977). However, global market structure and transfer cost penalties arising from long freight hauls, tariffs, and lack of close communication with customers made the export strategy riskier and less remunerative than—where country size permitted—production for domestic markets.

Export markets for RBI products

Table 4.4 shows the relationship between a worldscale plant and two markets: the world market (column 2) and the domestic market of a large developing country (column 3). At the global level, the table shows that worldscale plants are large relative to the world market for LNG (16 per cent) and methanol (7 per cent), small for aluminium and ethylene (around 1.3 per cent), and smaller still for ammonia and DRI/ steel. However, these simple ratios understate the potential market barrier because of distance-dictated fragmentation of the global market into regional markets and the resultant producer/consumer concentration.

Producer concentration was highest in the aluminium industry where declining partial oligopoly left the six largest producers still responsible for more than half global output in the late 1970s. Through the post-war period the vertically integrated aluminium majors sought to replicate their original national production chains by linking new African and Latin American mines to North Atlantic markets and Australian mines to those of the North Pacific. Mindful of anti-trust legislation, the MNRCs attempted to smooth the addition of new capacity along the production chain through target pricing, barometric price leadership, and the reallocation of profits between production stages (Auty 1983*b*). However, the six producers failed to prevent the emergence of surplus alumina capacity in the early 1970s which, together with substantial energy price changes, lowered entry barriers for aspiring new producers at locations offering cheap energy and bauxite. Stuckey (1983) has argued that the established producers sought to reconcile their interests with those of new entrants through increased recourse to risk-sharing, joint-venture partnerships premissed on access to MNRC technical skills and thereby to retard the decline of orderly marketing.

LNG markets also tended to be regional rather than global, and they too exhibited concentration (this time consumer concentration, in which Japan was pre-eminent). As with aluminium, multi-firm partnerships were usual in LNG, prompted by the desire to reduce risk. Such partnerships secured orderly marketing and satisfactorily screened new LNG projects.

Industry concentration was lower in the ethyelene market than in either aluminium or LNG, though vertical integration was still an important strategy for producers. The first and second oil shocks caused feedstocks to displace capital as the dominant determinant of ethylene competitiveness and caused resource-based producers heavily to discount their capital cost and transfer cost disadvantages. Consequently, even Malaysia aspired to the construction of an ethylene cracker, despite surplus capacity in neighbouring Singapore and a domestic demand which was one-quarter the output of a worldscale unit (Auty 1987*b*). However, apart from Saudi Arabia (which did build for export), the security of producing for a large domestic market proved the key attraction for ethylene projects and ethylene crackers figured prominently from an early date in the RBI strategies of the two medium-large countries in the sample group, Nigeria and Indonesia.

Domestic market constraints on RBI

Reliance on domestic markets promised higher margins than exports through lower transfer costs, the absence of tariffs, and superior customer communication. Some insurance against poor RBI viability was also offered by the prospect of monopolizing the domestic market. However, other cushions against low viability included the availability of feedstocks at discretionary prices and the steady erosion of high sunk capital costs by inflation. As a result, burdening domestic consumers with the costs of misconceived RBI projects seemed a last resort.

Table 4.1 shows domestic demand for selected RBI products in the sample countries during the early 1980s. It suggests that sufficient domestic demand existed in the mid-sized countries to support competitive integrated steel plants; and in the medium-large countries for oil refineries, fertilizer plants, and ethylene crackers, though not for methanol plants and aluminium smelters. Closer inspection reveals that the scale barrier is once more understated. There are two principal reasons for this. First, the statistics for domestic demand are inflated because they reflect markets during the peak of the second 1979–81 oil boom rather than a more 'normal' long-term trend. Second, the size of effective demand in developing country markets is diminished by product differentiation. For example, although Venezuelan demand for aluminium had expanded very rapidly to almost 100,000 tonnes by the early 1980s some 50,000 tonnes of this comprised canstock which is most competitively produced in mills of twice that scale. Similarly, a suboptimal 40,000 bpd oil refinery constructed by Cameroon produced too high a fraction of heavy products so that export markets for relatively small volumes of fuel oil were required while imports of lighter products persisted.

A final example of how market fragmentation reduced economies of scale is provided by fertilizers: despite the high aggregate volume of its agricultural production, Malaysia's ammonia demand remained insufficient to support a worldscale plant because the country's diversified agricultural production created very varied fertilizer requirements. Small and medium-small countries therefore clearly faced heavy dependence on export markets. In this context it is interesting to note that an analysis of the industrialization of Latin America's two largest countries (Brazil and Argentina) by Teitel and Thoumi (1986) found that intermediate industries like RBI appeared in the final stage of the industrialization process.

New entrants also underestimated the barrier to market exit (Vernon 1983a) as well as market entry. This arose partly from the inertia of large sunk capital costs and partly from the volatility of the post-1960s international economy. As noted earlier, the proliferation of new entrants—many with access to public or parent company financial

TABLE 4.5. *Revenue retention in large and small countries (%)*

Sector	Operating cost		Total cost	
	L	S	L	S
Ammonia	72	60	72	68
Steel	74	32	73	42
Aluminium	84	22	80	38

Notes: L = large country; S = small country.
Source: Auty (1986*b*).

resources—reduced the pre-1970s homogeneity of producer goals and further increased market rigidity.

REDUCED REVENUE RETENTION AND STUNTED
LINKAGES IN SMALL COUNTRIES

The barriers to entry faced by oil-exporting countries seemed low, given expectations of rising real energy prices. Even small countries could aspire to the implementation of a mix of large and small RBI projects, although they were more dependent on MNRC assistance and export markets than large countries. Smaller countries would also experience greater revenue leakage and more stunted linkages than larger countries.

Assuming efficient project implementation and prices which covered the replacement costs of greenfield producers, Table 4.5 shows the decrease in the domestic revenue retention coefficient (RRC) for ammonia, aluminium, and steel projects experienced by small countries. The principal differences between sectors result from operating costs since, for the purpose in hand, flows to service capital are assumed identical for large and small projects. The reduction in the RRC is smallest for ammonia because, unlike the metals, it uses few inputs other than gas and labour. The fraction of domestic revenue from operating costs drops from 72 per cent for the large country to 60 per cent. However, the inclusion of capital charges narrows the difference to only 4 per cent.

Steel production shows a similar total cost RRC to that of ammonia for the large country (73 per cent) but a much lower one (42 per cent) for the small country. This reflects both the higher share of operating costs in total costs and also the sizeable non-labour input requirements of steel production. For aluminium smelting the difference in the two

RRCs is much larger at 58 per cent (i.e. 80 per cent compared with 22 per cent) even though capital costs—at one-third of total costs—are more significant in aluminium production than in steel production. Leakages for major input purchases are the key factor.

Clearly, the underlying assumption that the smaller country has fewer opportunities to internalize domestic production implies that its final demand and fiscal linkages will also be characterized by a higher import content and loss of potential stimulus. Although the exact magnitude of loss involved cannot be calculated from the available data, some indication of forward linkage losses can be given. In the case of DRI/ steel, a tiny market such as that of Trinidad and Tobago could absorb 60,000 tonnes albeit with negligible further processing while that of a medium-small country, Cameroon, was around twice as big. Consequently, such countries must export 80–90 per cent of production at margins trimmed 15 per cent and upwards by freight costs, tariffs, and penalties against offshore suppliers. The mid-sized and larger countries could expect to dispose of all sales domestically and around half would go into further processing—albeit of a rudimentary nature—rather than into construction. However, such an advantageous scenario assumes that there are no existing domestic finishers of imported billet to compete with—a rare occurrence even in the smallest country.

In the case of aluminium domestic demand would absorb an even smaller fraction of the production of a worldscale smelter. Even a mid-sized country with a relatively high per caput income like Venezuela could not dispose domestically of more than one-third the output of a worldscale smelter. Around one-third of such domestic sales would comprise relatively high added value products generating revenues twice those of ingot, but most would secure smaller price premiums only one-fifth higher than ingot. Nor would aluminium exports realize greater added value: the bulk of the exports would occur as ingot since higher added value products such as extrusions tend to be market orientated. For example, the main fabricated aluminium export of Venezuela in the early 1980s was cable, which attracted prices less than 20 per cent higher than ingot sales.

Similar conditions apply in the case of olefins where the output of a worldscale plant is likely to exceed domestic demand in a medium-large country. For olefins exports, proximity to cheap raw materials becomes less advantageous moving along the production chain and convenient customer access becomes dominant (Banque Indosuez 1985). The relatively small size of RBI labour costs (5 per cent of total fob costs for ammonia and less than 4 per cent for metals) mean that even if RBI workers capture wages no higher than the base case (a rare outcome in reality) export penetration would be little improved.

The benefits enjoyed by the larger country over the smaller one require an important qualification. Capture of the scale-related economic stimulus is not automatic: capture of productive linkages requires additional *prudent* investment so that resources are not denied to more productive uses or—worse yet—sunk in poorly executed projects triggered by an ill-conceived RBI strategy. Just as expansion can compound the benefits from the initial investment in a well-executed RBI project so too the disbenefits associated with a poorly conceived and executed RBI strategy can be multiplied.

RBI's scale-driven pressures for further outlays—either to enhance expected benefits or to retrieve a substandard outcome—risk transforming the RBI strategy into a 'big push'. While such risks are greater the smaller and less diversified the economy, the actual scale of the 'big push' RBI strategy means that even the largest countries in the sample could be severely affected by a poorly conceived and executed RBI strategy. Moreover, there is evidence of the operation of an X-inefficiency factor in scale-sensitive industries whereby large producers (countries) may squander their size advantage through overambitious strategy design or rash implementation (Auty 1986*b*).

CONCLUSION: PRESSURE FOR PREMATURE ENTRY AND OVERAMBITIOUS RBI

The economies of scale are substantial in most RBI projects, increase moving upstream from fabrication to resource extraction in many, and are reinforced by agglomeration economies as well as vertical integration (in the cases of aluminium, ethylene, and LNG). Nevertheless, even the tiny oil-exporting countries could hope to implement a mix of large and small RBI projects since technological barriers to entry could be removed through joint-ventures with MNRC partners while investment barriers were shrunk by the oil windfalls.

Yet smaller countries still remained potentially disadvantaged compared with the mid-sized and medium-large countries. Their politically costly dependence on MNRCs was higher; their reliance on export markets for largely unfabricated products was almost total; and their RRCs and domestic linkages were significantly smaller, especially for metals.

However, if technological and investment barriers could be easily surmounted, market barriers were less easily overcome. This was so even for countries with sizeable domestic demand, because product differentiation stunted potential forward linkages and shrank the effective size of such markets. This increased dependence on exports where margins were lower and risks greater.

Cost reductions from brownfield expansion, agglomeration economies, and vertical integration interacted with subtler pressures for the enhancement of existing projects through investment in product diversification to increase the scale of commitment. The persistence of scale economies exerted pressure for premature entry and over-expansion. The first (refining) RBI investment assumed the character of a 'hump' to be overcome in order to link extraction operations with the smaller and less risky downstream investments. The initial RBI project had the capacity to trigger a Hirschmanian chain of unbalanced growth. Pushed to its logical conclusion the capture of internal economies of scale, vertical integration benefits, and agglomeration economies imparted a 'big push' character to RBI.

However, the triggering of linkages which made RBI so attractive, especially to the larger countries, held the potential for negative compounding if the RBI strategy was ill-conceived or poorly executed. While such disadvantageous compounding of inefficiency was inherently more threatening for the smaller and less diversified country, poorly implemented and overambitious RBI strategies could overwhelm the capacity of even large countries to mute their unfavourable spillover effects.

Under such circumstances the scale disadvantage might even be reversed. It is not uncommon where economies of scale exist for an X-inefficiency factor to operate whereby larger firms (countries) trade their size advantages for bolder and/or less rigorously implemented strategies while smaller ones, wary of their greater risk, offset the size disadvantages through more prudent strategy design and execution. The overoptimistic assumptions of the RBI feasibility studies examined in Chapter 5 created conditions conducive to overambitious RBI.

5

Extent and External Causes of RBI Resource Rent Overestimation

Chapter 3 showed that the anticipated benefits from RBI rested heavily on the capture of resource rents. Most RBI feasibility studies indicated that RBI resource rents would be forthcoming. They encouraged the oil-exporting countries to discount the risk associated with RBI and to frame ambitious RBI strategies. However, the feasibility studies employed price projections which proved universally optimistic, especially after the abrupt puncturing of the second oil boom. Consequently, the actual price out-turn caused the expected resource rents to shrink substantially, or—in many cases—to be eliminated entirely. Depressed prices placed a premium on the resilience of individual RBI projects. The efficiency of project execution and operation therefore assumed a critical role in minimizing the potentially damaging negative spillover effects of the RBI projects.

Before turning to evaluate the importance of internal (efficiency) constraints on RBI (Chapters 6 to 9), it is necessary to isolate the impact of external factors outside individual country control such as market and interest-rate shifts. This is accomplished in four steps. First, the potential resource rents are estimated under the base case assumptions. Second, the extent of the actual shortfall in price projections and its effect on resource rents is measured. Third, the flaws in the feasibility studies (especially the sensitivity tests) are analysed; and, finally, the explanations advanced for the sizeable market miscalculation are reviewed.

THE CENTRAL IMPORTANCE OF RESOURCE RENTS

The Displacement Factor: Mid-1970s Rent Projection

In a pioneering mid-1970s analysis of the potential for energy-intensive industrialization in the Persian/Arabian Gulf Stauffer (1975) compared the netback for gas used in indusrial exports with that for gas used in support of crude oil exports. He evaluated five gas-based export options (fertilizer, methanol, DRI/steel, aluminium, and LNG) along with two applications of gas that support crude oil exports (reinjection to improve oil well yields and substitution for fuel oil in oil refineries). His findings are summarized in Table 5.1.

The netback is the sum remaining per thousand cubic feet of gas input after deducting transformation and shipping costs but before deducting the costs of gas exploration and extraction. In order to derive the resource rent, the costs of gas exploration and extraction must be deducted from the netback. Such discovery and exploration costs might range from nothing where the gas occurred as associated gas and/or gas liquids covered extraction costs, up to more than $3/MCF (thousand cubic feet) for small or deep-drilled gas fields. Typical costs in the mid-1970s ranged from $0.25 to $0.75/MCF. Table 5.1 indicates that few RBI projects promised significant resource rents in the 1970s.

An important conclusion of Stauffer's analysis is that the potential netbacks per unit of heat value on gas-based industrial exports are significantly lower than those for more easily transportable crude oil exports. Table 5.1 shows that, among the gas-based export products, the netback on fertilizer would be superior to that on aluminium and LNG, while the netback on steel would be the least attractive. However, even the netback for fertilizer would be inferior to that generated by gas used to increase the volume of crude oil exports either through reinjection to boost reservoir output or through substitution for oil used as oil refinery fuel.

The sizeable difference between the netbacks on gas used for energy-intensive export products and those from its use in support of crude oil exports reflected the high costs per unit of heat value required to transform gas into a transportable (marketable) form. The cost per unit of heat value of getting crude oil to distant markets was much lower than that for petrochemicals or metal. After deducting discovery and extraction costs from the netback, few RBI projects yielded large resource rents at mid-1970s prices.

The second important conclusion from Stauffer's paper concerns the displacement effect of (low-rent) gas-based industrial exports on (high-rent) exports of crude oil. On the assumption that gas-based industrial exports would reduce production of such goods in the industrial countries and thereby correspondingly reduce the industrial countries' demand for imported crude oil. Stauffer incorporated the loss of future oil revenue streams into the netback estimates (column C in Table 5.1 compared with column A). The high displacement factor in column C reflects conditions faced by the low-absorbing oil exporters with large oil reserves who would be most affected by lower future oil export

TABLE 5.1. *Netback to alternative gas uses. Persian/Arabian Gulf 1975*

Gas use	Gas input (MCF/tonne)	Investment ($/MCF/Yr)	Transport cost ($/tonne)	Transport cost ($/MCF)	Gas value[a] ($/MCF)		
					A	B	C
Servicing oil export							
Reinjection	n/a	n/a	—	—			
Refinery fuel	4.00	18.00	0–1.5	0–0.33	1.68	1.39	0.70
Gas export products							
LNG	59.00	2.35	90.00	1.58	0.89	0.60	(0.09)
Methanol	19.50	4.65	n/a	n/a	n/a	n/a	n/a
Intermediates							
Sponge iron	16.00	5.00	25.00	1.50	0.60	0.31	(0.38)
Steel	21.00	n/a	25.00	1.10	—	—	—
Aluminium	113.00	14.00	25.00	0.22	0.94	0.65	(0.04)
Ammonia	39.00	4.30	n/a	n/a	1.10	0.81	0.12

[a] The displacement of future oil export income streams is incorporated by assigning a discounted value to long-term oil revenues. The displacement impact is allowed to vary as follows:

A. Unadjusted Project Netback: expressed per MCF of gas input after deducting the costs of freight, processing (where applicable), and gathering.

B. As A, but with a small displacement deduction to reflect a relatively short lifespan for oil exports under the assumption of a high ratio of gas to oil reserves. The calculations reflect low opportunity costs for gas exports in terms of future oil revenues foregone.

C. As A, but with a high displacement factor for future oil-based income, reflecting the assumption of relatively large oil reserves.

Source: Stauffer (1975: 6, 43, 44).

revenues. The reduction of future oil income streams would be less damaging to the high-absorbing oil-exporters with more limited oil reserves. Column B of Table 5.1 reflects this difference.

Stauffer held back from concluding that the low absorbing oil-exporting countries should not pursue a strategy of energy-intensive industrialization. He noted that the overall benefits from industrialization might offset the displacement effect in the low absorbing countries, though he made no attempt to quantify such compensatory effects. Despite his remarkably insightful analysis, Stauffer did not anticipate how the displacement factor might interact with price-induced oil conservation to erode the oil windfalls.

For the present purpose it is sufficient to note that energy-intensive RBI projects, whether for export or import substitution, were means for the oil exporters to sell more energy and, as such, were potential competitors for crude oil exports. Judged from this perspective, RBI emerges as a minimalist diversification strategy: like crude oil exports it was heavily dependent on resource rents. However, RBI proved more vulnerable than crude oil exports to falling energy prices because it had inherently lower resource rent.

The large resource rents projected in the second boom

The euphoric second oil boom of 1979–81, when many RBI projects were under construction or sanctioned, eliminated any lingering caution engendered by the tapering of the first oil boom. Table 5.2 shows the estimated mid-1980s netbacks on RBI projects under two sets of prices. The first set of prices is a 1980 projection that reflects the pervasive optimism of the second oil boom and yields very large netbacks. The second set of prices in Table 5.2 comprises actual mid-1980s prices and generates much lower gas netbacks than the first set. It was not possible to generate a set of 1980 price projections for all the RBI products in Table 5.2 from a single source, so that some of the variation in the projected netbacks reflects differences in price projection assumptions. It should also be noted that the relatively small energy input per unit of physical output for urea and steel production heightens the sensitivity of their netbacks to price changes *vis-à-vis* the other products.

A comparison of the projected netbacks for the mid-1970s and mid-1980s (Table 5.1, column A and Table 5.2) shows sharply higher netbacks for the later period. A small part of the difference arises from assuming that the mid-1980s projects are implemented in a large efficient developing country (the base case) rather than Stauffer's Persian/Arabian Gulf locale, but the main cause of the higher netbacks is

TABLE 5.2. *Base case netbacks to alternative gas uses, projected and actual 1985 prices*

| Gas use | 1985 price ($/tonne) | | Gas input | FOB cost | Freight | Gas netback ($MBTU) | |
	Projected	Actual	(MCF/tonne)	($/tonne)	($/tonne)	Projected	Actual
Gas product exports							
LNG	382.00	241.90	59.0	162.80	44.30	2.96	0.59
Methanol	321.17	150.00	42.6	77.70	30.00	5.01	0.91
Intermediates							
Steel	361.00	259.00	21.00	173.60	30.00	7.51	2.64
Aluminium	2402.10	1081.20	113.00	1218.30	30.00	10.25	(1.44)
LDPE	1401.00	590.00	65.70	408.60	40.00	13.37	2.15
Urea	342.60	148.70	23.70	86.30	20.00	9.97	1.79
Crude oil							
export	323.70	203.77	—	3.01	1.50	6.84	3.84

Source: World Bank (1980 (2nd edn. 1985)) projected prices escalated from 1980 constant dollar prices by 6 per cent/annum 1980–5 for LNG, oil, urea, and aluminium; Rischard (1982) for methanol; Mobil Chemical Company (1985) for LDPE; Industry sources for steel.

the more optimistic price projections of the second oil boom. The central assumptions of the 1980 oil price projections were that rapid economic growth, continuing high inflation, and real price increases in energy and energy-related products would coexist. If gas discovery and extraction costs are assumed to have doubled from the mid-1970s in line with underlying inflation (i.e. so that they ranged from $0.50 to $1.50/MCF), then the potential RBI resource rents were very large indeed.

Actual mid-1980s resource rents

The second oil boom price projections overestimated actual mid-1980s prices for oil and LNG (tied to the oil price) by a factor of 1.6. This was the case even before the sharp 1986 oil price decline. Prices for methanol, urea, and aluminium (calculated along with that of oil from the same source, the World Bank 1980 and 1985) and also LDPE (Mobil Chemical Company 1985) were overestimated by a factor of 2.2. The lower ratio for steel, at around 1.4, reflects the more conservative assumptions about links between existing and future prices in this sector.

The variation among netbacks for products produced under base case assumptions using actual mid-1980s prices is less than that based on the 1980 price projections. In particular, the actual base case netback for steel (Table 5.2) is high in relation to alternative RBI investments because the steel production cost estimates contain a stronger efficiency bias than the other cost models. It is also high in comparison with the actual returns on the projects which were implemented in the eight oil-exporting countries because the steel plants that were built performed significantly worse than any other RBI sector. This serves as a reminder that the base case assumptions were invariably superior to actual operating conditions.

As with the mid-1970s calculations (Table 5.1) the actual RBI gas netbacks (Table 5.2) are lower than those from oil. RBI projects could still generate a positive netback on the energy input, albeit a much more modest one than that calculated from the 1980 price projections, with the exception of aluminium. However, after deducting $0.50 to $1.50/ MCF for the gas discovery and extraction cost, resource rents were negligible or eliminated entirely. Since the RBI projects that were implemented invariably had higher costs than those assumed in Table 5.2, their resource rents in the mid-1980s were frequently negative. A review of RBI feasibility studies shows why the risks associated with RBI were underestimated and points to the importance of demand mis-calculations for the disappointing outcome.

THE FEASIBILITY STUDY SENSITIVITY TESTS

The role of feasibility studies

As well as quantifying the projected returns and testing their sensitivity, rigorous feasibility studies provided an important check on the fuzzier, less tangible economic objectives (such as technology transfer) used by governments to discount unwelcome cautious financial advice. The execution of a feasibility study for a large RBI project requires careful evaluation of the technical specifications, production costs, market prospects, and rates of return.

No matter how carefully the data are compiled, many unknown variables remain. Some are potentially under the investor's control, like the quality of the project construction and operating management team. However, there remain key external parameters which are unknown and cannot be controlled. Some of these—such as long-term trends in demand, inflation, and interest rates—have become increasingly difficult to determine since the 1960s. Although sensitivity analysis can explore the penalties for miscalculation, it does nothing to remove uncertainty. The potential for error in the most meticulous of feasibility studies is substantial.

Moreover, even a carefully executed feasibility study could not prevent governments from manipulating the figures to make a favoured policy choice appear more desirable. Although a figure of 8 per cent appears to have been widely accepted as the minimum return most governments were prepared to accept in sanctioning low risk projects, laxness occurred in the rigour with which projected lower targets were accepted as cut-offs for RBI investment. For example, relatively low returns could be improved by widening the definition of government cash flows to include taxation and the margin on gas sales, as in the example of the Trinidad and Tobago steel plant (Table 5.3). Or again, depreciation and operating costs were included in the 8 per cent 'return' sought by the Venezuelan government on the large Guri hydroelectric project. Shadow pricing was also employed on occasion to augment the national benefit, though the limited importance of factors like labour costs which were sensitive to such changes meant the divergence between adjusted and unadjusted rates was slight (UNICO 1974).

Consensus, commitment, and feasibility study reliability

The international business community relied heavily on consensus about future trends in face of the heightened uncertainty of the post-1960s period. It believed that high oil prices would generate large oil windfalls

TABLE 5.3. *Scenarios for Trinidad and Tobago DRI/steel plant, July 1981 ($468 million investment)*

Performance Index	'Minimum'	'Optimistic'
Cumulative net cash flow to 1990 ($b.)	0.658	1.159
Discounted cash flow on equity 1977–95 (%)	13.00	20.00
Cumulative accrual ($b.)[a]	1.818	2.318
Cumulative discounted return on equity (%)	22.00	30.00
Payback period (years)[b]	9.0	7.0
Payback period (years)[c]	7.0	6.0

Notes: Details on price assumptions etc. not available.
[a] Net cash flow + corporation taxes + gas margin.
[b] Based on cumulative net cash flow.
[c] Based on cumulative accruals.

Source: National Energy Corporation press release, 8 July 1981.

which would be difficult to recycle so that real interest rates would remain low and permit rapid economic growth to coexist with rising real energy costs. A crucial factor was the 1979 oil shock which swept away the mounting caution engendered by the fading first oil boom and replaced it with an optimistic consensus about RBI prices.

The RBI projects spawned by the first oil boom began to come on stream against this background and even the least successful projects burdened with sizeable cost overruns could look forward to rising profitability as inflation pushed prices ever higher. The less prudent observers urged the commencement of uneconomic projects on the grounds that by the time such projects were completed and inflation-proofed, they would be cheap relative to the cost of executing the same project at that time. Projects already in the pipeline which had been delayed as the 1974–8 oil boom faded were started during the 1979–81 boom and new ones added.

The firms which drew up the feasibility studies for RBI projects in the developing countries were of three types, with differing degrees of commitment to the actual performance of the proposed project. Some feasibility studies were produced by firms which would reap no further benefits from either the construction phase or the production phase. While these studies were potentially the most objective, such firms escaped lightly from major error, especially in the context of the international consensus.

Other feasibility studies were executed by firms which were prepared to take a modest equity stake in anticipation of receiving the order to supply the bulk of the machinery. In such cases the initial equity stake was often small and shrank as a fraction of the total cost, as cost overruns necessitated expansion of the equity (invariably declined by the technology partner) or the loan capital. For example, in Venezuela Reynolds and Alusuisse provided the technology for an aluminium smelter expansion and greenfield alumina refinery, respectively. In the case of the Venezuelan alumina refinery, Alusuisse ended up with less than 4 per cent of the equity in place of the original 10 per cent, while Reynold's share of the smelter's equity shrank from half to less than a fifth in the course of the expansion.

In a seller's market, such as that for technology during each of the two oil booms, such small equity stakes could easily be recouped by boosting the margin from the technology sale. There is also evidence that feasibility studies undertaken by equipment suppliers were linked to inhouse technology and carried options for expansion in multiples peculiar to the suppliers' technology. In addition, the technology purchased was often more elaborate than required in contrast to deals struck by more experienced purchasers who built to the leanest specifications.

The third option in drafting feasibility studies was to involve a reputable equity partner, or partners, who would also take a substantial part of the output, usually in proportion to the equity stake. The resulting benefits of an assured market, an experienced partner, and shared risk which such a high equity commitment entails proved substantial when the optimistic conditions engendered by the second oil boom abruptly evaporated in 1981. Unfortunately, such agreements tended to be more difficult to negotiate and often proved politically less palatable than the alternatives. For example, the breakdown of joint-venture negotiations in 1976 led the government of Trinidad and Tobago to enter export steel markets on its own. Governments tended to discount RBI risk more than private partners and consequently undertook projects which potential private partners eschewed.

The relative importance of natural resources and markets

Figure 5.1 illustrates the sensitivity of the returns on an Indonesian olefins complex proposed in the mid-1970s to price, energy cost, scale, capacity utilization, and construction cost changes. It reveals the fragility of the natural resource advantage. Under assumptions appropriate to conditions in the first oil boom, it is clear that a given percentage change in the feedstock cost had a considerably smaller impact than any

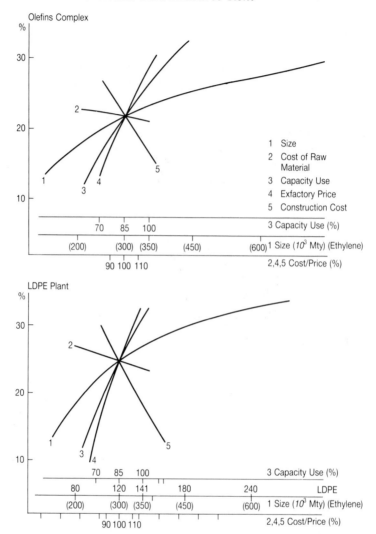

FIG. 5.1. Sensitivity analysis: Indonesian olefins complex and LDPE plant

of the other factors considered. In particular, the olefins project was more sensitive to price variations: markets potentially played a bigger role in determining profitability than raw materials.

The extent of the departure of actual prices from those projected by the feasibiltiy studies underscores the importance of the market factor. The departure ranged from around two-fifths in the conservatively estimated case of steel to more than half in the more typical instances

TABLE 5.4. *Mobil sensitivity test for a US Gulf Coast petrochemical complex*
(a) Performance index

	1981 projection	1985 projection
Total capital investment ($ billion)	1.40	1.10
Discounted cash flow return (%)	13.00	Negative
Return on total assets (%)	11.00	Negative

(b) Sensitivity index (% return)

	Discounted cash flow	Total assets
Capital costs +/- 10%	+/- 1.00	+/- 1.50
Product prices +/- 10%	+/- 3.00	+/- 4.00
Feedstock cost +/- 10%	+/- 1.50	+/- 2.00
Plant capacity only 75%	- 3.5	- 5.00

Note: Ethane-fed Gulf Coast petrochemical complex (410,000 tonnes ethylene cracker, 270,000 tonnes polyethylene, and 204,000 tonnes ethylene glycol annual capacity) ordered in 1981 for 1985 start-up. Return on assets based on 100% capacity utilization by the fourth year of operations.

Source: Mobil Chemical Company (1985).

(methanol, LDP, urea, and aluminium). The amount of that departure attributable to the unexpectedly abrupt slowdown in the underlying general rate of global price inflation was less than one-fifth. The bulk of the RBI price decline therefore reflected the failure of energy and energy-intensive product markets to command the substantial resource rents expected.

The role of the price shortfall is compounded because of the simultaneous deterioration of other related factors. In particular, depressed markets not only dampened prices, they also invariably reduced capacity utilization, thereby causing a further shrinkage in revenues as well as a rise in unit costs. Table 5.4 uses a second sensitivity test on a polyolefins complex to confirm the greater relative importance of price and capacity changes compared with feedstock cost and shows how even modest reductions in price and capacity utilization could halve the discounted cash flow. Yet the feasibility studies did not consider price declines of the magnitude which actually occurred (more than 50 per cent for ethylene, for example) let alone the simultaneous deterioration of several parameters which the depressed markets triggered.

Interest-rate changes and capital structure

A second unfavourable external factor which depressed returns on the RBI projects in addition to market failure was the abrupt rise in real interest rates as the second oil boom receded. As an index, the nominal value of money market rates in the US averaged between 6 and 7 per cent during the first boom, compared with more than 13 per cent during the second oil boom (Amuzegar 1983: 16). When global inflation is taken into account, as measured for example by the rate of inflation in OPEC imports, then real interest rates were negative in the late 1970s, but became strongly positive in the early 1980s. This cycle in interest rates initially worked simultaneously to discourage oil windfall saving, encourage domestic investment, and stimulate heavy recourse to loan finance through the second oil boom. Thereafter, as real interest rates rose sharply, the heavily front-loaded RBI projects lacked the flexibility of more conservatively geared producers to absorb lower prices.

In place of the prudent 50/50 debt/equity finance assumed in the base case, many RBI projects were financed with 70 per cent or more debt. The high-absorbing oil-exporting countries invariably denominated the bulk of such debt in foreign currency so that the RBI projects were used in effect to amplify the oil windfall. Suppliers' credits from OECD countries, which typically bore nominal interest rates of 7–8 per cent and were repayable over eight years, played a central role in encouraging such incautious gearing (Wilson 1985). Moreover, extra capital was raised via medium-term and long-term loans with volatile interest rates, rather than through bonds which provide a more appropriate financial instrument for projects with long payback periods. Worse still, short-term loans with floating interest rates were frequently used to cover cost overruns, rather than equity. This mismatch of capital to risk reduced the flexibility of the RBI projects to cope with low prices: the interest and debt repayment burden was highest during the difficult start-up period.

Low real interest rates had a second important, albeit less direct, impact on the RBI projects. Easy access to foreign borrowing encouraged many high-absorbing oil-exporting countries to allow their exchange rate to appreciate rather than face less popular measures to restore competitiveness such as devaluation and deflation. By the late 1970s, foreign borrowing in Latin America exceeded the region's rate of investment as external resources were used to sustain consumption (Enders and Mattione 1984). Where sustained currency appreciation occurred it promised to reduce the local currency cost of interest payments on loans besides lowering the cost of amortization.

TABLE 5.5. *Impact of 30% and 70% capacity utilization and interest rates on Delta Steel costs*

| | Costs ($/tonne) | |
	30%	70%
Variable costs	351.00	351.00
Labour	155.00	76.00
Plant overhead	140.00	33.00
Overhead for employee's town	40.00	11.00
TOTAL OPERATING COST	686.00	471.00
Depreciation	339.00	145.00
Interest	505.00	217.00
TOTAL COST[a]	1530.00	833.00

Notes:
1. Actual revenue estimated at cost of imported steel = $405/tonne.
2. At 70% capacity utilization, operating costs alone remain 16% above estimated revenues.
3. Total production costs are reduced by 16% and 30% at 30% and 70% capacity, respectively, by a halving of interest rates.
4. A shift from 30% to 70% capacity utilization reduces total production costs by 45%.

[a] Excluding return on equity.

Source: Industry sources.

When real interest rates turned strongly positive and global inflation slowed at the close of the second oil boom, there were four important consequences for the RBI projects. First, falling real energy prices eroded expected returns; second, the cost of debt service became greater than envisaged; third, the drastic macro-economic corrections required by past financial imprudence severely depressed domestic markets and increased RBI dependence on exports. Finally, where devaluation occurred and a sizeable fraction of the debt was denominated in OECD currencies, real depreciation further boosted the debt/equity ratio.

Cost estimates for a Nigerian steel plant allow comparison of the impact of interest-rate changes with capacity utilization and poor execution (Table 5.5). If labour is assumed part of the fixed costs, then the variable costs alone were almost 85 per cent of the cost of imported steel, a figure indicative of basic flaws in project design. Interest charges accounted for almost one-third of plant costs at 30 per cent of capacity so that halving the interest rate would shave around 15 per cent off the average total cost of production. In contrast, the shift to a more efficient level of capacity utilization would cut average total costs by 45 per cent.

Figure 5.1 confirms the importance of capacity utilization for the return on RBI investment: it shows the high sensitivity of the IRR to low capacity utilization. Since underutilization of capacity as well as lower prices was a result of glutted markets, marketing problems imparted a double blow to the base case IRR, underscoring the primacy of the market factor in determining project performance. Burdensome as it was, the RBI debt repayment problem caused by the unexpected change in interest rates was a far less important factor than the market in depressing project returns.

The neglected importance of plant vintage

The optimistic consensus assumed that the price of energy-intensive products in a rapidly expanding market would be set by the cost of new capacity at the margin rather than the cash costs of established producers (Crowson 1985). The importance of plant vintage during a period of high inflation was underestimated. Capital service charges formed a significant part of production costs for new RBI plants, but a decreasing share of the costs for plants of older vintage which had been heavily depreciated and/or constructed at lower nominal cost. All else being equal, the faster and more persistent the rate of inflation, the higher the rent on the older plants (as their historic capital costs shrank further) and the greater their capacity to ride out price falls and pass the burden of adjustment onto greenfield producers.

The resulting vulnerability of new RBI entrants was significantly increased in the case of the developing countries by their higher costs of constructing new capital-intensive factories which arose from the lack of infrastructure, distance from machinery suppliers, and lack of indigenous skilled workers. Overelaboration of plant design compounded this tendency towards higher capital costs. It will be recalled that UNIDO (1981) estimated that during the second oil boom the cost of constructing greenfield chemical plants in Mexico, Saudi Arabia, and Indonesia was higher than costs in the US Gulf by 20 per cent, 60 per cent, and more than 100 per cent respectively. The consensus view (that inflation would persist alongside burgeoning demand for energy-intensive products) therefore strongly discounted the importance of plant vintage in determining price.

Table 5.6 illustrates the relative importance of major cost components (including plant vintage) through a comparison of aluminium production costs for three older plants and three greenfield ones. The potential advantage of cheap energy resources is clearly illustrated: for example, electricity generated from oil accounted for more than half the total

TABLE 5.6. *Aluminium smelting costs, by location and plant vintage 1982 ($/tonne)*

	Canada 1943 hydro	France 1970 hydro	Japan 1972 oil	USA 1982 hydro	Oceania 1982 coal	Venezuela 1982 hydro
Alumina	404	404	395	404	395	482
Carbon	142	132	115	132	115	153
Other materials	110	110	110	110	110	132
Electricity	69	366	1039	446	386	73
Direct labour	169	102	60	292	85	190
Maintenance	110	78	58	167	70	183
Administration	53	26	16	92	23	87
Total variable cost	1039	1218	1793	1643	1174	1300
Capital service (historic cost)	75	183	212	330	360	413
Total cost/tonne	1114	1401	2005	1973	1534	1713
Capital service (replacement cost)	360	360	380	330	360	413
Total cost/tonne	1399	1578	2123	1973	1534	1713
Percentage cost breakdown						
Materials	57	46	31	33	40	45
Electricity	6	26	52	23	25	4
Labour, Administration, Maint.	30	15	7	28	12	27
Capital service charge (historic)	7	13	10	16	23	24
Relative costs, Canada = base = 100						
Total cost (historic Base)	100	126	180	177	138	154
Total cost (replacement Base)	100	113	152	141	110	122
Electricity cost (mills/kWh)	4	22	70	26	24	5
Cost of new capacity ($/tonne)	2400	2400	2200	2200	2400	2750

Notes:
1. Column headings give date and power source of smelters.
2. Percentage cost breakdown
3. Relative costs, Canada = base = 100
4. Electricity cost (mills/kWh)
5. Cost of new capacity ($/tonne)

Sources: Anthony Bird Associates (1983); Hashimoto (1983: 1–102); Industry sources.

costs of a Japanese smelter in the early 1980s. However, the capacity for some established producers to offset their higher energy cost penalty is also shown in Table 5.6. More typical OECD electricity costs based on non-captive hydro (i.e. hydro power bought at arm's length) or coal in OECD countries accounted for 25 per cent of production costs.

New smelters with access to low opportunity cost hydro in Canada or Venezuela could secure a 20 per cent cost advantage over such plants. However, the low capital service charges for plants of older vintage using non-oil power (and historic cost accounting) could eliminate two-thirds of such a cheap power advantage. Moreover, the rest of the cheap energy smelter's advantage could (and did) evaporate through over-manning and inefficient administration. Market penalties such as tariffs and higher freight charges also eroded the competitiveness of the new resource-orientated producers. More significantly, those new-developing-country aluminium smelters which derived their competitiveness from cheap power were vulnerable to the post-1981 decline in real energy prices.

Cheap energy pricing

The cheap energy advantage of the oil-exporting countries rests on the assumption that the energy resources have low opportunity costs. While this assumption may be valid, as in the case of large reserves of associated natural gas, it is not necessarily the case. For example, the cheap power advantage enjoyed by the Venezuelan plant modelled in Table 5.6 resulted from overestimation of domestic electricity demand. Once the domestic market has absorbed the surplus hydro capacity, the real opportunity cost of power will rise. Moreover, if the Venezuelan state oil corporation was permitted to price domestic fuel oil sales close to their opportunity cost the necessary tariff increase would be very high. A second example of the transitory nature of cheap energy is provided by Saudi Arabia: when Saudi oil production shrank in the early 1980s and associated gas production fell below domestic needs, the real opportunity cost of Saudi RBI gas supplies rose significantly (Stauffer 1983).

If energy pricing is discretionary, rather than based on its real opportunity cost, it becomes vulnerable to pressure to absorb any cost cuts needed to maintain the competitiveness of the project. This raises the possibility that the benefits from cheap resources will be passed on to industrial country consumers of the product through lower prices during downswings. For example, the price of Venezuelan electricity shown in Table 5.6 reflects a very low return on the capital invested in the hydro project.

Stauffer's concept of the displacement factor identifies the wider implications of such a substitution of low-rent RBI exports for high-rent crude oil exports. Razavi and Fesharaki (1983) sought to quantify the effect with reference to the impact of surplus oil refining capacity on crude oil prices. They estimated that a one million barrel per day increase in refined oil exports, all else being equal, would reduce crude oil (and product) prices through the short term by around $2.20/bl.; and by $4.80/bl. over the long term. The actual expansion in oil product exports was expected to be greater than one million barrels per day.

The erroneous demand forecasts had a cumulative effect on the oil-exporting countries. They not only shrank potential rents on the vulnerable highly levered new RBI projects. By bringing energy into glutted world markets in new forms, they contributed to the decline in crude oil prices on which the oil-exporting countries depended for much of their foreign exchange and government revenues. The Achilles heel of RBI as a diversification strategy is that it is an insufficiently bold move away from energy dependence.

CAUSES OF THE ERRONEOUS PRICE FORECASTS

A new forecasting consensus emerged based on expectations of continued slow global economic growth accompanied by a shift towards less materials- and energy-intensive GDP (Auty 1985*b*). For the industrial countries the pre-shock ratio between energy growth and GDP growth was close to unity: by the 1980s it had fallen below two-thirds, implying a more frugal use of energy to generate economic growth. Similarly, key materials such as steel, aluminium, and plastics experienced sharp reductions in demand growth, partly on account of slower economic growth and partly owing to conservation (Tilton 1985). These shifts may have started prior to the 1973–4 oil shock, but they were at once masked and accelerated by the erratic behaviour of the international economy through the remainder of the 1970s so that their significance was not immediately recognized.

Confusion over changed global demand trends

The lag in the conversion of the forecasting consensus from high to lower rates of global economic growth explains part of the error in the feasibility studies made during the two oil booms. But despite the new mid-1980s forecasting consensus, there was no agreement on the specific causes of the deceleration in demand. This raises doubts about the reliability of the present consensus and helps to explain the reluctance of producers in industries with high barriers to exit to close marginal capacity. These two aspects of the market, the unexpected downturn in demand and the rigidity of producer adjustment, make the market the critical factor responsible for the poor performance of the RBI investments (Auty 1987a).

Theories on the causes of changed international demand range from those which view it as a consequence of an unusually prolonged extension of the downturn in the business cycle (Bruno 1984, Lawrence 1984) through those which postulate the existence of Kondratiev long waves (Sterman 1985) and product cycles (Auty 1984c) to those suggesting fundamental structural change linked to the increasing competitiveness of the newly industrializing developing countries (Beenstock 1983, Krugman 1979). The speculative element in these theories increases moving from Bruno to Beenstock: the theories postulating an extended slowdown are the most conservative and have the highest probability of being correct.

Market rigidity in steel, aluminium, and petrochemicals

The fact that there is as yet no accepted explanation for the unexpected slowdown in the demand for the products of the RBI plants during the 1970s underlines the uncertainty still faced by producers in the mid-1980s. Radetzki and van Duyne (1983) suggest that the adjustment to an unexpected downturn in demand in relatively rigid markets may be easily achieved in a market of profit maximizers. Using copper as an example, they argue that the adjustment could be achieved in less than five years by deferring planned expansions and stretching out the completion of those under way. That the markets have taken longer than this to adjust arises from their need to adjust simultaneously to two other changes in addition to the downturn in long-run demand. These are, first, the abrupt and unstable changes in regional competitiveness; and second, the absorption of many new entrants comprising both state enterprises and the subsidiaries of diversifying natural resource corporations, most notably the oil majors.

The fundamental problem in the steel, aluminium, and petrochemical markets lies in the need to absorb lumpy increments in capacity while avoiding the wide price swings associated with excess or deficient capacity. The concept of the strategic group in the theory of the firm (Broadman 1981) suggests that an important reason for the exceptionally slow adjustment and persistent overcapacity in such markets lies in the sharp reduction in producer homogeneity, and therefore in the shared objectives of producers, which accompanied the proliferation of new state enterprises and subsidiaries of diversifying MNRCs through the 1970s (Auty 1987*a*). In contrast to conditions in the 1980s, the pre-shock oil and aluminium markets absorbed new entrants and rapidly expanded supply at declining real prices without yielding excess profits. These markets were characterized by a declining partial oligopoly of vertically integrated producers which used target pricing and barometric price leadership (Auty 1983*b*, 1983*c*) to facilitate the absorption of lumpy new increments to capacity.

The pre-shock copper market was different: it exhibited more erratic price behaviour, which reflected greater producer diversity and weaker target pricing than in the pre-shock steel and oil markets. Post-shock conditions in the aluminium, steel, and petrochemicals industries more closely approximate those of the pre-shock copper market. The emergence of sizeable unstable differences in competitiveness linked to energy-price, interest-rate, and exchange-rate volatility made it unclear which enterprises were marginal through the long term. Consequently, the barriers to exit that arose from high capital costs were reinforced. The reduction in producer homogeneity caused by the proliferation of new entrants compounded market rigidity.

It is tempting to ascribe the increased post-shock market rigidity to the proliferation of state enterprises alone (Prain 1975, Mikesell 1979, Vernon 1983*b*), since there are strong theoretical arguments for expecting state enterprises to be characterized by a more rigid response than private profit-maximizing firms (Shirley 1983), and state enterprises significantly increased in importance during the 1970s. Such a view overstates the case. The nickel industry, which experienced little expansion by state enterprises, nevertheless exhibited increased rigidity in adjusting to post-shock market changes (Stobart 1984). Even the aluminium industry, which had hitherto been regarded as having maintained a relatively high level of producer homogeneity (and therefore common interest) by successfully absorbing the new entrants through establishing joint ventures with them, has subsequently experienced difficulty in adjusting capacity to demand. Moreover, the diversification of the oil majors into non-fuel minerals production meant that their newly acquired subsidiaries, like the state enterprises, had access to large external financial resources which reduced their market sensitivity.

Rather, a number of variables increased the uncertainty about underlying competitiveness and exacerbated the problem of apportioning market share among producers during the period of unexpected demand deceleration. Reduced producer homogeneity (due to the increased range and volatility in key cost elements as well as to producer proliferation) is at the root of the problem. Consequently, unless there is some reduction in the volatility of the international economy and/or an increase in recourse to joint-ventures, market rigidity may depress RBI prices for some considerable time.

CONCLUSION: THE IMPORTANCE OF RBI PROJECT RESILIENCE

The RBI feasibility studies projected sizeable resource rents which encouraged the oil exporters to discount risk. Many RBI projects were highly levered, a step encouraged by the ready availability of suppliers' credit loans bearing low or negative rates of interest.

The feasibility studies were based on a forecasting consensus which assumed continuing inflation, rising real energy prices, and rapid global economic growth. They overestimated the benefits of cheap natural resources and undervalued market access. The feasibility-study sensitivity tests focused on changes in single parameters while the actual outcome was for a combination of market-related parameters to fall well below expectations. Actual mid-1980s prices were between two-thirds and half the levels projected.

In glutted markets, prices were set by the cash costs of established producers with heavily depreciated plant so that the highly levered greenfield RBI projects were marginalized. Higher interest rates and low capacity utilization further eroded competitiveness. It is ironic, but apparently the case, that market access is the dominant requirement for successful RBI, a strategy which has generally been presumed to draw its strength from access to cheap resources.

RBI, far from capturing resource rents for the oil-exporting countries, may transfer them to industrial country consumers through lower prices while saddling domestic enterprises with uncompetitive sources of key materials. Worse, expanded energy-intensive exports may simply compound the problems of glutted energy markets through their displacement effect on crude oil exports. This may undermine not only the rationale for many of the RBI projects, but also the oil windfall on which the oil-exporting countries remain dependent for foreign exchange and government revenues. The Achilles heel of RBI as a strategy for economic diversification is that it is an insufficiently bold departure from energy dependence.

The reasons why RBI product markets fell so far short of the universally overoptimistic feasibility projections remain controversial.

Reduced producer homogeneity impeded efforts to adjust to changed demand so that market rigidity increased substantially. Whatever its cause, price depression severely tested the resilience of the highly levered RBI projects so that much depended on the efficiency with which they had been executed. This subject is now addressed in Part 3.

PART 3.
Implementation Efficiency

6

Political Constraints on Macro-economic Efficiency: Oil Windfall Deployment in the Low-Absorbing Countries

MACRO-ECONOMIC CHALLENGES OF THE OIL WINDFALLS

After infrastructure, RBI was the second largest investment application of the oil windfall by the oil-exporting countries. Efficiently implemented, RBI promised to absorb a significant fraction of the oil windfall with minimum inflationary risk (Alam 1982). However, for the RBI investment to be productive, it required appropriate macro-economic measures, and herein lay the challenge of oil windfall deployment. Effective windfall deployment is difficult to achieve on account of strong political pressure for overrapid absorption (Gelb 1988).

A prudent policy for the deployment of oil windfalls is premised on a clear distinction between the volatile and finite minerals sector and the sustainable non-oil economy. In order that the non-oil economy should escape severe distortion by overrapid absorption and/or withdrawal of the oil windfall it is necessary first to sterilize the windfall by allocating it to special development accounts. In the absence of viable domestic investment opportunities a significant fraction of the windfall may be held overseas to accumulate interest until barriers to effective investment such as transport bottlenecks and shortages of skills are removed.

The injection of the oil rents into the domestic economy may then take the form of investment in infrastructure and directly productive activity. If the boom is not thought to be transitory, consumption may be increased either by higher current spending in the public sector or through price and exchange-rate controls which boost private purchasing power over domestic and foreign goods respectively.

The deployment problem is particularly acute when—as in the case of oil—the mineral resource is characterized by a series of booms. Mineral booms tend to foster patterns of consumption and investment which are difficult to curb during subsequent downswings (Wheeler 1984). Worse, 'Dutch disease' effects triggered by the boom may be severe enough to weaken the non-minerals tradeables sector (agriculture and manufacturing) and so work against diversification efforts. The abrupt termination of a boom compresses the period of adjustment to mineral export decline. This renders the required expansion of foreign exchange and tax revenues from the non-mining tradeables sector difficult to achieve. The downward shift in exchange rate and factor remuneration is painful and often resisted (Gelb 1988).

Economic policy must create three conditions if the harmful negative spillover effects from overrapid windfall absorption are to be avoided and RBI projects are to be effectively implemented. First, price distortions must be minimized to facilitate the accurate comparison of prospective returns from RBI investment with alternative opportunities, including savings overseas. The reduction of price distortions also promotes the development of a healthy diversifying non-resource tradeables sector—an essential source of employment and an important safety-net against cyclical downturn in the oil and RBI sectors. Monetary, exchange-rate, and subsidy policies all play critical roles in this respect.

Second, absorptive capacity must be increased through carefully sychronized investment to remove social and economic infrastructure bottlenecks and contain inflationary trends. Such investments are usually lumpy with long payback periods so that fostering ease of entry (and exit) for foreign workers and firms fills gaps in domestic capacity and enhances flexible adjustment over the interim.

Third, prompt response to cyclical downturn requires bold exchange-rate, interest-rate, and budgetary adjustments. Clearly, fiscal policies which promote the accumulation of a cushion of overseas savings, the steady diversification of revenue sources, and the prudent targeting of subsidies during boom periods help smooth the adjustment to the downswing. RBI benefits from full capacity utilization and this requires sustained expansion of domestic markets and/or competitive access to export markets. Of all the macro-economic measures, Pinto (1987) concluded that maintaining foreign exchange convertibility and broad fiscal balance were most important.

Many developing-country governments have overestimated their capacity to formulate and implement economic policy (Lal 1983). Clear evidence emerged through the 1970s that overextension of government activity could create resource sinks. If unchecked, the cumulative effect of such resource sinks could severely depress the overall productivity of

TABLE 6.1. *Sectoral shares in non-mining GDP, by country 1972 (%)*

Country	Agri- culture	Manufac- turing	Construc- tion	Services	(Mining)
Low-absorbers					
Bahrain	2.9	19.0	6.6	71.5	66.0
Saudi Arabia	10.3	21.3	10.1	58.1	54.1
High-absorbers					
Indonesia	45.1	11.0	4.3	39.7	12.1
Nigeria	39.2	5.1	10.7	45.0	15.1
Cameroon	31.4	12.1	3.8	52.7	0.2
Malaysia	31.0	17.3	4.3	47.4	6.2
Venezuela	7.6	19.5	6.0	66.9	20.5
Trinidad and Tobago	5.8	22.0	8.0	64.2	8.8

Sources: Gelb (1986*a*); Kubursi (1984); Ministry of Planning (1986); World Bank (personal communication).

domestic capital within little more than a decade (Gelb, Knight, and Sabot 1986).

The political constraints on the effective deployment of the oil windfalls for RBI are explored here first with reference to Saudi Arabia and Bahrain. The relatively small size of their non-oil tradeables sectors appeared to restrict their absorptive capacity, earning them the designation of 'low-absorbers'. In contrast, the more diversified economies of the 'high-absorbing' countries analysed by Gelb (1988) had greater ability to deploy large capital inflows (Table 6.1). The performance of the 'high-absorbing' oil-exporting countries is discussed in Chapter 7. However, before analysing the windfall deployment patterns of Saudi Arabia and Bahrain, a simple model is constructed which links a country's capacity to formulate and pursue a long-term national development strategy to the type of political regime.

POLITICAL CONSTRAINTS ON PRUDENT OIL
WINDFALL DEPLOYMENT

A framework for cross-country comparison

As noted in Chapter 2, Haggard (1986) developed a useful framework for cross-country comparison of the political constraints on economic policy. The constraints are conceptualized as working on three levels:

the international level, the country level, and the government level. It is on the third (governmental) level that Haggard's approach is of most use to the present study. Haggard ascribes an active role to government élites who determine the extent to which pressures for short-term goals prevail over long-term developmental objectives. Two constraints are paramount: first, the ability of bureaucrats to formulate a coherent long-term development policy geared to broad national interests and, second, the degree to which they can effectively implement such a policy, i.e. the administrative efficiency. It is here that the nature of the political regime plays a prominent role.

The successful deployment of large windfalls for RBI calls for disciplined long-term planning and timely skilful adjustments to upside and downside shifts in the boom. This requires an effective professional bureaucracy which, in turn, requires a regime which eschews the temptation to expand the public sector simply to generate patronage. It is easier to postulate regime/performance relationships than it is to operationalize them. The number and diversity of factors responsible for departures from prudent economic management in particular countries makes generalization difficult. Nevertheless, while recognizing that unique conditions may overwhelm more general factors in specific instances, systematic links exist between regime types and the capacity of government élites to arbitrate effectively between conflicting social demands.

Table 6.2 attempts to link political regimes via bureaucratic constraints to macro-economic policy, a specific objective (here prudent windfall deployment) and sectoral characteristics. A basic distinction between stable and unstable regimes is elaborated by subdividing each into authoritarian and pluralistic types. Of the stable regimes in the eight oil-exporting countries, the paternalistic autocracies proved more capable of pursuing a long-term national development strategy than the mature democracies. Nigeria most clearly illustrates the difficulties encountered by weak regimes—whether unstable autocracy or fragile democracy—preoccupied by the politics of survival.

Schafer (1983) notes that insecure governments effectively trade long-term national economic benefits for specific political support. Strong governments retain institutions which insulate key policy instruments from corrosive internal (and external) political pressures. Bureaucrats in weak regimes are subject to intense pressures to provide short-run favours to potential government supporters. The prevailing clientelistic ethic discourages professionalism, encourages personal power-building, and undermines efficiency. Such conditions are incompatible with the

TABLE 6.2. *The effects of political constraints on windfall deployment*

	Effectiveness	
	Low	High
Political System		
Authoritarian	Unstable	Secure paternal
Pluralistic	Fragile democracy	Mature democracy
Bureaucracy		
Ethic	Rent dispensing	National welfare
Efficiency	Low	High
Welfare Perspective		
Temporal	Short-run	Long-run
Distribution	Sectional	Society-wide
Economic Management		
Trade:		
Reserves	Overextended	Cushioned
Export range	Narrowing	Widening
Exchange rate	Overvalued	Timely Adjustment
Financial:		
Prices	Severely Distorted	Flexprice
Money supply	Loose	Accommodatory
Interest rate	Capped	Competitive
Fiscal:		
Tax base	Narrowing	Widening
Subsidies	Ballooning	Tightly targeted
Balance	Growing deficit	Broadly neutral
Windfall Deployment		
Overseas saving	Negative	Positive
Rent sterilization	Minimal	Development accounts
Investment criteria	Socio-political	Economic return
SOC provision	Uncoordinated	Synchronized
Consumption	Rising subsidies	Targeted low
Sectoral Character		
Private	Pirate capitalism	Competitive market
Public	Commissar fiefdoms	Technocrat autonomy

effective pursuit of a coherent long-term development policy in the broad social interest.

Table 6.2 also suggests links between the type of regime and the prevailing character of enterprises in the public and private sectors. The public sector enterprises in the stronger regimes encourage an autonomous technocratic management capable of distancing itself from short-run political pressures. In contrast, weaker regimes favour a more centrally controlled commissarial management (Escobar 1982) which more effectively distributes benefits through clientelistic networks. For the private sector a distinction is made between the adaptive competitive enterprises of the secure regimes and rent-seeking enterprises in weak regimes. According to Schatz (1984) the behaviour of private firms in weak regimes may reach an extreme form which he describes as pirate capitalism. Under pirate capitalism, entrepreneurial skills throughout society are directed at capturing immediate advantages through the exploitation of inefficiencies in the system rather than at building up the means for the long-term creation of wealth.

Some qualifications to the postulated regime–policy links are in order. First, the regime distinctions and sector characteristics in Table 6.2 are clearly polar types designed to suggest the essence of the observed differences rather than their precise nature. For example, particular regimes may exhibit hybrid sectors, as the private sector in Indonesia's paternalistic autocracy shows (Flatters and Jenkins 1986). Second, the relationships between regime types and economic policy or deployment strategy are similarly impressionistic. Yet a review of the political constraints on reform (Grindle 1986) suggests that there is little consensus on more rigorous regime categorizations.

With these qualifications in mind, four hypotheses concerning the effectiveness of windfall deployment for RBI are explored here in Chapters 7–9.

- capital surplus oil-exporting countries have low effective absorptive capacity for RBI;
- continuity of political regime is positively correlated with effective windfall deployment for RBI;
- RBI enterprise efficiency and sectoral performance are sensitive to macro-economic policy, underlining the importance of sound macro-economic management to RBI;
- significant performance differences between RBI projects reflect the operation of the above factors.

SAUDI WINDFALL DEPLOYMENT OPTIONS

Saudi deployment options: capital and efficiency constraints

The oil shocks combined with expanded oil production to yield a windfall to Saudi Arabia equivalent to just over twice its non-oil GDP during the first oil boom and around 180 per cent of a greatly expanded non-oil GDP during the second boom (Table 6.3). Such sharply increased revenues, backed up by vast oil reserves, meant that the option

TABLE 6.3. *Saudi Arabian absorption 1969–72 to 1982–5*

	1969–72		1974–8		1978–82		1982–5	
	(1)	(2)	(1)	(2)	(1)	(2)	(1)	(2)[a]
Non-mining GDP	8.341		49.690		144.917		204.5	
Oil windfall	—		102.064		258.740		152.169	
Absorption								
Private consumption	6.393	(76.6)	26.702	(53.7)	102.900	(71.0)	138.057	(67.5)
Public consumption	3.837	(46.0)	28.543	(57.4)	89.977	(62.1)	121.519	(59.4)
Investment	2.977	(35.7)	35.444	(71.3)	100.603	(69.4)	114.081	(55.8)
Total	13.207	(158.2)	90.689	(182.4)	293.480	(202.5)	373.657	(182.7)
Budget balance	0.344	(4.1)	7.537	(15.1)	15.132	(10.4)	-6.479	(-3.2)

Measures: (1) Billions of Saudi Riyals; (2) Percentage of non-mining GDP.
  [a] Absorption break-down available for 1982–4 only.

Source: Saudi Arabian Monetary Authority.

of accumulating overseas savings and drawing on the rents to boost domestic consumption was a real one for Saudi Arabia. Kuwait did favour such a strategy and, with a population less than one-fifth that of Saudi Arabia, it had accumulated overseas assets of a similar magnitude to Saudi Arabia (over $80 billion) by the mid-1980s. Stauffer (1985) contends that the dependence of Kuwaiti economic growth on depleting capital assets (whether oil or overseas investment) had declined substantially by the early 1980s.

However, the rentier strategy implied continued reliance on imports for goods and skills. Instead, the Saudi government chose to develop domestic productive capacity in order to equip its people to exploit the most modern technology and wrest its benefits for themselves. Evaluations of Saudi oil windfall deployment range from the uncritical review of Johany *et al.* (1986) to the caustic appraisal of Kanovsky (1986). In broadbush terms the strategy displays strong positive aspects. Absorptive capacity was expanded with speed and technical (if not economic) efficiency. Meanwhile the accumulation of overseas assets and liberal recourse to imported skills provided insulation against external shocks and permitted incremental adjustment when oil prices dipped in the mid-1980s. More detailed examination reveals less desirable features, notably a reluctance to broaden the tax base, increasing recourse to subsidies, and overexpansion of the bureaucracy. The other oil-exporting countries shared such flaws, but lacked the margin of tolerance which Saudi Arabia's windfall gave for such political sweeteners.

The Saudi windfall deployment strategy was largely directed at a once-for-all boost to social and economic infrastructure. The development of a competitive non-oil tradeables sector relied heavily on RBI (with petrochemicals as the lead sector) to provide the catalyst for change. Iran amply demonstrates the risks arising from such a strategy (Gelb 1988), yet Saudi Arabia proceeded with remarkable speed, consistency, and technical efficiency. First, the Saudi government accumulated sizeable overseas assets as domestic absorptive capacity was steadily expanded through the provision of modern infrastructure, both social and economic. Then, from the early 1980s, it efficiently constructed the petrochemical plants through joint-ventures with experienced MNRC partners. Meanwhile Saudi entrepreneurs cut their teeth on the easy profits from import businesses, construction, and domestic manufacturing. Finally, the government planned to reduce its role from the mid-1980s as the private sector completed economic diversification by exploiting the expanding investment opportunities which RBI and burgeoning domestic demand were expected to trigger. The relative success of Saudi efforts was rooted in an unusually favourable combination of windfall size and regime type. The large windfall on its own could not ensure success, but it created conditions in which a prudent government could reconcile competing interests without corroding implementation capacity. Saudi planners enjoyed greater continuity than those of other countries in expanding infrastructure and pursuing RBI. As a stable paternalistic autocracy, the Saudi government did not face electoral pressure to pursue short-run objectives at the expense of long-term development goals. However, it did have to make concessions to the interests of the princes, middle class, and poorest people. Modern infrastructure provision, social as well as economic, was the main response to these interests but its rapid expansion was also compatible with the government's long-term goal of industrialization. The windfalls were large enough to accommodate the build-up of overseas savings simultaneously with the expansion of efficient infrastructure and competitive RBI—but only because project implementation was superior to that of most oil-exporting countries.

A second reason for Saudi success lies in its readiness to shun the prevailing 'go it alone' fashion of other developing countries. Saudi Arabia did not seek overrapid indigenization of management and productive assets, preferring to absorb skills and technology over a generation rather than overnight. Deficiencies in implementation capacity were flexibly filled through liberal recourse to skilled foreigners, rather than to inadequately trained locals. Implementation efficiency was further enhanced through the retention of traditional values among key civil servants which muted the potentially corrosive effect of political patronage on windfall deployment.

An important consequence of Saudi windfall deployment for managing the mid-1980s downswing was the accumulation of several buffers (overseas savings, large once-for-all SOC expenditures, and foreign companies and workers) between the non-oil economy and the deteriorating external environment. These layers provided considerable latitude for smooth incremental adjustment to external shocks, as is shown in Chapter 10.

Windfall sterilization measures

The Saudi government captured the bulk of the oil windfalls through taxation and in order to avoid overrapid absorption it accumulated large reserves overseas. By the early 1980s the accumulated overseas assets were estimated by the IMF to have peaked at around $170 billion

(Financial Times 1986*a*), the equivalent of almost one-third of the windfall from the two oil booms. American, Japanese, and West German bonds were strongly favoured. Private overseas funds held by Saudi nationals were estimated at $40 billion. The savings were one of the three cushions which the government used to smooth out fluctuations in the windfall, covering modest budget deficits 1977–9 and larger ones which absorbed an estimated $46 billion of the reserves 1983–6 (Economist Intelligence Unit (EIU) 1987, Kanovsky 1986).

Even so, during the oil booms of 1974–8 and 1979–81 more than two-thirds of the oil windfall was absorbed into the domestic economy. Investment, especially public investment, rose sharply in the mid-1970s from a level of one-third of non-oil GDP to slightly over two-thirds of non-oil GDP, a rate sustained for the next decade (Table 6.3). Construction activity accounted for four-fifths of capital accumulation, machinery and transportation equipment for the remainder. Total construction investment from the mid-1970s to the mid-1980s was estimated at more than $270 billion, most of it through the public sector. Aramco (1984 and industry sources) calculated that 90 per cent of government investment was expended on infrastructure as opposed to directly productive activity.

Disappointing real returns on overseas holdings through the late 1970s together with Iran's problems in gaining access to its overseas holdings after the Shah was deposed further encouraged rapid domestic absorption. The creation of the national physical infrastructure was viewed as a once-for-all requirement which was especially well suited to windfall absorption. It provided a second cushion between the domestic economy and fluctuating oil revenues since it could be flexibly adjusted. The principal burden of cut-backs in infrastructure spending would be absorbed by foreign construction firms and workers.

In order to distinguish the potentially transient windfall revenues from funding for routine expenditures, the Five-Year Plans expressly recognized development expenditure as a separate category. Table 6.4 summarizes the planned development expenditures for each of the Five-Year Plans covering the period 1970–90. In aggregate terms, development expenditures increased their share of the total planned allocation during the Second and Third plans (1975–85) before falling back. At the sectoral level, the early concentration on investment in physical infrastructure gave way to greater emphasis on directly productive investment, before both these sectors shrank as the major programmes were completed and mounting financial constraints caused the government to hasten the planned reduction of its role within the economy.

TABLE 6.4. *Planned financial allocations, Saudi Arabia 1970–1990 Five-Year Plans (%)*

Plan	(1) 1970–5[a]	(2) 1975–80[b]	(3) 1980–5[c]	(4) 1985–90[d]	(5) 1987 Revision
Development					
Economic Resources	6.5	18.5	32.8	13.1	5.0
Human Resources	17.9	16.1	16.7	13.5	14.0
Social	4.7	6.6	7.1	8.9	6.5
Physical Infrastructure	29.2	22.7	33.3	14.4	2.5
TOTAL	58.3	63.9	89.9	49.9	28.0
Other					
Administration	18.7	7.6	5.3	n/a	6.0
Defence	23.1	15.7	n/a	n/a	35.7
Miscellaneous	—	12.7	4.8	n/a	30.3
TOTAL	41.8	36.0	10.1	50.1	72.0

[a] Total allocated US $9.2 billion.
[b] Total allocated $141.7 billion.
[c] Total allocated $222.0 billion.
[d] Total allocated $227.0 billion.

Sources: (1)–(2) Nyrop (1977a): 240, 242; (3) Economist (1982: 70); (4) Financial Times (1985a); (5) EIU (1987).

Public spending on construction shrank from $50 billion in 1981 to $19 billion in 1985 while the rate at which new public contracts were awarded declined even faster from $20 billion to $4 billion over the same period (Financial Times 1985b). From the mid-1980s, the main thrust of public investment was directed at improving the level of skills and living conditions in an expanding network of cities.

Liberal policies towards migrant labour, foreign construction firms, and imported goods comprised the third layer of protection against oil revenue downswing. They also played an important role in containing inflationary pressures associated with the huge windfall injection. The remarkable expansion of the construction industry, which doubled its workforce to 460,000 1976–8, did so largely through foreign or joint-ventures (led by the South Koreans) which took 70 per cent of the work (Aramco 1984). By 1980 the total number of immigrant workers was estimated at two million, the equivalent of between one-quarter and one-third of the Saudi population. Official figures suggest that the percentage of non-nationals in the workforce rose from 8 to 43 between 1975 and 1980 (Harvey 1982) and to just over half by 1983.

Migrant workers, notably Yemenis, Filipinos, Koreans, Palestinians, Pakistanis, and Indians, dominated employment in the manufacturing sector as well as construction. Around 200,000 Syrians, Lebanese, and Egyptians filled gaps in clerical and administrative positions while about half that number of Americans and Europeans supplied more sophist-icated skills. Saudi workers showed a distinct preference for govern-ment, trade, and service jobs and their early dominance in agriculture declined. The large pool of immigrant labour lubricated the expansion of absorptive capacity through the oil booms and cushioned Saudi against the subsequent downswing.

Systematic SOC provision: the 1975–85 construction boom

Saudi Arabia's rapid infrastructure expansion may be traced through the Aramco index of construction expenditures and contract awards (Aramco 1982, 1984). The awards index jumped from 40 in May 1975 to 305 in July 1976 and after a fourteen-month pause which successfully tempered inflation rose to 600 in mid-1978. There followed a further pause in contract awards as the Second Plan was completed before the index jumped again to peak at 650 in 1982. The index fell steeply to more normal pre-1976 levels, reaching 90 by 1985. The pattern of actual construction expenditures (as opposed to contract awards) described a smoother trend. It lagged the contract awards, rising fourfold 1976–9 to a plateau which averaged $3 billion per month until late 1981. Thereafter, the awards made at the beginning of the Third Five-Year Plan fed through to push the monthly expenditures to a $4 billion peak in 1983.

Absorption initially did proceed too rapidly and serious bottlenecks pushed the inflation rate above 30 per cent 1975–6. The index of consumer prices shows that house prices (non-tradeables sector) rose 460 per cent 1970–8 compared with 240 per cent for goods represent-ative of the tradeable sector such as clothing and footwear (Alam 1982). However, even though the rate of absorption of the oil windfall remained high through the second oil boom, sound macro-economic management ensured that it did not overtax the non-oil sector. A combination of tight monetary control, price subsidies, and the elimination of infrastructural bottlenecks brought inflation below 3 per cent in the early 1980s (Amuzegar 1983, IMF 1984).

Public expenditure in the Second Five-Year Plan (1975–80) was more than ten times as large as that in the First and the development of infrastructure accounted for around half the increase (Table 6.4). Actual expenditure exceeded the 1975 budgeted allocation by some 20 per cent, reflecting higher-than-expected inflation 1975–7. Even though inflation was subsequently curbed, construction costs remained high relative to the industrial countries because of the dependence on imports and foreign skills, the difficult work conditions on site, a marked preference for state-of-the-art technology, and elaborate design and margins of 5 per cent and more to secure mandatory local Saudi participation. UNIDO (1981) suggests Saudi construction costs were 50 to 70 per cent above those of the US Gulf Coast and 30 per cent above those of a Latin American country during the 1979–81 oil boom. Consequently, although Saudi Arabia's anti-inflation policies minimized unexpected cost overruns compared with most oil-exporting countries, the efficiency of capital was still lower than that of the industrial countries so that the global investment of around $300 billion overstates the physical accomplishment during the oil booms (Johany *et al.* 1986).

The apparent lack of capital constraints during the oil booms is illustrated by Saudi Arabia's readiness to provide infrastructure well ahead of demand. Saudi infrastructure investment was remarkable for its systematic and well-synchronized implementation. The emphasis on infrastructure investment steadily shifted under the Second, Third, and Fourth Five-Year Plans from communications and hydrocarbons distribution to housing and then to education. Communications received first priority under the Second Five-Year Plan and two new ports were built at Jubail and Yanbu while the existing major ports of Jeddah on the Red Sea and Dammam on the Gulf had their capacity boosted fourfold. The Third Five-Year Plan called for the addition of 50 per cent more capacity.

The country's airport system was similarly overexpanded, with major new facilities constructed at Jeddah and Riyadh (costing more than $10 billion and $15 billion respectively). The road network was also improved and by the mid-1980s 30,000 km. of paved roads connected the main economic centres on the Red Sea coast and around Dammam with the capital city and neighbouring oasis towns. A further 25,000 km. of rural roads linked 7,000 villages to the major highway network. Under the Third Plan the paved road network was expanded by one-third and the entire system by more than 50 per cent as part of the $45 billion allocated to communications improvements (Harvey 1982, Duncan 1986).

The second investment priority of the 1975–80 Five-Year Plan was to make more efficient use of the hydrocarbon resource and to diversify its markets. The first phase of the $12 billion Master Gas System was designed to handle 3.5 bcfd of gas. It commenced in 1975 and was completed in 1982. The second phase boosted the capacity of the system to 5 bcfd by 1986 for a further $8 billion. This ensured that reduced oil production levels did not constrain the availability of gas for RBI and other uses (Stauffer 1983) by linking the system to offshore gas and non-associated gas from fields some 5000 m. below the Ghawar oil field. Additional pipelines were also built to transport gas liquids to Yanbu and Jubail with an oil pipeline running parallel to the Yanbu gas liquids line (Economist 1982). The timely provision of the large new economic infrastructure underpinned the efficient start-up of the RBI projects in the Al-Jubail and Yanbu industrial growth poles.

The early 1980s softening of prices for light crude reinforced the post-nationalization strategy of Aramco to boost the proportion of heavy crude extracted. Depletion of the large Ghawar field, the main source of light crude, was slowed while offshore fields with more diverse, but generally heavier, crudes were either expanded or opened up. The result was the addition of an extra 1.4 mbpd of medium/heavy crude for Saudi use. Five new refineries were planned in order to boost domestic capacity to 1.29 mpbd by the late 1980s, in addition to the expansion of export capacity to 1.32 mbpd. The delay and cancellation of refinery contracts (one 50 per cent complete) during the mid-1980s downturn illustrates Saudi ability to make difficult cuts in project—if not recurrent—spending.

Accommodation and urban services provided the third focus of the Second Plan and the percentage of the rapidly rising population housed in large cities increased from one-fifth in 1970 to two-fifths by 1980. The percentage dwelling in the desert declined from around 60 to 45 per cent. The capital city of Riyadh, with 1.6 million residents, was virtually built from scratch in the middle of the desert, some 900 km. from Jeddah, through which the bulk of its import requirements both before and after completion were drawn. Jeddah, with a population of one million, was subject to a massive rebuilding programme while considerable progress was made in establishing two new industrial cities at Jubail on the Gulf coast north of Dammam and Yanbu on the Red Sea north of Jeddah. Much of the urban water consumption was supplied by desalination, requiring a capacity of more than 1.6 bcmd, still well short of the 5.5 bcmd built to supply water to improve the efficiency of oil extraction from the Ghawar field.

Under the Third Five-Year Plan, some $40 billion was allocated to education, almost as much as that assigned for completion of the country's communications network. For although many Saudis entered the middle class during the 1970s, relatively few possessed basic education. As the construction boom wound down (new contracts were running at less than one-third of their peak level by 1983) the Saudi government was anxious to see the repatriation of immigrant labourers and the replacement of more skilled workers with Saudi nationals. One-third of the expenditure on education was allocated to post-secondary school training and the educational system assumed an increasingly important role as the relative size of the oil sector declined, government expenditure tapered off, and the burden of sustaining economic growth fell on the non-oil private sector.

The expenditure on social and economic infrastructure dwarfed that on the RBI projects (examined in detail in Chapter 9) and was the key factor behind economic growth during the Second and Third Five-Year Plans. At one point the construction industry accounted for almost one-third of non-oil GDP and was still responsible for one-seventh in the mid-1980s. As the basic infrastructural expansion neared completion the government's deployment of oil revenues shifted to the maintenance and operation of the new facilities. This required the wind-up of many (mostly foreign) construction firms and the birth of new firms in maintenance services. Given a total investment of over $300 billion, annual operation and maintenance expenditures have been variously estimated at $6 billion plus/minus 50 per cent, one-sixth the rate of public expenditure absorbed at the height of the construction boom.

Consumption

Non-oil GDP expanded by 13 per cent annually in real terms during the two oil booms and by 4 per cent per annum 1981–4. Consumption increased its share of non-oil GDP from 120 to 133 per cent over the same period. While private consumption remained equivalent to three-quarters of non-oil GDP, public consumption increased from 46 to 62 per cent. Although income distribution remained highly skewed, these gains were reflected to improving social indicators as Saudi Arabia caught up with and exceeded the middle-income country average in terms of health care and life expectancy. The provision of heavily subsidized water, food, and electricity supplies even to remote areas was an important means of diffusing the oil benefits throughout Saudi society.

Educational attainments, however, remained below average with only 69 per cent enrolled in primary schools and 36 per cent at secondary schools in 1983 (World Bank 1986*b*). Service jobs accounted for the bulk of the increase in total employment which expanded by more than 50 per cent 1975–85 (Johany *et al.* 1986). Although Saudis showed a marked preference for civil service and commerce, some evidence of a shift towards semi-skilled and skilled manual jobs began to emerge among the young during the mid-1980s (Financial Times 1985*b*).

The pattern of consumption revealed some disturbing features about Saudi windfall deployment. The government failed to diversify its revenue base and remained heavily dependent on oil revenues and portfolio income. Personal income tax was not levied (though individuals were expected to contribute 2.5 per cent of their income to the community) and seemed unlikely to be so. Nor did direct taxation appear more acceptable: value added tax was negligible while import duties were also very light. Far from raising broad-based taxation above such minimal levels, the Saudi authorities preferred to retain the government function as a distributor of largesse. For example, basic services were provided to the remotest communities, even though the marginal cost of such provision was often high.

Subsidies ballooned to 20 per cent of recurrent non-military expenditure by the early 1980s. Agriculture proved particularly costly, as fixed wheat prices rose to five times import levels, producing an embarrassing surplus. Meanwhile, large capital-intensive farms captured most of the benefits and even began importing fodder crops in order to concentrate on wheat. Similar rent-seeking behaviour was evident in the bureaucracy: government employment doubled to 450,000 between 1978 and 1983 with ample evidence of slack work habits (Kanovsky 1986).

However, the Saudi government displayed a commitment to fiscal balance and currency convertibility through both oil booms. It preferred to stimulate private investment in manufacturing through infrastructure provision, licensing, and cheap loans rather than tariff protection. Yet macro-economic management during the economic downturn, examined in more depth in Chapter 10, revealed disturbing weaknesses. Burgeoning recurrent expenditure proved difficult to curb. Rather than implement unpopular measures such as increased domestic taxation and major subsidy cuts, the government resorted to drastic project spending curbs, delays in contractual payments, seizure of public sector company reserves and large drawdowns on overseas savings. Military spending, which was twice as large as other recurrent expenditures, was untouched. Tariffs were eventually raised in order to boost revenue and protect domestic producers, but the widely expected sizeable exchange-rate devaluation in response to the 1986 oil price fall did not occur. Instead the rate was reduced by a token 2.5 per cent.

Such a response confirms the view that the downswing of a boom is harder to manage than the upswing. It suggests that the scale of the Saudi windfall was a very important factor in Saudi deployment successes. The decline and collapse of oil prices associated with the mid-1980s downswing tested the insulation provided by the layers of foreign labour and overseas savings which the Saudi government had built up during the booms (Chapter 10).

BAHRAIN: A SMALL COUNTRY'S MORE
CAUTIOUS APPROACH

Table 6.1 shows that Bahrain was even more dependent than Saudi Arabia on oil revenues on the eve of the first oil shock. However, Bahrain did not consider the rentier strategy as a long-term option because it lacked the vast hydrocarbon reserves of its larger neighbour. Indeed, the country had pioneered RBI in the late 1960s, using its combined advantages of cheap energy *and* labour (national per capita income was still around $500 in the mid-1970s, much lower than the Gulf region average) to establish a aluminium smelter. Although the contribution of oil to GDP shrank sharply during the two oil booms (from more than two-thirds to less than one-third), the economy remained heavily dependent on the trickle-down of Gulf oil benefits—from aid as well as oil-related business—especially from Saudi Arabia and Kuwait.

Bahrain's political regime was similar to that of Saudi Arabia—a brief experiment with democracy was abandoned in 1975—and the pattern of windfall absorption shared important features with that country. Bahrain accumulated overseas savings as a cushion against downswings; expanded its infrastructure with liberal recourse to foreign workers and firms; looked to the private sector for long-term diversification; and adopted a paternalistic stance towards its people, providing many basic services free or at nominal cost. Economic management also shared favourable features with Saudi Arabia during the oil booms: trade and capital movements were relatively unfettered; emphasis was placed on fiscal prudence, with minimal recourse to deficit financing; and inflation was tightly controlled after an initial surge. These measures created a macro-economic environment conducive to effective RBI project execution and the foundation was laid for on-going economic diversification—provided injections of oil revenues continued through RBI's long gestation period.

There were also differences with Saudi Arabia. Bahrain made less effort than Saudi Arabia to sterilize its accounts and resorted to extra-budgetary means for aid receipts (more than one-tenth of the total) as well as for some expenditures. One consequence of this is that the absorption of Bahrain's windfall is difficult to trace accurately. Another data problem arises from revision of the national accounts: the more recent figures, covering the period since 1977, differ significantly from earlier ones. Comparison between the two booms must therefore be based on the earlier unrevised data set (Kubursi 1984). These indicate that aggregate investment was more modest than in Saudi Arabia: although investment rose to the equivalent of one-third of non-oil output during the first boom it never exceeded one-fifth of total absorption and its share shrank to one-eighth of total absorption during the second boom. Moreover, public investment accounted for a smaller share of the total investment than in Saudi Arabia and was more heavily concentrated on social infrastructure such as housing, power, and water supply rather than the economic infrastructure emphasized by Saudi Arabia.

The structure of Bahrain's non-oil economy—initially so similar to that of Saudi Arabia—diverged increasingly from that of its larger neighbour as the relative size of Bahrain's oil sector rapidly declined. The ratio of oil sector output to non-oil GDP initially expanded from a pre-shock one-third to almost 60 per cent during the first oil boom. Thereafter, it declined to around half during the 1979–81 oil boom and to less than one-quarter by 1984. Yet Bahraini agriculture and manufacturing continued to generate only modest fractions of non-oil GDP as they did in Saudi Arabia. Bahrain's agriculture employed a much smaller fraction of its population and—despite Bahrain's pioneering role in RBI within the Gulf—its manufacturing sector remained dominated by oil refining.

Construction played a less prominent role in Bahrain than in Saudi Arabia, reflecting the reduced emphasis on investment in Bahrain's windfall absorption. Although construction's share of Bahraini non-mining GDP jumped to 15 per cent during the first oil boom it fell back to 10 per cent during the second boom and into the mid-1980s. Banking and insurance, especially offshore banking, emerged as the most important contributor to Bahrain's economic growth as the Gulf region's financial explosion combined with the political disintegration of Lebanon to open new opportunities.

The fact that Bahrain pursued tighter fiscal policies than Saudi Arabia and commenced economic diversification earlier meant that its less construction-dependent economy was in a better position than that of its larger neighbour to adjust to the mid-1980s downswing. Expenditures were quickly matched to revenues based on $20/bl. oil by stretching out developing expenditures, initiating annual recurrent expenditure cuts of 5 per cent and raising the price of public services. The country's overseas holdings, estimated at between $2 and $4 billion (Far Eastern Economic Review 1986*b*), were considered sufficient to underwrite several years of revenue diversification even if oil prices fell to $10/bl.

Although Bahrain's per caput income matched that of Saudi Arabia, its earlier and less conservative social reforms resulted in superior social indicators (life expectancy twelve years higher, infant mortality one-third as high) while its citizens, female as well as male, made more progress during the downswing in shifting into non-office urban employment of the type normally shunned by Gulf region nationals.

CONCLUSION: 'LOW-ABSORBER' PARADOXES

The standard assumption that capital-surplus oil-exporting countries have low absorptive capacity is clearly erroneous. Paradoxically, such countries proved capable of absorbing capital at an extraordinarily rapid rate. The autocratic character of the Arabian Gulf regimes provided the long-term time horizon and insulation of government élites from short-term political pressures which an effective absorption required. However, the character of the regime and the scale of the windfall were symbiotic. The successful deployment of the large oil windfall simultaneously demanded prudent management and created the wherewithal (through paternalistic measures) for such regimes to defuse discontent.

Prudent economic management during the two oil booms sought to maintain fiscal balance, restrain inflation, and sustain currency convertibility. It established three cushions against shrinking oil revenues through overseas saving, once-for-all infrastructure spending (especially favoured by Saudi Arabia) and liberal recourse to foreign workers and firms. A readiness to make full use of foreign firms and workers to fill gaps in domestic skills is one important cause of the Saudi regime's technical success in deploying the windfalls which it shared with Bahrain. Saudi Arabia proved remarkably effective at implementing the many large and complex projects which required careful synchronization (Chapter 9).

Unfortunately, the diversification strategies adopted by both Arabian countries were predicated upon the long-term availability of oil rents—directly in the case of Saudi Arabia and increasingly indirectly (via trickle-down effects from its larger neighbours) in the case of Bahrain. Even the vast foreign capital reserves of Saudi Arabia, equivalent to more than twice non-oil GDP at their peak compared with one-half for Bahrain, were strained by the scale of the mid-1980s collapse.

A second paradox now emerges: despite efficient absorption the RBI projects chosen could scarcely generate sufficient revenues to service the capital invested, let alone recoup the massive outlays on the large complementary infrastructure investments they required. This disappointing outcome discouraged private investment in linked industries so that the anticipated large multiplier effects from RBI failed to materialize. The two weaknesses of RBI as an economic diversification strategy are clearly demonstrated: its minimalist diversification from hydrocarbon dependence and its long gestation period.

Saudi Arabia proved more adept at windfall deployment during the upswing than during the downswing, whereas Bahrain adjusted more expeditiously to the latter. This suggests that the combination of earlier diversification and a smaller windfall—akin to the conditions experienced by the high absorbing oil-exporters—might favour a more resilient outcome from oil windfall absorption. Gelb (1988) has examined why this did not occur in depth. The consequences for RBI of the inability of most high-absorbers' political regimes to resist political pressures for overrapid oil windfall absorption is analysed next, in Chapter 7.

7

Macro-economic Constraints on the 'High-Absorbing' Oil-Exporting Countries

THE 'HIGH-ABSORBING' OIL EXPORTERS' WINDFALL DEPLOYMENT PROSPECTS

The oil windfalls of the 'high-absorbers' were relatively small compared with Saudi Arabia. Standardized as a fraction of non-oil GDP, they ranged from one-fifth (Trinidad and Tobago) to one-twentieth (Venezuela) the size of Saudi Arabia's windfall. It might be expected that the smaller windfall of the 'high-absorbing' countries would be easier to deploy. However, this was not the case because pressure for overrapid absorption hampered efforts to cushion against downswing through the accumulation of overseas reserves, once-for-all infrastructure provision, and the build-up of sizeable guest workforces. It also depressed absorptive efficiency.

In all six 'high-absorbing' countries, the intended deployment was different from the actual outcome, and this is only partly attributable to the unanticipated swings of the booms. For example, the rate of domestic absorption was affected by unforeseen factors which could work both to mute it (as with Indonesia's Pertamina scandal during the first boom) and boost it (as with the Venezuelan state enterprises' largely unmonitored overseas borrowing through the second boom). Most important, intense pressures for overrapid absorption taxed the strength of political regimes in all six countries. The euphoric second oil boom proved especially difficult to manage since projections of rapid global economic growth alongside sustained real energy price increases reversed the caution engendered by the tapering first oil boom.

This was the case even though five of the six 'high-absorbers' had relatively stable governments. Only Nigeria experienced continuous political instability as a brief period of democracy 1979–83 interrupted a series of coup-terminated military regimes. In contrast, Indonesia and Trinidad and Tobago had unbroken government. The paternalistic autocracy of General Soeharto ruled Indonesia for more than two decades from 1966 while a single dominant political party governed Trinidad and Tobago from 1954 to 1986, with a strong, cautious prime minister (Dr Eric Williams) in control for all but the final six years. Both late-starters, Malaysia and Cameroon, were also dominated by a single political party and an austere capable ruler held power in Cameroon for an unbroken twenty-one years until 1982.

However, it proved unfortunate that new heads of state had to establish themselves in all three small democracies (Trinidad and Tobago, Cameroon, and Malaysia) 1979–82, during—or shortly after the termination of—the second oil boom. In Venezuela, a change of leadership also coincided with the second oil boom and the newly elected president was seriously weakened by conflicts between his office and that of the opposition-dominated congress.

In the absence of an adequate cushion (via overseas saving and guestworkers) against an oil price downswing, sound macro-economic management for the 'high-absorbers' required attention to the resilience of the non-oil tradeables sector. Yet all six countries experienced difficulty in fostering a competitive manufacturing sector, resource-based or non-resource-based. Consequently, it fell to the agricultural sector to provide foreign exchange and tax revenues to offset decline in the oil sector. The more successful 'high-absorbing' countries were those with a sizeable and resilient agricultural sector. Table 6.1 shows that the lower-income 'high-absorbers' were in a better position at the outset of the oil booms in this respect than either the mid-income 'high-absorbers' or the 'low-absorbers'.

The pre-shock non-oil tradeables sectors of Venezuela and Trinidad and Tobago, which had exported oil for a longer period than the other 'high-absorbers' and had higher per capita incomes, were about two-thirds the size of the Chenery and Syrquin norms for countries of their size and level of development, with agriculture especially shrunken (Table 6.1). In contrast, the non-oil tradeables sectors of both Indonesia and Nigeria were large and dominated by agriculture. Finally, the pre-shock economies of Malaysia and Cameroon exhibited little distortion since hydrocarbons production did not reach significant proportions until the late 1970s. However, in the absence of prudent fiscal and exchange-range policies, even strong agricultural sectors proved quickly vulnerable to 'Dutch disease' effects during the oil booms.

Summarizing, among the 'high-absorbers' Indonesia possessed the most favourable combination of regime and initial economic conditions for effective windfall deployment for RBI. Venezuela had the least favourable combination. Nigeria's strong pre-shock position was undermined by weak government while Trinidad and Tobago's leadership advantage was offset by its poor pre-shock economic structure. Trinidad and Tobago also experienced an unfortunately timed leadership change—as did Malaysia and Cameroon. However, Malaysia and Cameroon had compensating advantages through their strong pre-boom economic performance and late-start. A priori, the absorption prospects for the two south-east Asian countries and Cameroon were superior to those of Nigeria and the two South American countries.

The relationship between regime type and macro-economic performance is now examined in detail for the six 'high-absorbing' countries. Particular attention is given to the capacity of different governments to maintain financial discipline and a competitive exchange rate. These macro-economic goals underpin the price stability, sustained domestic demand, and export competitiveness which successful RBI requires. Indonesia and Nigeria, the two populous low-income autocracies, are analysed first since they span the full range of regime effectiveness. Venezuela and Trinidad and Tobago, the two mid-income democracies which also had the longest dependence on oil, are next examined. Finally, the ability of Malaysia and Cameroon to take advantage of their late-start is assessed.

THE LARGE LOW-INCOME AUTOCRACIES: INDONESIA AND NIGERIA

Regime and absorptive efficiency

Indonesia and Nigeria shared important pre-shock characteristics. Both were large populous countries, with resilient agricultural sectors that were recovering strongly from internal political disturbances. Their potentially large domestic markets provided favourable conditions for RBI. Despite these promising similarities, the oil booms were associated with sustained rapid economic growth in Indonesia whereas in Nigeria real per caput incomes declined below pre-shock levels. The divergent performance is rooted in differences in the strength of political regime and attitudes towards the rural sector.

Indonesia benefited from the continuity provided by the Soeharto regime with its commitment to the pursuit of prudent fiscal and exchange-rate policies (Pinto 1987, Gillis 1984). The Five-Year Plans drafted by the Indonesian government were indicative rather than a precise blueprint. They provided a long-term (three decades) framework for development in which the emphasis evolved from basic agriculture via agro-industry to basic industry and finally balanced and self-sustaining growth in all sectors (Bunge 1983).

In contrast, the increasing frequency of regime changes in Nigeria heightened uncertainty, shortened time horizons, and inhibited implementation of unpopular policies such as fiscal restraint and devaluation. Successive Nigerian governments, military and civilian, increased state intervention, whether to boost public expenditure during the booms or to ration resources during downswings. Regulation burgeoned and simultaneously overloaded the bureaucracy and expanded the opportunities for corruption. As the overburdened civil service increasingly assumed the role of arbiter in rent-seeking behaviour so its capacity for effective administration declined. Schatz (1984) characterized the Nigerian economy as 'pirate capitalism' in which enterprise is devoted to extracting short-term gains from government largesse rather than to creating the means for the long-term generation of wealth.

The Indonesian civil service, which had been so faction-ridden as to be almost incapable of action under Sukarno, became more effective under Soeharto. Even though rent-seeking flourished and political fiefdoms persisted at local and national levels (in both the public and private sectors, notably in industry), a bureaucratic pluralism existed (Emmerson 1983). Able technocrats retained sufficient independence from the military to prevent key development ministries (Finance, Mines and Energy, Industry, and Public Works) from being wholly dominated by considerations of patronage. Although the balance of power shifted between two polarized technocratic factions, one comprising sectoral, statist nationalists and the other pragmatic, market-orientated technocrats (Gillis 1984), the latter faction was effectively used during the two oil booms to realign the economy periodically to real external constraints.

The Soeharto regime's commitment to fiscal balance and exchange-rate convertibility reinforced the pragmatic incrementalists' ability to implement unpopular measures. Luck also played a part. The Pertamina scandal helped mute Indonesian absorption during the first oil boom and provided a timely warning on the dangers of mismanagement and overrapid absorption which Nigeria lacked. Indonesian readiness to use foreign assistance (until *effective* indigenization could occur) further enhanced the country's administrative efficiency. It echoed the strategy of the 'low-absorbers' and contrasted with that of most 'high-absorbing' oil exporters.

The Nigerian and Indonesian regimes also diverged in their attentiveness to the rural sector, especially peasant farming. The Soeharto government, conscious of the role of food riots in the downfall of its predecessor, paid particular attention to foodgrain production and rural welfare. Indonesia diverted substantial resources to output- and productivity-boosting irrigation, input, and extension services. Nigeria made smaller allocations which were targeted at large farms and were used far less effectively.

Nigerian rural neglect requires explanation since Nigeria had, like Indonesia, experienced serious political upheaval over the previous decade—the 1967–9 Biafran War in Nigeria and the forcible overthrow of Sukarno in Indonesia—and faced a real threat of political disintegration. Both countries had to be more mindful of their rural constituencies than either Venezuela or Trinidad and Tobago. However, Nigeria had no counterpart to Java's timely new high-yield rice strains. Nigeria therefore sought to gain rural support through spending on infrastructure, notably on roads and education, rather than on agricultural production. Rural Nigerians welcomed this emphasis on education and roads since they favoured an urban life for their children and saw education as the means of achieving that goal. In the absence of strong class divisions, tribal considerations were dominant in Nigeria (Bienen 1983) and it was necessary to demonstrate conspicuously that the windfalls were being widely deployed. General infrastructure provision proved the most convenient vehicle.

Indonesia was transformed from a major foodgrain importer to self-sufficiency during the period of the two oil booms, whereas Nigeria moved in the opposite direction. Given the relatively underdeveloped manufacturing sectors of both countries, Indonesia's robust agricultural sector proved an important stabilizing element during the economic downswing of the mid-1980s. Nigeria's lack of a robust agricultural sector was the more damaging since its RBI projects were poorly implemented, while many Indonesian RBI projects—most notably the large export-earning LNG plants—were well implemented. Nigerian agriculture still employed two-thirds of the workforce in 1980 (World Bank 1986*b*).

Indonesia: cautious and fortunate deployment

A method for tracing oil windfall deployment has been developed by Gelb (1988) with reference to Indonesia, Nigeria, Venezuela, Trinidad and Tobago, Algeria, and Ecuador. His method is used here. It compares actual trends in absorption patterns, economic growth, and structural change with projections from the pre-shock period. The resulting divergence, corrected for differential inflation and growth rates and

TABLE 7.1. *Oil windfalls and their uses, four 'high-absorbers' 1974–1978 (%
non-mining GDP)*

Country	Indonesia	Nigeria	Trinidad and Tobago	Venezuela
Domestic oil windfall	15.9	22.8	38.9	10.8
Real	1.6	−2.3	2.3	−20.5
Price	14.3	25.1	36.6	42.3
Absorption effects				
Trade and NFS	5.3	2.8	27.2	−1.0
Current balance	2.1	5.6	27.2	3.8
Non-oil growth effect	−2.4	−1.5	−7.8	5.9
Allocation effects				
Values				
Private consumption	2.1	2.9	7.1	1.9
Public consumption	2.4	4.2	6.9	1.6
Private investment	−1.7	−6.6	−2.6	3.3
Public investment	7.9	19.5	7.3	4.9
Prices				
Private consumption	−1.1	1.2	−18.4	−10.1
Public consumption	0.7	−0.1	—	3.5
Investment	−0.5	3.8	0.0	4.4
Real				
Private consumption	3.3	1.7	25.6	12.1
Public consumption	1.7	4.3	—	0.8
Private investment	−1.3	−9.5	−2.6	1.8
Public investment	8.0	18.6	7.3	2.6
Real allocation + growth effects				
Private consumption	−1.5	7.6	19.4	15.8
Public consumption	1.5	4.2	—	1.8
Private investment	−3.4	−9.8	−4.6	3.3
Public investment	7.9	18.5	5.5	3.3

Note: Trinidad and Tobago public consumption included under private consumption, aside
from nominal value data.

Source: Gelb (1986*a*): 62–3.

standardized through expression in terms of non-oil GDP, is attributed
to the impact of the oil booms.

Although Indonesia's oil windfall, relative to non-oil GDP, was two-
thirds that of Nigeria during the first oil boom, Indonesia was more
cautious and saved one-third abroad (Table 7.1). Indonesian absorption
was further muted during the first boom by the scandal which engulfed
Pertamina, the state petroleum corporation. Pertamina's military director

overexpanded the company and resorted to short-term loans in order to circumvent a 1972 presidential decree which ordered that long-term international loans must be approved by the Finance Ministry and the Bank of Indonesia. The 1974–5 global recession slowed Pertamina's cash flow and precipitated a repayment crisis which revealed corporate debts of $10 billion on top of the country's $8 billion official public foreign debt.

The crisis drew down the country's foreign exchange reserves and required rescheduling of debt repayment to foreign creditors (Economist 1979). This slowed down the rate of Indonesian oil rent absorption and helped to halve inflation from 33 per cent. It also delayed many of Indonesia's RBI projects until the second boom. A further significant consequence of the Pertamina crisis was to temper the government's anti-foreign investment stance which had hardened in 1974 in response to public protests against Japanese investment.

During the first oil boom, public consumption increased by the equivalent of 1.5 per cent of non-oil output in real terms (Table 7.1) while private consumption shrank by a similar proportion from the pre-shock trend. Although private investment declined from its relatively high pre-shock trend, public investment more than offset this, for a net increase in the rate of capital formation over the pre-shock rate equivalent to 4.5 per cent of non-oil GDP. Two large LNG projects were successfully initiated as joint-ventures with MNRCs during this period and helped to expand and diversify hydrocarbon markets.

At first sight Indonesia's prudent, if somewhat fortuitous, windfall deployment continued through the second oil boom and into the post-boom adjustment period. The overall pattern of development expenditure supports this view: more than 40 per cent of the second windfall was saved abroad. Two-fifths of all development investment was allocated to the hydrocarbon sector to prolong oil production and diversify both foreign exchange earnings and tax revenues through LNG exports. Less than one-sixth of development expenditure went into the metal industries, compared with two-fifths in the case of Venezuela, and much of that resulted from the unsanctioned scaling up of the Krakatau steel plant. A similar amount was invested in the non-metals industries to broaden the manufacturing sector. Lastly, around one-quarter of the development investment went on infrastructure, much of it dispersed through the sprawling chain of islands and targeted at rural improvement, in an attempt to narrow the income gap between Java and the less-developed Outer Islands.

Closer inspection of the planned absorption pattern during the second oil boom, however, reveals a less flattering appraisal of Indonesia's economic management. First, private consumption, public consumption, and investment all increased sharply so that inflation accelerated. It exceeded that of the country's regional competitors and eliminated the benefits of the 1979 devaluation. Second, subsidized consumption expanded so much during the second oil boom that it threatened to undermine the competitiveness of the erstwhile efficient foodgrains sector. Fuel subsidies promised to reduce future export earnings by accelerating domestic consumption of the oil resource. Third, Indonesia announced a $10 billion list of RBI projects in 1982 which included many large ones at a time when clear evidence was emerging of reduced efficiency in its own RBI investment. Similar projects in other 'high-absorbing' oil-exporting countries such as Venezuela and Nigeria were already facing chronic global overcapacity and severe operating difficulties.

Even Soeharto's Indonesia found the pressures for overrapid absorption created by the euphoric second oil boom difficult to resist (Auty 1987c). Indonesia's reputation for the prudent deployment of its oil revenues owes much to the ability of the incremental technocrats to restrain the high-spending sectoral nationalists. The commitment to fiscal balance and currency convertibility permitted the incremental technocrats to make bold and effective adjustments to the budget and exchange rate in line with external constraints. Such timely shifts were made after unexpected negative shocks, such as the Pertamina scandal and the collapse of the first and second oil booms. Indonesia executed moderate devaluations in 1979, 1983, and 1986 in contrast to the massive exchange-rate adjustment required of Nigeria in 1986. A start was also made on broadening the tax base and on dismantling industrial protection. The latter move was long overdue, but Indonesian agriculture proved sufficiently resilient to underpin its implementation. Nigeria had no such cushion.

Nigeria's overrapid domestic absorption

Table 7.1 shows that Nigeria's first oil windfall was larger than that of Indonesia relative to non-oil GDP, but the second windfall was of similar magnitude (around 22 per cent of non-oil GDP). Unlike the Indonesian government, Nigeria saved little. After an initial sharp increase in foreign exchange reserves as the revenue was deposited abroad the Nigerian deployment swung strongly towards domestic absorption. Overseas savings were quickly run down and by 1978 the country became a net borrower, a condition to which it soon returned after a brief respite provided by the second (1979) oil shock. Nigeria used its oil revenues as collateral for foreign borrowing, effectively bringing forward consumption and boosting the rate of absorption. Such absence of fiscal prudence made bridging loans difficult to secure when sharply declining oil revenues pushed the country's debt/service ratio above 40 per cent in the mid-1980s (Harman 1986).

Investment dominated Nigerian absorption, accounting for almost two-thirds of its first windfall and one-half of the second. The greatly increased scale of public sector investment was sufficient to offset a decline from the pre-shock trend in private investment (Gelb 1988). The more modest share of consumption in windfall absorption, equivalent to 7 per cent of non-oil output during the first boom and 10 per cent during the second, was also dominated by the public sector. However, both investment and consumption figures are based on nominal prices: after adjusting for changes in relative prices and allowing for the sharp departure from the underlying pre-shock trend in economic growth during the second boom, the increase in Nigerian investment from the pre-shock trend was negligible 1979–81 while private consumption actually declined sharply (Table 7.2). This disappointing outcome reflected the severe supply-side failure of Nigerian windfall absorption (Gelb 1986*b*).

The large capital sums absorbed were poorly invested (Auty 1988*a*). Although plans for domestic steel, petrochemicals, and paper projects were already under consideration when the first oil shock occurred, Nigeria was slow to move from the feasibility stage to implementation so that the launch of its RBI strategy was delayed until the second oil boom. Instead, the first oil boom (which broadly overlapped the Third Five-Year Plan 1974–9) used a rapid expansion of infrastructure as the principal vehicle for domestic investment. Transportation accounted for one-third of government allocation 1974–9 and education for one-ninth. Although this deployment pattern drew broad popular support and conspicuously displayed the widespread and equitable distribution of oil windfall benefits, its economic utility is uncertain and the payback—at best—will be very long term (Gelb 1988).

The Fourth Five-Year Plan (1981–5) shifted emphasis to directly productive investment and emphasized RBI for import substitution. It projected an annual rate of investment exceeding one-third of GDP with steel accounting for one-third of planned expenditures, petrochemicals for one-fifth, and large pulp and agro-industry projects for one-tenth. Sustained domestic economic growth was crucial to full RBI capacity utilization but the oil glut caused oil revenues to decline and quickly

TABLE 7.2. *Oil windfalls and their uses, four 'high-absorbers' 1979–1981 (% non-mining GDP)*

Country	Indonesia	Nigeria	Trinidad and Tobago	Venezuela
Domestic oil windfall	22.7	21.9	34.7	8.7
Real	−2.5	−6.1	−7.4	−28.0
Price	25.2	28.0	42.1	36.6
Absorption effects				
Trade and NFS	9.6	0.1	16.8	1.1
Current balance	6.1	3.9	19.2	7.0
Non-oil growth effect	−3.5	−29.8	0.6	−6.6
Allocation effects				
Values				
Private consumption	1.2	4.1	8.6	9.4
Public consumption	3.7	5.6	—	0.7
Investment	8.1	12.1	9.3	−2.5
Prices				
Private consumption	−9.3	−4.1	−18.2	−14.7
Public consumption	0.3	0.6	—	0.4
Investment	−0.5	4.8	−2.6	1.1
Real				
Private consumption	10.5	8.2	26.7	24.1
Public consumption	3.4	5.0	—	−0.3
Investment	8.6	7.3	12.0	−3.5
Real allocation + growth effects				
Private consumption	7.7	−15.3	27.2	20.0
Public consumption	3.0	2.3	—	−0.7
Investment	7.9	0.4	12.2	−6.0

Note: Trinidad and Tobago public consumption included under private consumption.
Source: Gelb (1986a): 64.

rendered key assumptions of the plan unrealistic. The plan details were never published (Stevens 1984). Nevertheless, dominated by RBI, manufacturing absorbed one-third of total federal expenditure 1975–83 and the public sector accounted for two-thirds of all Nigerian manufacturing investment over that period. The quality of directly productive investment in the public sector was uniformly low. Large projects dominated manufacturing allocations and experienced big cost overruns and severe operating difficulties and failed to achieve satisfactory capacity utilization (Chapter 9).

Unlike Indonesia, Nigeria had no resilient agricultural sector to cushion it against declining oil revenues. The modest sums invested on small rural projects during the booms yielded a poor return. They improved the lot of administrators and contractors rather than farmers (Harman 1986). Meanwhile, severe 'Dutch disease' effects eroded agricultural competitiveness. The exchange rate appreciated from its 1970–2 base by 30 per cent during the first boom and 70 per cent during the second boom—an overall rise of 110 per cent by 1982–3—as successive governments postponed devaluation. Unlike Indonesia, the Ministry of Finance in Nigeria was not called upon to make timely exchange-rate adjustments. Despite sharply rising prices, agricultural production failed to keep pace with demand. Meanwhile, manufacturing became increasingly import dependent so that an estimated three-quarters of the sector's inputs were imported in the early 1980s. Acute operational difficulties therefore occurred as the foreign exchange earnings from oil contracted.

Yet Nigeria's urban-dominated public opinion strongly opposed devaluation. The country increasingly resorted to government controls to allocate scarce foreign exchange, despite mounting administrative problems. Abuse of the system was so widespread that it was estimated that less than one-quarter of Nigeria's scarce foreign exchange was expended on the imports for which it was allocated—a revealing index of government inefficiency.

THE PIONEERING DEMOCRACIES: VENEZUELA AND TRINIDAD AND TOBAGO

Saving the windfall

Venezuela and Trinidad and Tobago were pioneers of RBI with many similarities arising from their common lengthy experience as petroleum economies. Their per capita incomes were significantly above those of the other 'high-absorbers' and the structure of their economies diverged more sharply from the Chenery and Syrquin norms for countries of comparable size and level of development (see Table 10.2, below). Neither economy was underpinned by a sizeable agricultural sector so that diversification into competitive manufacturing was more urgent.

Democracy based on universal suffrage was relatively new in both countries but resulted in weaker regimes in Venezuela. Whereas political power in Venezuela alternated between the two main parties and could produce stalemate between an executive and legislature controlled by differing parties, Trinidad and Tobago's Westminster-styled government allowed a single party to dominate and within that party a single leader held extraordinary authority. However, the Trinidad and Tobago government's strong parliamentary majority proved difficult to translate into prudent long-term windfall deployment. Extra-parliamentary disturbances in 1970, including an abortive coup, shook the confidence of the Trinidad and Tobaco government, rendering it more receptive to radical demands for national ownership and income redistribution (Auty and Gelb 1986).

Table 7.1 shows that Venezuela received windfalls from the oil shocks equivalent to 10 per cent of non-oil GDP 1974–8 and 8 per cent 1979–81. However the size of the windfall experienced by Trinidad and Tobago relative to its non-oil economy was around four times that of Venezuela in each case. Both governments sought to sterilize the revenue inflow by building up overseas reserves and establishing special development funds. Trinidad and Tobago was more successful in accumulating foreign reserves: 70 per cent of Trinidad and Tobago's first oil windfall was saved abroad and almost half the second windfall. By 1981 its reserves totalled more than $3 billion, equivalent to half the country's non-oil GDP, and provided a sizeable cushion against declining oil revenues.

Although the Venezuelan government earmarked half the oil revenues for long-term saving and established the Fondo de Inversiones Venezuela (FIV) as a repository, actual saving fell far short of this goal. FIV received only 35 per cent of windfall revenues in 1974, less in 1975, nothing in 1976, and 10 per cent in 1977. By that year the seeds of the early 1980s financial crisis had been sown. To avoid delays imposed by the opposition-dominated congress, the state enterprises resorted to overseas financing on a mounting and imprecisely monitored scale, thereby effectively undoing the executive's efforts to control the pace of windfall absorption. Instead of saving half the windfall from the first oil shock 1974–8, Venezuela absorbed virtually all of it and also expanded its foreign debt (Gelb 1988). Imprudent borrowing and huge capital flight left Venezuela with debts exceeding $26 billion by 1984.

Overambitious public investment

Table 7.1 shows that Venezuela invested a larger fraction of the oil windfall during the first oil boom than its smaller neighbour, since Venezuela simply scaled up its existing diversification programme while Trinidad and Tobago was still publically debating its deployment options. Venezuela specialized heavily in steel and aluminium production in Ciudad Guayana which absorbed nine-tenths of its RBI investment. The RBI investment in turn exceeded that expended on oil and gas exploration and development and also that on infrastructure, the other major applications of investment from the oil windfalls.

By contrast, Trinidad and Tobago was initially cautious in allocating its oil windfall. Real private investment actually declined from the pre-shock trend, though this reflected the relatively high pre-shock levels associated with the development of new hydrocarbon resources off the island's east coast. A public debate on the allocation of the windfall ended in 1976 with the decision to construct a gas-based industrial complex at Point Lisas. Investment thereafter picked up and intially concentrated on the elimination of the infrastructural backlog which had built up since the late 1960s—notably in transport, power, and water—as the major RBI projects were planned and launched (Auty and Gelb 1986). During the shorter second oil boom Trinidad and Tobago boosted investment by the equivalent of 12 per cent of non-oil GDP above the pre-shock trend as the RBI projects were completed.

Poor implementation, aggravated by nationalistic reluctance to take full advantage of MNRC assistance, rendered the large capital infusions both low in quality and inflationary. Trinidad and Tobago invested the equivalent of one-fifth of its GDP 1974–82, more than twice the rate of Venezuela. The scale of investment overstretched transportation facilities and the construction sector; skilled labour shortages were exacerbated; poor project synchronization caused delays so that by the late 1970s public sector infrastructure projects were costing two to four times pre-boom levels. This, together with the diversion of a rapidly increasing share of government 'investment' to cover losses in state industries acquired during the two booms (in response to populist demands for greater economic autonomy) significantly depressed investment quality.

In Venezuela, the Ciudad Guayana industrial complex also experienced strong inflation and large cost overruns, exacerbated by its isolated location which made labour difficult to attract and retain (Auty 1986*b*). In 1979 the newly elected COPEI government anticipated accelerating inflation as production from the new RBI investments came on stream and so it introduced deflationary measures. Unfortunately, production from the overambitious and poorly implemented RBI strategy was much delayed. This delay combined with the sudden onset of the second oil boom to prompt the COPEI government to draw back in midstream from the prudent measures it had introduced to liberalize the domestic economy and spur private investment. The Trinidad and Tobago government similarly downgraded the more prudent policies championed by its Finance Ministry. High levels of protection in the private manufacturing sector and further corrosion of agricultural efficiency left both countries overdependent on oil and RBI for revenues and foreign exchange.

Burgeoning consumption patterns

Ironically, it was the mid-income democracies among the 'high-absorbing' oil-exporters which diverted the largest fraction of their windfall to consumption (Tables 7.1 and 7.2). Higher consumption absorbed a substantial fraction of the windfalls through subsidies and price controls. After correcting for prices and growth effects, real consumption was boosted by 19 per cent of non-oil GDP in Trinidad and Tobago during the first oil boom compared with the pre-shock trend and by just over 17 per cent in Venezuela (Table 7.1). Consumption gains were even greater during the second boom (Table 7.2), despite the deflationary package introduced by Venezuela's COPEI government.

Both governments used widespread price controls to curb inflation. One consequence of this was that Trinidad and Tobago experienced a modest 1.4 per cent appreciation in its exchange rate during the first oil boom whereas the Venezuelan currency depreciated 3 per cent. Unfortunately, price controls depressed investment in private industry and helped retard diversification towards a more competitive non-oil economy. Worse, public expenditure on subsidies proved unsustainable beyond the second oil boom and fuelled inflation. The exchange rate appreciated rapidly in both countries after the 1979–81 oil boom.

Although both countries did redistribute income towards the poorer people and pushed unemployment to low levels during the boom periods, the scale was small and proved unsustainable. In Trinidad and Tobago, increasing subsidies to high-paying public works programmes adversely affected the supply of rural labour to agriculture. Subsidies to failing public corporations, such as the state sugar industry, also proved counter-productive. Unit wage costs rose fivefold 1977–82 in the state sugar industry as production costs soared to almost ten times those of an efficient producer (Financial Times 1985c). Similar levels of inefficiency permeated the Venezuelan economy: the investment and rapid expansion of the labour force during the two oil booms generated only half the output which could reasonably have been expected.

Prudent measures designed to curb consumption and boost the neglected non-RBI sectors as the first oil boom faded in 1978–9 were swept aside as the 1979 oil shock overrode the arguments for caution. Ominously, the accelerating appreciation of the real exchange rate in both countries through the second boom simultaneously expanded each country's import capacity and further undermined their weak non-oil tradeables sectors. Exchange-rate correction was delayed until late 1983 in Venezuela and late 1985 in Trinidad and Tobago, and the adjustment proved too modest in each case. Venezuela resorted to prolonged and severe deflation while Trinidad and Tobago exhausted its sizeable foreign exchange reserves in the vain hope of an oil price upswing. Elections in Trinidad and Tobago replaced the ruling party with a government open to the pursuit of less statist policies. However, Venezuela remained locked into corporatist policies, ostensibly prompted by fears of extremist intervention but—perhaps, more significantly—underpinned by the clientelism of both major political parties (Scott 1986).

THE LATE-STARTERS: MALAYSIA AND CAMEROON

Leadership changes promote overrapid absorption

Prior to the second oil boom, hydrocarbon exports were of negligible importance to either Cameroon or Malaysia. Both countries had acquired reputations for prudent economic management which was reflected in favourable sustained rates of economic growth (Acharya 1981, Benjamin and Devarajan 1984, Bunge 1984).

Cameroon benefited from membership of the CFA Franc Zone, since that reduced the risk for foreign investors and encouraged fiscal prudence to maintain currency convertibility (Devarajan *et al.* 1986). During the lengthy and cautious paternalistic leadership of its first president Cameroon steadily increased the share of investment in GDP (simultaneously reducing dependence on aid) and lifted its rate of economic growth, based largely on competitive agriculture and modest import substitution industry. A tree-crop boom in the mid-1970s was successfully managed (Devarajan *et al.* 1986). Malaysia also benefited from continuity of government and began promoting manufactured exports so that, reflecting its faster economic progress, manufacturing's share of GDP jumped from 12 to 22 per cent through the 1970s while the sector's share of exports, spearheaded by electronics, jumped to one-quarter.

Conditions for prudent windfall deployment were propitious for both countries. Since oil did not assume a dominant role in their economies until the second boom, each country had ample opportunity to learn from the mistakes of its large 'high-absorbing' neighbour. However, neither was successful, even though Cameroon sought to follow an unusual and extraordinarily cautious deployment strategy. The immediate cause of the problem was a change of leadership in both countries but more fundamental difficulties lay in ethnic strife and government inefficiency.

The two countries shared the prospect of ethnic strife. Historically, Cameroon met this by a sustained commitment to small-scale agriculture which employed the vast majority of the workforce (irrespective of tribe), whereas the Malaysian government sought to increase the economic participation of Malays at the expense of the Chinese minority by expanding parastatals and legislating ethnic shares of equity ownership (Mallon 1982). Change in political leadership as oil production grew had important consequences for each country. Malaysia's new prime minister proved an impatient authoritarian and committed his government to massive expansion of the economic role of the public sector. By contrast, the new Cameroon president who took office in 1982 was weaker than his long-established predecessor and sought to consolidate his position with political favours.

The oil windfalls proved timely for both new leaders. Oil production expanded rapidly in the two countries through the early 1980s: rising volumes offset declining prices to boost revenues and prolong the second oil boom until the price collapse of 1986. The Malaysian windfall rose to around 15 per cent of non-oil GDP while the Cameroon windfall expanded from the equivalent to 10.5 per cent of non-oil GDP 1979–81 to almost 19 per cent 1982–5. Unfortunately, both the timing of the late-starters' windfall and data deficiencies preclude the use of Gelb's methodology to trace their windfall deployment.

Malaysia's cavalier deployment

Whereas Cameroon resorted to extraordinary secrecy over its windfall deployment strategy, Malaysia deployed its oil windfalls in a well-publicized diversification into heavy industry. Unfortunately, the strength of the Malaysian economy in the late 1970s had been overestimated: a marked improvement in Malaysia's terms of trade masked a significant weakening in agricultural performance and in the economy as a whole. The World Bank estimated that favourable trading trends accounted for half the unusually high rate of economic growth (around 11 per cent per annum). The late 1970s' boom was associated with 'Dutch disease' effects as productive resources shifted into the non-tradeables sector and unsustainable patterns of expenditure were established.

Under the aegis of the future prime minister, the Malaysian government determined on a large-scale expansion of heavy industry at

TABLE 7.3. *Malaysian absorption 1979–1985 (% total GDP)*

	1979	1980	1981	1982	1983	1984	1985
Private consumption	48.3	50.5	53.1	53.1	51.7	49.8	50.0
Public consumption	13.9	16.5	18.1	18.3	17.5	14.8	15.3
TOTAL CONSUMPTION	62.2	67.0	71.2	71.4	69.2	64.6	65.3
Private investment	17.5	19.5	19.9	18.2	17.3	16.8	14.0
Public investment	8.9	11.6	16.1	18.2	18.0	15.1	15.8
TOTAL INVESTMENT	26.4	31.1	36.0	36.4	35.3	31.9	29.8
TOTAL ABSORPTION	88.6	98.1	107.2	107.8	104.5	96.5	95.1
TOTAL PUBLIC ABSORPTION	22.8	28.1	34.2	36.5	35.5	29.9	31.1

Note: Oil as % total revenues: (1979) 14.0; (1980) 23.0; (1981) 32.0; (1982) 34.0; (1983) 30.0; (1984, 1985) n/a.

Sources: Ministry of Finance (1986); Petronas (1984) for oil as % total revenues.

the close of the 1970s, after the Korean development model. Ironically, the South Koreans were then beginning to doubt the wisdom of their heavy industry drive. The commencement of Malaysia's heavy industry programme increased its rate of domestic investment to more than 30 per cent of GDP. The oil windfall was used to boost capital inflows and much of the heavy industry programme was financed in yen with Japanese suppliers' credits. The output generated by these investments was disappointing, while the mid-1980s appreciation of the yen exacerbated burdensome capital service charges.

In addition to its central role in funding heavy industry Malaysian government undertook other expenditures in the early 1980s designed to offset the commodity downturn. The public sector's share of GDP jumped from 40 to 60 per cent while the budget deficit rose to 20 per cent of GDP. The current account, which had recorded sizeable surpluses in the mid-1970s, was transformed into a deficit of around 10 per cent of GDP. Private capital formation declined (Table 7.3) and growth decelerated sharply as deflationary measures were introduced as part of a stabilization package. However, Malaysia's export agriculture and diversifying competitive manufacturing proved adequate cushions during the country's painful mid-1980s adjustment.

Cameroon's secretive deployment

In contrast to Malaysia and the other 'high-absorbers', the Cameroon government, mindful of the experience of neighbouring Gabon and

Nigeria, sought to escape pressures for rapid absorption by deliberately understating the size of its oil windfall. One estimate in the mid-1980s suggested that Cameroon saved as much as three-quarters of the oil windfall overseas (Benjamin and Deverajan 1986), but more recent figures suggest the outcome was one-third that level (Institute for International Finance (IIF) 1986). The secrecy surrounding the oil windfall in Cameroon made its size and allocation difficult to gauge and this was ultimately the policy's undoing.

Successive Five-Year Plans saw a steady rise in the proportion of GDP allocated to investment from 14 per cent in the late 1960s to more than 25 per cent in the early 1980s, the first years of Cameroon's oil boom. Three large RBI projects commenced at the close of the Fourth Plan but they were disappointing (Auty 1988a). Although Cameroon's Fifth Plan (1981–6) envisaged an exceptionally large increase in overall investment the priority switched away from industrial projects. Less than one-fifth of planned total investment was earmarked for manufacturing (including the oil sector) under the Fifth Plan compared with almost half under the Fourth Plan, while rural and social investment each expanded to around one-quarter, on a par with infrastructure. However, the scale of investment projected for the Fifth Plan proved beyond the country's implementation capacity: public sector projects were often vaguely specified and unimplemented while private investors were untempted.

The cooling of Cameroon's appetite for new RBI projects was in contrast to Nigeria, and is consistent with the pursuit of a prudent deployment policy. However, the momentum of overambitious decisions made in the Fourth Plan (1976–81) and the need of the new president who came to power in 1982 to use extra-budgetary spending to establish his authority worked against the goal of slow absorption. Official figures point to a sharp increase in public expenditure from the early 1980s while unofficial estimates suggest additional large sums were expended by the presidency from extra-budgetary sources (IIF 1986). These extra funds were allocated to infrastructure projects and to service the foreign debt of ailing parastatals.

As elsewhere, the Cameroon oil windfall was overrapidly absorbed. Oil revenues expanded to account for more than two-fifths of total government revenues (Table 7.4) while non-oil revenues fell back to 16 per cent of non-oil output—their level in 1971. By the mid-1980s, losses from state enterprises were estimated to account for almost half the total oil revenues, with much of that funding coming through extra-budgetary sources. Worse, as a relatively high-cost oil producer (Cameroon oil costs more than four times that of Nigeria), the 1986

TABLE 7.4. *Cameroon: absorption, structural composition, and revenue sources 1978 and 1985 (% non-oil GDP)*

	1978	1985
Absorption		
Private consumption	72.0	67.3
Public consumption	11.1	11.3
Investment	25.2	30.0
Total absorption	108.3	108.6
Sectoral composition		
Agriculture	31.7	25.3
Manufacturing	9.0	14.5
Other non-oil	59.3	60.2
Government revenue		
Total revenue	20.6	29.1
Oil revenue	1.2	13.1

Notes: Non-oil GDP: (1978) 1,113.0 CFA billion; (1985) 2,975.0 CFA billion; Non-oil GDP as % total GDP: (1978) 97.1%; (1985) 82.8%.
Sources: Cameroon government sources.

decline in oil prices sharply reduced the Cameroon government's receipts. Unable to square public pronouncements on windfall savings in the mid-1980s with the actual situation, the country drifted. It was left to the still large and resilient agricultural sector to smooth the country's adjustment to lower oil revenues.

CONCLUSION

The smaller windfalls of the 'high-absorbing' oil-exporters meant they lacked the 'low-absorbers' fortunate symbiosis of plentiful resources and strong paternalistic governments. They could not defuse conflicts by simultaneously building up a large cushion of overseas reserves, expanding social and economic infrastructure, and diversifying the non-oil tradeables sector. The macro-economic prerequisites for effective RBI launch (price stability, sustained domestic demand, and a competitive exchange rate) therefore proved elusive.

Although most governments sought to pursue prudent policies, none successfully resisted pressure for overrapid absorption. Only Indonesia emerged from the oil booms with its reputation for sound macro-economic management intact. Absorption tended to be wasteful. Competitive structural diversification decelerated or even regressed—

most dramatically in Nigeria, but also in Venezuela and Trinidad and Tobago. The two late-comers, Malaysia and Cameroon, learned little from the mistakes of others.

Only Trinidad and Tobago (which experienced a relatively large windfall) and Indonesia (which had high spending plans fortuitously curbed) accumulated significant overseas savings. Saving and sterilization efforts by Cameroon failed as did those of Nigeria and Venezuela which accumulated burdensome debts beyond their capacity to service unaided. Public investment absorbed sizeable fractions of the oil windfall in all countries, but overtaxed the government's implementation capacity so that its quality was poor—especially in Nigeria, Venezuela, and Cameroon. Consumption rose to unsustainable levels, notably in Trinidad and Tobago and Nigeria, boosted by subsidies and exchange-rate overvaluation.

Regimes able to pursue long-term development policies, notably those of Indonesia and Trinidad and Tobago, but also the late-starters, had the advantage of consistency. However, leadership changes in both the South American and late-starter countries during the second oil boom weakened their capacity to pursue prudent policies—a course already strained by the euphoria which that boom engendered. Like the weak Nigerian regimes, they lacked the ability to make timely and bold macro-economic adjustments to the exchange rate and public spending in line with changing external constraints. Cameroon's potentially advantageous links to the CFA Franc Zone in this regard were undermined by its secretive deployment strategy. Only Indonesia (and Malaysia, to a lesser extent) appeared to possess the required macro-economic discipline and skill for the successful pursuit of RBI.

The disappointing overseas saving and investment results increased the importance of a sizeable and resilient agricultural cushion against windfall contraction. Prolonged exposure to 'Dutch disease' effects before the two oil booms left the two South American countries disadvantaged here, a condition worsened by their failure to make a compensating expansion of competitive manufacturing. Of the four other countries, Nigeria neglected its smallfarm sector and thereby squandered an important source of economic and political stability.

The inability of governments to fulfil a dominant role in windfall deployment is clear. Even the long-running and cautious Indonesian regime's reputation for prudent deployment owed something to fortuitous spending curbs. The 'high-absorbers' might have benefited by drawing on skills from the developed countries—as the 'low-absorbing' countries so obviously did—but pressure for domestic spending made such a course difficult. Macro-economic effectiveness varied and was reflected in the performance of specific RBI projects (Chapter 9). In general, the 'low-absorbers' outperformed the 'high-absorbers' and within the latter group the south-east Asian countries sustained the most favourable macro-economic environment and Nigeria the least favourable. The RBI launch enterprises tended to reflect macro-economic performance, as Chapter 8 demonstrates.

8

Micro-efficiency: Firm Performance in RBI

MACRO- AND MICRO-EFFICIENCY LINKS

This chapter explores the extent to which the differences in the macro-economic effectiveness of the eight oil-exporting countries were mirrored by their RBI firms and hence amplified. It asks whether the performance of particular RBI firms was significantly better than or worse than that predicted by a country's macro-economic performance, and why. It will be recalled that effective macro-economic policy for RBI required price stability through prompt removal of inflation bottlenecks during construction (to contain capital costs), sustained rapid growth in the domestic economy (and therefore, in high-margin domestic sales), and maintenance of a competitive exchange rate (to permit profitable non-oil exports). The ability of governments to meet these requirements proved highest in the Middle East, slightly lower for South-east Asia, disappointing for South America, and lowest for Nigeria.

The product strategy and organizational structure of firms normally has a strong effect on their performance. However, for the RBI firms in the eight oil-exporting countries, the autonomy of the firm proves more critical. The autonomy of RBI firms is shown to have little relationship to internal organizational structure, but to influence product strategy. Firm autonomy is strongly and positively related to multinational resource corporation (MNRC) equity participation. MNRC participation is, in turn, positively related to country macro-economic performance and completes a virtuous circle of efficiency.

In developing countries state involvement is usually required to secure sizeable domestic participation in RBI. This is because the scale of investment and risk associated with most RBI projects is too great for domestic private firms to bear. Such market-failure arguments for state involvement are reinforced by political considerations which include the potential divergence between private corporate and state interests, accelerated technology transfer, and the extension of political patronage. Ideology may also play an important role, as in the case of Algeria among the oil-exporting countries as a whole (Conway and Gelb 1988).

The benefits from the pursuit of such non-commercial objectives are difficult to quantify and monitor. Most RBI projects were conceived in the mid-1970s when the developing-country backlash against MNRCs was at its height and experience with state-owned enterprises (SOEs) in developing countries was limited. The benefits from employing SOEs was expected to outweigh any costs arising either from the learning experience or the broadening of corporate objectives (Radetzki 1985). Yet few mechanisms for isolating the cost of pursuing non-commercial objectives (such as formal contracts between the SOE and the state for their performance) were adopted. The option of confining the role of the state to that of an investor in an MNRC subsidiary was universally rejected in favour of either joint-ventures between SOEs and MNRCs or wholly state-owned firms. The expected high returns from RBI may have seemed to offer an ample margin with which to absorb any net costs arising from the pursuit of socio-political goals.

By the mid-1980s SOEs had accumulated a disappointing record in the developing countries, though not universally so (Auty 1986c, Jones 1982, Nellis 1986, Shirley 1983, Radetzki 1985, Trebat 1983, World Bank 1983a). The generally poor performance of SOEs in developing countries arises from five basic problems: the imposition of multiple, and sometimes contradictory, goals, the absence of a single performance measure such as profitability, the distorted use of factors of production (through preferential access to overseas capital and domestic finance and through pressure for employment maximization), the low expectation of enterprise liquidation, and insufficient managerial autonomy (Shirley 1983). The prominent role assigned to SOEs in RBI ran the very real risk that macro-economic inefficiency in the deployment of the oil windfalls would be compounded by inefficiencies at the micro level.

Shafer (1983) has explored the link between SOE efficiency in particular countries and the political stability of the governing regime, drawing examples from the international copper industry. He contrasts the poor performance of the state copper firms in Zambia and Zaire with the superior performance of Codelco in Chile. He finds that weak regimes are likely to trade the economic efficiency of SOEs for short-term political gain. Shafer suggests that developing country governments failed to appreciate the extent to which MNRC ownership can insulate economic enterprises from the debilitating effects of both predatory domestic political pressures as well as external financial and market difficulties.

The experience of the oil-exporting countries with RBI broadly supports Shafer's findings. However, some qualification of the direct link between strength of political regime, macro-economic efficiency, and SOE performance is required since efficient SOEs can coexist with inefficient ones within the same country (Trebat 1983). Escobar (1982) offers a sophisticated explanation of such divergent performance through a comparison of SOEs in Brazil and Venezuela. She views SOEs as evolving coalitions of efficiency-orientated engineers and politically sensitive commissars. The balance between the two groups—which can change in response to specific policy issues—determines enterprise performance.

Although SOEs can pursue efficiency criteria in Escobar's model, it is clear that the SOE's attraction as a source of political patronage tends to deflect them. This tendency may be checked with adequate (not excessive) managerial autonomy. The managerial autonomy required may be secured through personal leadership or the leverage which a dominant enterprise wields on account of its central role in the economy. However, neither of these factors safeguards the required autonomy: an institutional mechanism is needed to ensure that commercial goals are not subverted either by excessive government intervention or secretive autocratic management. Ayub and Hegstad (1986) consider organizational structure to be effective in this regard, but their findings are not supported by the present study. Rather, MNRC equity participation is found to be closely associated with satisfactory RBI enterprise autonomy.

The argument is developed through a series of case studies, the data for which were collected from documentary sources and through interviews with SOE and private executives, government officials, consultants, and academics in the eight oil-exporting countries. The conclusions are based on the experience of the twenty RBI firms and more than fifty projects in the eight countries studied. But first, a classification of SOEs is required.

CLASSIFICATION OF RBI ENTERPRISES

Rumelt's classification: project strategy

In his seminal analysis of the performance of large enterprises in the US, Rumelt (1974) uses two classification criteria, product strategy and organizational structure. Product strategy emerges as the critical characteristic. Of special significance is the degree of dependence on a single product and the extent to which diversification, when it occurs, is into products which are related to the basic product line.

Organizational structure is subservient to product strategy. For

Rumelt, the key to organizational structure is the manner in which field units are integrated into the corporate system. The two principal modes of organization are divisional (by product line) and functional (by central service across product lines).

Rumult showed that the 500 largest US firms exhibited a pronounced product diversification trend 1949–69, with a sharp decline in the number of firms in the single product category balanced by a rise of conglomerates to form 12 per cent of the total and, most important of all, by related diversified firms (which moved away from a dominant vertically integrated strategy by building on a single resource or strength) to 45 per cent. The performance of the related diversified firms was superior to other groups. Single product firms tended to stagnate. Conglomerate diversifications were beset by problems of overextension beyond the core of skills possessed by the firm.

The dominant product vertically integrated strategy favoured by established MNRC firms involved in RBI also performed below average. This resulted from their need to commit a large fraction of their resources to risk-reducing investment along the vertical chain. The firms which pursued this strategy were far less able than diversified firms to take advantage of new high-growth products.

The overall diversification trend noted by Rumelt appears to reflect changes in the North American market's regional product cycle (Auty 1984c). As advancing maturity causes a deceleration in the regional growth rate of their lead product, single and dominant-product firms need to merge or diversify if they are to retain a growth dynamic at the level of the firm (Auty 1983a, Auty 1984c). This suggests that a specific product strategy will perform differently, according to the particular stage of the product style reached in its principal market (Table 8.1).

Rumelt's classification: organizational structure

Rumelt found that major changes in organizational structure reflected trends in product strategy. The firms using a product division organization expanded from one-fifth to almost three-quarters of the total. The functional organizational structure declined in approximately the inverse of these same ratios. The divisional structure is of particular interest to SOEs spawned by the large public sector bureaucracies because it postpones the onset of diseconomies associated with administering large organizations. It does this by passing day-to-day decisions to the field units, leaving the head office to monitor returns from the divisions with an eye to long-term strategy. The divisions thus compete with each other for the allocation of investment since this will

TABLE 8.1. *Some characteristics of product life-cycle stages*

Stage	Growth	Corporate risk	Market structure	Product strategy
Pioneer	high/ erratic	high/ falling	monopoly	single
Maturity	high/ easing	low	oligopoly	dominant
Eclipse	slow/ negative	increasing	concentration/ state monopoly	diversifying/ subsidized single

Source: Auty (1984c: 328)

go to existing or new product lines promising the highest rate of return beyond the short term. While the divisional structure is triggered by the pressures of administering a large business, it has been noted by Chandler (1962) that—once established—the multidivisional structure institutionalizes a strategy of product diversification (Auty 1981).

Further elaboration is required in order to extend Rumelt's classification to embrace SOEs. His geographical organizational category is excluded since only two SOEs studied were permitted to invest overseas (and then, on a relatively minor scale). More fundamentally, Rumelt's functional and divisional structures appear to have little bearing on the crucial relationship between the SOE and the government. Consequently, these structures are relegated to a passive role and a new subdivision based on autonomy is adopted, recognizing two polar types: (low autonomy) bureaucratic firms and (high autonomy) commercial firms. In the eight oil-exporting countries, the extent of private MNRC participation proved the most important determinant of enterprise autonomy.

Specifically, a joint-venture with an MNRC can reduce socio-political corrosion of efficiency criteria—provided the private equity stake crosses a threshold level around 25 per cent of total equity in a prudently levered project. In other words, the MNRC partner has sufficient capital at risk to press for efficiency goals. Moreover, MNRCs restrict the scope for secretive SOE partners to abuse their autonomy because most industrial countries require MNRCs to make prompt and extensive disclosure of their financial operations.

Three qualifications concerning the value of MNRC partners are in order. First, SOEs can effectively launch RBI in countries pursuing efficient macro-economic policies, though they may lack adequate

TABLE 8.2. *Product strategy and autonomy of RBI firms*[a]

	High autonomy	Low autonomy
Single product	AISCO(B)[b] ALBA(B)[d] Inalum(I)[b]	Nafcom(N)[c]
Single product (horizontal integration)	PT Pusri(I)[e]	SDD(N)[e] PT Krakatau(I)[e]
Dominant product (vertical integration)	PDVSA(V)[e]	Pertamina(I)[c] NNPC(N)[e] Petromin(S)[c] SNH(C)[d] Petronas[e]
Diversified: related	SABIC(S)[c] GPIC(B)[b]	
Diversified: conglomerate	NEC(T)[d] HICOM(M)[c]	CVG(V)[d] SGI(M)[e] SNI(C)[d]

Notes:
[a] Country of operation shown by brackets: B = Bahrain; C = Cameroon; I = Indonesia; M = Malaysia; N = Nigeria; S = Saudi Arabia; T = Trinidad and Tobago; V = Venezuela.
[b] More than 50% privately owned;
[c] Between 25 and 50% privately owned;
[d] Less than 20 per cent private;
[e] Wholly state-owned.

safeguards against the long-term political corrosion of performance. Second, the consortia of MNRCs favoured by Japanese investors may result in each firm's stake being too small to maintain the required pressure for commercial goals. Third, MNRC partners do not guarantee a superior allocation of national resources: ineffective governments may be as incapable of handling private firms as they are SOEs (Svejnar and Harigu 1987).

Rumelt recognized that several of his product strategy classes were redundant and, for the more specialized group of enterprises analysed here, the nine categories he adopted in his study can be further reduced to five. Table 8.2 summarizes the classes remaining and they are:

- single product with horizontal integration;
- single product without horizontal integration;
- vertically integrated dominant product;
- related diversified;
- unrelated diversified (or conglomerate).

Each category can be further subdivided by degree of autonomy.

The potentially most dynamic enterprise is the high autonomy joint-venture, which is divisionally organized and pursuing a related-diversified product strategy in a dynamic regional market. The least resilient firm is the functionally organized, low autonomy bureaucratic firm pursuing a single product strategy in a mature (slowing) regional market. It may be noted that the base case (Chapter 3) assumes a high autonomy joint-venture pursuing a *de facto* vertically integrated dominant product strategy in a high-growth market.

MNRCs as a model for SOEs

The fledgling state oil corporations provided an obvious RBI launch vehicle and one for which the oil majors served as a model. In the post-war years the oil majors embarked on a long-term strategy of dominant product vertical-integration. This was supplemented by diversification into related product lines, such as coal and minerals, and also into unrelated businesses like retailing and electric motors (Auty 1983c). The leading aluminium MNRCs also pursued a vertically integrated dominant product strategy into high-growth regional markets. They too briefly attempted rapid diversification when demand in those markets unexpectedly slowed down in the late 1950s and again in the mid-1980s. The aluminium majors responded to decelerating aluminium demand and the proliferation of new materials by seeking to transform themselves into diversified materials producers. In contrast, the leading steel firms traditionally emphasized horizontal integration orientated towards national markets. They accelerated their product diversification when those markets experienced an unexpectedly sharp decline in the early 1980s.

Vertical integration reflects efforts to internalize firm-specific advantages in the face of imperfect markets (Dunning 1980). It can also reduce risk during periods of heightened uncertainty such as the 1970s (Rugman 1978). The continuing strategic benefits of vertical integration are amply demonstrated by the sharp oscillations in the relative profitability of the oil majors' upstream and downstream operations through the 1980s. Horizontal integration buttressed vertical integration as a defence against heightened uncertainty. It often involved geographical diversification into new regional markets, a strategy which new-developing-country entrants found hard to emulate. The divisional structure adopted by most MNRCs to achieve diversification goals was most commonly based on product lines, and only occasionally on a functional or geographical structure (Auty 1983a, 1983b, 1983c, 1984c).

The mixed success of the MNRC's diversification efforts confirmed the weakness of conglomerate diversification into unrelated products. However, the expected symbiotic gains from shifts by the oil majors into related product lines such as other minerals yielded few of the expected benefits (Auty 1983c). Fundamental demand changes during the two oil booms had pushed most RBI away from the leading edge of industrialization in the advanced economies. Although developing country RBI product markets were in earlier stages of the product cycle and could therefore look forward to a decade or more of rapid growth, materials-conserving and materials-diversifying technological change may shorten the product cycle for them. However, this is more an argument against entry into those industries in the first place, rather than against a particular product strategy.

The state oil corporations represented one important potential vehicle for RBI project launch. They were the largest domestic enterprises engaged in activities with clear links to the energy-intensive RBI projects. They are therefore examined first. A second option, extensively used by Venezuela, Saudi Arabia, Malaysia, and Trinidad and Tobago (Table 8.2), was the diversified non-oil resource corporation. The single product firm, analysed last, was less common.

THE STATE OIL CORPORATIONS

The years 1969–75 were the critical formative ones for the state oil corporations (apart from Petromin and SNH which were established in 1962 and 1980 respectively). During those years, anti-MNC feeling ran high in many developing countries (Williams 1975). Nationalist pressures for sovereignty over natural resources blocked a more gradual extension of state ownership. The state oil corporations in the eight oil-exporting countries ranged from large and highly autonomous entities such as Venezuela's PDVSA and Indonesia's pre-1975 conglomerate, Pertamina, to simpler configurations which were little more than extensions of the head of state's office like Petronas in Malaysia and SNH in Cameroon. The state oil firms rarely proved effective vehicles for RBI launch: high autonomy related diversified RBI firms performed better.

The overwhelming importance of oil to the domestic economy was a force promoting commercial efficiency over socio-political corrosion. Yet few state oil firms were able to emulate MNRC efficiency levels and their very sizeable profits earned during the booms helped mask inefficiency. Whatever the intended degree of autonomy and the safeguards initially granted, state oil corporations tended to be deflected from the pursuit of efficiency goals. The combination of legitimate watchdog functions with the commercial operations of a state oil corporation, intended to reduce the duplication of scarce domestic expertise, proved an uneasy alliance. It enhanced political control over the resources required for the efficient performance of the firm's commercial function. Most governments resolved such conflict by effectively leaving the MNRCs to handle exploration and international marketing, while the state corporations focused on domestic supply.

Three types of state oil corporation may be recognized: the large vertically integrated firms modelled on the oil majors (which were, however, rarely permitted to integrate into overseas markets), the extensions of the bureaucracy, and the unintegrated firms. Because of their role as government watchdog for the oil industry, few state oil firms were able to escape bureaucratic sclerosis. The most effective oil firms for RBI launch were the high autonomy integrated oil corporations. Ironically, the most efficient wholly state-owned oil corporation, PDVSA, was the least active in RBI project launch. Consequently, the high autonomy-related diversified petrochemical/metals firms like SABIC, free of government watchdog functions, had most success in establishing RBI.

Large integrated state oil corporations

Venezuela recognizes the potential inefficiency of SOEs and makes a common distinction between nationalized SOEs, which are considered to retain their pre-nationalization efficiency levels, and grassroots SOEs, which are considered less efficient (Escobar 1982). In the oil sector, PDVSA, the nationalized firm is contrasted with Corpoven and Pequiven, the grassroots oil and petrochemical firms respectively. Similar contrasts are found in power generation, mining, and aluminium. Venezuela's cautious nationalization of the multinational oil corporations in the mid-1970s included management contracts with the former owners for transport, marketing, and distribution. Many expatriate staff were retained from the MNRCs and there was continuity in remuneration levels. The constitution pledges autonomy for PDVSA management to pursue efficiency objectives (Sigmund 1980, Martz 1984). Yet PDVSA still experienced corrosion of its autonomy.

PDVSA adopted a divisional organizational structure that both maintained continuity and retained a strong interdivisional competitive element. The original twenty-two pre-nationalization firms were consolidated into fourteen, with PDVSA as the holding company. This was later consolidated into four major subsidiaries based on the three largest private oil firms and the grassroots state oil firm. A third merger created three major subsidiaries based partly on geographical location. The product stategy continued that of the oil majors: it was one of dominant product vertical integration, with steady diversification into other product divisions concerned with petrochemicals (through management revitalization following the 1978 acquisition of the ailing state petrochemical company), gas and international operations.

Despite a promising start, PDVSA's performance disappointed, largely because of external factors. It commenced a massive investment programme to expand proven conventional oil reserves, raise extractive efficiency, enhance refinery flexibility, and develop the massive (but costly) Orinoco tar sands. From 1979 the programme was predicated on oil prices of $45 per barrel and investment efficiency was therefore depressed when oil prices unexpectedly declined. As the Venezuelan economy deteriorated, government agencies—notably the Central Bank and Ministries of Energy and Planning—sought increased control over PDVSA (Martz 1984). Directives were issued in 1981 requiring PDVSA to expand its socially orientated programmes and to increase spending on domestic goods and services (already 60 per cent) irrespective of competitiveness. The corporation's autonomy was dealt a severe blow in 1982 by government annexation of much of its retained earnings. PDVSA no longer deployed its post-tax earnings as it wished and after 1984 Central Bank authorization was required for foreign exchange expenditures in excess of $200 million. In 1986 almost 90 per cent of PDVSA's remaining financial reserves were menaced by government reluctance to cut oil royalties (EIU 1986). The annexation of its financial reserves threatened the efficiency of PDVSA. The company halved its capital expenditure 1982–5 but shrank its labour force, which doubled in size after nationalization, by only 4 per cent (PDVSA 1985).

Despite such corrosive intervention, PDVSA pursued a prudent product strategy. It secured markets for 600,000 bpd (one-third of its exports) through vertical integration into North America and North-West Europe despite fierce domestic opposition to such offshore investment. It also wisely blocked expansion of the overextended domestic chemical industry until its subsidiary achieved a positive cash flow. When new chemical investments were planned in the mid-1980s they were modest in scale and joint-ventures with experienced private partners. Despite the corrosion of its autonomy, PDVSA remained the most commercially orientated state oil corporation. It is therefore ironic that, oil refinery expansion aside, the company played a minor role in

Venezuelan RBI. The main thrust of Venezuelan RBI was in metals processing under the aegis of CVG, a highly politicized grassroots state conglomerate.

The early experience of Indonesia's Pertamina cautions that large state oil corporations may enjoy too much autonomy. Pertamina pursued a strategy of conglomerate diversification with disastrous consequences. Its rapid growth commenced in 1969 with the merger of two existing state oil firms, one of which had bought out the Indonesian operations of Royal Dutch Shell three years earlier. Directed by a close military colleague of President Soeharto, the newly formed state oil corporation had the character of an economic fiefdom. Initially a downstream firm running gas stations, oil trucks, and a tanker fleet, Pertamina diversified rapidly into both related and unrelated businesses. The latter included fertilizer, steel, real estate, air travel, data processing, and rice estates. As noted in Chapter 7, Pertamina sought to evade ministerial efforts to oversee SOE finance by borrowing short and medium term instead of long term (Glassburner 1983). A severe cash flow squeeze in 1975 caught Pertamina with $10.6 billion of foreign debt which required rescheduling by the central authorities and took almost ten years to repay.

Pertamina spun off most of its unrelated activities (notably PT Krakatau Steel) and concentrated on the production, processing, and distribution of hydrocarbons. Three product divisions were established to oversee each of the principal activities, while three functional divisions handled telecommunications (including transport), general affairs (including international marketing, project execution, and subsidiaries), and finance. However, high risk operations such as oil and gas exploration and LNG were prudently assigned to MNRCs. Pertamina handled domestic refinery upgrading, distribution, and fertilizers (US Embassy 1985).

A board of commissioners was established to determine government policy for Pertamina, comprising key figures from the Ministries of Mines, Planning, Finance, Research and Technology, and Foreign Affairs. A Directorate of Oil and Gas (MIGAS) was also established in the Ministry of Mining and Energy to perform the government watchdog functions of national oil and gas policy, including production, pricing, and manpower. It also compiled statistics, distributed licences to foreign oil companies, and oversaw the operations of foreign contractors.

The reformed Pertamina was bureaucratic. It proved an important source of government patronage via employment. The workforce expanded through the second oil boom to 54,000 in the mid-1980s, with 24,000 more employed by exploration and production contractors. Paperwork was slow and accountability was weak since the diverse accounting systems inherited from the pre-Pertamina companies proved difficult to fuse. The blurring of domestic and export sales made cross subsidization and efficiency difficult to monitor. In 1984 the new director declared the accounts inauditable and set the compilation of reliable profit and loss accounts as an important goal.

Pertamina's RBI performance reflected these problems: whereas the large joint-venture LNG projects were efficiently implemented, the execution of the ambitious wholly state-owned refinery and fertilizer projects deteriorated through the second oil boom after a promising start (Auty 1987c). As commercial pressures increased in the mid-1980s some improvement occurred as the government sought a better balance between too much and too little autonomy. Four of the firm's seven directors were replaced by senior Pertamina staff, the operating terms for foreign contractors improved and an MNRC was hired to resolve the severe technical problems of the refinery expansion (Far Eastern Economic Review 1986a).

The large Nigerian state oil corporation was even less successful than Pertamina in escaping burdensome bureaucracy and, in addition, suffered from frequent major restructuring. The Nigerian National Oil Corporation was established as a grassroots vertically integrated SOE in 1971 with a mandate to enter all sectors of the hydrocarbon industry, including allied industries such as fertilizer and petrochemicals. It was a holding company with a hybrid 'functional-with-subsidiaries' structure (Onoh 1984). The three functional units (finance, law, and administration) existed alongside five product subsidiaries (exploration and production, refining and petrochemicals, distribution and marketing, transportation, and material equipment and supplies). The holding company structure was intended to act as a buffer between the field units and the government, but it lacked the required autonomy. By law, NNOC was not allowed to raise finance or dispose of property without permission from the Commissioner of the Ministry of Mines and Power. Moreover, the disposal of surplus funds was directed by the Nigerian cabinet.

Dissatisfaction with NNOC's performance led in 1977 to its replacement by the Nigerian National Petrochemical Corporation (NNPC) which had a greatly expanded role. Positive aspects of the change included increased scope to raise finance and award contracts without prior approval of the cabinet. However, its bureaucratic functions were expanded as four new tasks were added, namely: oil industry monitoring, petroleum industry research, management of government exploration and production equity, and scrutiny of MNRC oil production contracts. Within three years of NNPC's formation a national tribunal (not NNPC management) concluded it was too large to be managed efficiently and recommended another reorganization. NNPC was alleged to have lost billions of dollars through poor monitoring and marketing, although the exact amount was never determined.

NNPC reverted to a holding company divisional structure with nine specialized, self-accounting subsidiaries. They comprised exploration and production, three separate subsidiaries for each of the refineries (which had 60 per cent of NNPC employment), pipelines, marine transportation, gas, petrochemicals, and research and engineering. Geographical dispersal reinforced the divisional separation: the subsidiary offices were moved out of Lagos as part of the government's decentralization policy. Unfortunately, the principal reforms included the formation of a Ministry of Petroleum and Energy (with the minister also the chairman of the modified NNPC). The new reforms seemed likely to bring about the very opposite of the needed change. The NNPC was unable to unable to insulate its RBI projects (mostly petrochemicals) from Nigeria's damaging macro-economic environment.

Smaller bureaucratic firms: Petronas and SNH

Petronas was established in 1974 in order to increase national control of the Malaysian oil industry. It oversaw producer contracts, trained nationals, and expanded local service and supply industries (Petronas 1984). The company was structured as a holding company with seven wholly owned subsidiaries (dealing with exploration and production, rig ownership, rig operation, gas distribution, refining, domestic marketing, and international marketing). In addition, three joint-venture companies handled domestic fertilizer, overseas fertilizer, and LNG production. In 1985, reforms created two divisions concerned with upstream and downstream operations. Ostensibly meant to improve co-ordination, there is evidence that the move reflected demotion for the finance director who championed commercial goals (Far Eastern Economic Review 1985*b*).

Petronas had insufficient autonomy to escape from being essentially an extension of the office of Malaysia's very powerful prime minister. Apart from the joint-ventures, many of Petronas's activities reflected nationalistic rather than commercial objectives. Petronas initially sought to increase government control of upstream activities. Arduous renegotiation of MNRC contract terms (92 per cent of profit was creamed off) proved counter-productive and required a dramatic climb-down by Petronas in 1976 (Gale 1981). An aggressive expansion down-stream into the domestic market occurred during the second oil boom and was spearheaded by the construction of an oil refinery and the capture of 25 per cent of the domestic gasoline outlets. The refinery was suboptimal in size, had an oversimple product mix and was remote from the country's main Klang Valley market.

By the mid-1980s Petronas had diversified into gas sales (over one-quarter of its revenues), employed more than 6,000 workers, but remained essentially a political instrument. Far from endeavouring to improve Petronas's operation during the mid-1980s downturn, the government used the state oil corporation to bail out ailing projects in unrelated businesses. Even though Petronas's constitution expressly precluded its participation in banking, the company was forced in 1984 to expend more than $1 billion (one-quarter of its reserves) to take over the Bank Bumiputra which had incurred bad debts in Hong Kong. Similar unrelated interventions involved a large government-owned conference centre and a proposed east–west railway.

While Petronas had the appearance if not the substance of an integrated oil corporation, Cameroon's SNH (Société Nationale d'Hydrocarbure) had neither. It was clearly an extension of the president's office. Established in 1980, SNH was the youngest, smallest, least commercial, and most secretive of the state oil corporations. Its mandate was loosely specified as management of the state interest in hydrocarbons. This meant monitoring oil company performance (in-cluding revenue transfers to the government), lifting and marketing the state's share of the oil, and developing long-term plans to become an integrated oil company in its own right.

The Cameroon president appointed the general manager and the board which comprised one representative each of the Ministries of Mines and Finance and eight to ten others whose terms were variable. The General Manager could appeal over the head of the board to the country's president. The appointment of SNH's 200 staff was often political and drew from the civil service so that important skills were deficient. The company was structured in five divisions (oil extraction, rig operation, refining, marketing, and long-term gas development). However, the primary function of SNH was as a conduit for extra-budgetary oil revenues, the chief vehicle for allaying pressure for overrapid windfall absorption (Chapter 7).

SNH took 60–70 per cent of oil production and paid 50 per cent of the exploration, development, and production costs. While corporation and other taxes levied on the oil industry went directly into national revenues, SNH held the proceeds of oil sales (estimated at 60 per cent of the total government receipts from oil) in extra-budgetary accounts. The low priority assigned by SNH to commercial criteria in its other operations is shown by its unwillingness to participate directly in exploration, its failure to liquidate an ill-conceived, majority-owned rig operation in order to preserve 300 jobs, and the poor product configuration and suboptimal size of its unprofitable majority-owned greenfield refinery. Nor, as Chapter 7 shows, did it prove an effective vehicle for sterilizing the extra-budgetary oil revenues.

Unintegrated state oil corporations: Saudi Arabia

Three of the oil-exporting countries (Saudi Arabia, Bahrain, and Trinidad and Tobago) did not establish integrated state oil corporations. They maintained separate firms for exploration and production, refining and marketing, and RBI. State control—and socio-political objectives— was more pervasive in the domestic refining and marketing arms where employment expansion outweighed profitability as the key objective.

Saudi Arabia clearly recognized the dilemma between the regulatory and commercial functions of state oil firms. Petromin remained essentially a domestic refiner-distributor and became an extension of the bureaucracy. Aramco was cautiously nationalized and maintained as a commercially orientated upstream producer while SABIC was spun off from Petromin in 1976 as a commercially orientated RBI firm. The scale of the oil industry in Saudi Arabia meant that even with such fragmentation, all three corporations were very large enterprises in their own right. Intended to shield the RBI projects and their hydrocarbon supplier, Aramco (responsible for the massive gas-gathering scheme which underpins Saudi RBI) from the blunted commercial efficiency of Petromin, the strategy was not totally successful.

Petromin was established as an arm of the Ministry of Petroleum and Mines in 1962 to increase domestic control of the country's mineral resources through manpower training programmes and investment. The Minister of Petroleum and Mineral Resources along with the 'governor' of Petromin chaired the board. The seven other directors comprised two additional representatives from the Ministry of Petroleum and Mineral Resources, one each from the Saudi Monetary Authority and the Ministries of Finance, Industry, and Planning and one representative from the private sector. Although free to engage in joint-ventures, Petromin was not financed as a company: its funding came directly from the national budget. Echoing the experience of PDVSA, more than $5 billion of its accumulated reserves were appropriated by the government in the mid-1980s (Ballantine 1985).

Petromin was organized as a holding company with a hybrid 'functions-with-subsidiaries' structure. The five functional units comprise planning, execution, co-ordination and control, international trading, and social services. The twenty subsidiaries were intended to be autonomous and profit-orientated. However, a substantial social welfare element intruded into domestic operations. For example, the Planning Ministry costed the provision of regionally uniform product prices at almost $500 million annually. Or again, the large export oil refineries, undertaken as MNRC joint-ventures, initially received managers from Petromin of disappointing calibre. Political considerations prevented Petromin from lifting its share of refined products so the refineries initially ran at unprofitably low capacity levels.

The principal refineries and the domestic marketing subsidiary dominated Petromin in terms of employees, accounting for one-quarter and one-third respectively of the 1985 total of 12,000. The remaining subsidiaries (in non-hydrocarbon minerals, drilling, and surveying) were of minor importance and gave priority to national production rather than commercial return (Barker 1982). Through the early 1980s, Petromin overexpanded its role in crude oil marketing and came into conflict with Aramco. The expansion of crude sales on a government-to-government basis during the second oil boom shrank Aramco's share of total export sales. It has been criticized for reducing efficiency by injecting yet a further (political) complication into oil marketing (Levy 1982, Vernon 1983a).

The management of Aramco (whose 170 billion barrels of oil reserves alone were valued at more than $1 trillion in terms of early 1980s North American finding costs) remained largely in the hands of the four US oil majors even after they had ceded full ownership to Saudi Arabia 1973–80. Aramco dwarfed Petromin in the early 1980s: its 55,000 workforce being more than eight times that of Petromin's (Petromin 1984) and its 1981 peak sales almost four times Petromin's $30 billion (Johany *et al.* 1986). Yet, despite cautious nationalization akin to that of PDVSA, Aramco did not escape political corrosion. It had long adopted a paternalistic stance towards the eastern region and this role accelerated through the oil booms. By the mid-1980s Aramco faced three serious problems: overmanning, marketing, and appropriation of financial reserves by the government.

Employment increased sixfold 1970–85, although productive capacity grew only two-and-a-half times. Operating costs reached almost $3/bl. in 1985. Cost-cutting efforts were implemented slowly and concentrated on the capital budget which fell by three-quarters 1983–6 amid doubts that funds would be sufficient even for that amount. The large workforce was cut by 10 per cent 1982–5, almost entirely at the expense of non-Saudi employees (Financial Times 1986*a*). Crude oil production halved over the same period. Plans to follow the product strategies of PDVSA and KPC (Kuwait Petroleum Corporation) through full vertical integration into overseas markets were delayed until 1988. Overall, the separation of Petromin and Aramco afforded some insulation against political corrosion for the upstream producer. However, the separation was more successful in the case of SABIC, where MNRCs had a major equity stake in most subsidiaries.

Summarizing the state oil corporations' experience, even cautiously nationalized ones like PDVSA and Aramco, which retained sizeable expatriate managements and were capable of efficient operation, experienced difficulty in reconciling socio-political and commercial interests. Their efficiency was reduced by government demands, even in countries which strove for macro-economic efficiency like Saudi Arabia and Indonesia. Low autonomy grassroots companies under direct political control like NNPC, Petronas, and SNH were even more handicapped. None of the diverse organizational structures adopted by the state oil corporations proved capable of restraining political corrosion. Yet the early experience of Pertamina cautions that the problem is not simply one of higher autonomy, but one of balance.

The state oil corporations' joint-venture export projects tended to outperform their wholly state-owned domestic ones (Chapter 9), reflecting the beneficial influence of MNRC equity. However, in most cases it proved better to implement RBI through high autonomy-related diversified SOEs pursuing jont ventures with MNRC partners than through state oil firms.

DIVERSIFIED SOES

The diversified SOEs could be as large as the state oil firms but they differed in other important respects. They performed fewer direct government functions since they were neither major tax collectors nor MNRC regulators. However, this inherent advantage for commercial operation was offset by their attraction as sources of political patronage. Despite differing organizational structures, the diversified SOEs invariably ended up performing important socio-political functions at the expense of commercial objectives, including prudent product strategy. Only where diversified SOEs made frequent use of joint-ventures, notably in the Middle East and to a lesser extent in South-east Asia and Trinidad and Tobago, were high standards of RBI project implementation and operation consistently achieved *and* maintained.

High autonomy-related diversified Middle Eastern enterprises

SABIC was established in 1976 to launch Saudi Arabia's gas-based industry. It was the most effective large RBI state enterprise in the eight oil-exporting countries. Although SABIC was closely linked to a government ministry, like Petromin, it used foreign consultancy firms liberally to screen projects and partners. It also secured experienced MNRCs with a 50 per cent equity stake in most of its projects and stressed commercial efficiency. Whereas Petromin's joint-venture oil refineries were initially adversely affected by ministerial interference in managerial appointments and marketing, this was not so with SABIC. SABIC was one of the few SOEs which published—and in timely fashion—annual accounts and quarterly summaries. The more secretive and bureaucratic Petromin did not.

SABIC was organized as a holding company with four functional divisions (planning and research, projects and implementation, finance and investment, and administration). These divisions proved flexible so that as the major construction phase ended, the implementation division took on maintenance while the planning division embraced product and market research. The composition of SABIC's board of directors reflected the firm's close affiliation with the Ministry of Industry and Electricity. The Minister was the non-executive chairman of the seven member board and three other (one each from Finance, Planning, and Industry) represented ministries. The three remaining board members comprised the managing director of SABIC and two private businessmen so that the civil service had a majority. However, the SABIC board set the highest professional standards from the outset and drew heavily on foreign assistance to do so. These two criteria of exacting initial standards and adequate foreign assistance to secure it are critical for successful enterprise launch in developing countries (World Bank 1986c).

The RBI projects functioned as subsidiary or associate companies with high levels of autonomy and, while SABIC pressed for the indigenization of management, the safe and efficient operation of the enterprise held priority. The twenty subsidiaries/affiliates were subdivided into seven categories:

- fertilizers (sulphuric acid and urea);
- petrochemicals (two methanol, two ethylene, and three polyetheylene plants);
- downstream industry (VCM/PVC and MTBE);
  - support industry (industrial gases);
- mineral industries (DRI/steel and steel milling);
- Bahrain affiliates (aluminium smelting, aluminium rolling, and methanol/urea production);
- marketing (industrial product marketing, market services, and aluminium sales).

The devolution of autonomy together with the concentration on petrochemicals (a steel plant aside) offset the potential disadvantages of large-scale operation. The high standards of the joint-ventures were emulated by the two large subsidiaries undertaken as 95 per cent (steel) or wholly state-owned (ethylene) ventures.

SABIC recognized the international trend towards diversified materials corporations, but its product strategy focused strongly on vertical integration. It is here that a significant clash arose between commercial and political interests. First, the constitution of SABIC expressly barred its participation in the production of goods for final demand, even though such products commanded far higher margins than basic products in the mid-1980s. Second, failure to invest in downstream plants in large OECD markets curbed SABIC's sales flexibility. Freed of such constraint, SABIC's MNRC partners could offset poor returns on basic petrochemicals against higher margin downstream sales.

The efficient implementation at Al Jubail of seven large RBI projects and their associated economic and social infrastructure testify to the effectiveness of SABIC as an RBI launch vehicle. Not only were most projects completed simultaneously on time and under budget, but they reached—and in some cases surpassed by an ample margin—their design capacities with remarkable speed. In 1985 the assets of SABIC exceeded more than $6 billion while the total project investment was almost twice that amount (excluding the $15 billion in infrastructure) with a further $4.5 billion in the pipeline. Yet, without integration into higher margin downstream plants, even the efficient start-up which SABIC achieved could do little better than break even with a 1985 profit of $15.5 million (Financial Times 1986c). However, that obstacle to commercial operation may weaken with the sale of 25 per cent of SABIC equity to the public.

SABIC held one-third of the equity in GPIC, a producer of methanol and urea in Bahrain, which commenced production on schedule and under budget in June 1985. Like the SABIC projects in Al Jubail, the new units quickly attained and surpassed full design capacity. Methanol marketing was undertaken by SABIC and ammonia sales by its Kuwaiti counterpart, PIC. However, GPIC did not have an experienced MNRC partner since SABIC's partners are the government of Bahrain and state-owned PIC.

High autonomy conglomerates

Trinidad and Tobago and Malaysia relied heavily on conglomerates to launch their RBI projects and both faced potentially high political interference reflecting direct interest by strong leaders. However, Trinidad and Tobago was least adversely affected. Trinidad and Tobago's RBI launch enterprise was the National Energy Corporation (NEC), a small team of technocrats headed by the prime minister's protégé which exercised considerable autonomy and relied on joint-ventures wherever possible. Malaysia's diversified enterprise (HICOM) also used joint-ventures, but was larger than NEC and experienced more direct intervention by the head of state.

Although the NEC was essentially an offshoot of the office of Trinidad and Tobago's autocratic prime minister, Dr Eric Williams, it proved an effective RBI launch enterprise—after a shaky start. Directed by a protégé of the prime minister, NEC enjoyed unusual independence and sought to achieve commercial autonomy for its projects by establishing them as self-contained joint-ventures. However, echoing the early experience of Pertamina, that same independence was responsible for costly errors with the NEC's first (and most ambitious) project, a DRI/steel plant.

The DRI/steel plant was initially planned as a joint-venture with three experienced MNRCs. The partners would supply one-third of the equity in a cautiously levered plant and market nine-tenths of the product. NEC sought to speed implementation and opted for a scaled-down wholly state-owned plant (Auty and Gelb 1986). NEC hired three MNCs, one responsible for each of market research, technology, and construction—but none held an equity stake nor marketing responsibility. A crucial, unrecorded decision taken by the NEC director to double the DRI capacity boosted capital costs by 26 per cent and unbalanced the production chain. Chronic marketing difficulties required a restructuring of capital and management by two European firms to turn the company round. It was then leased to an Indian firm for commercial operation in 1988.

NEC also launched two fertilizer plants during the first oil boom but both were undertaken as joint-ventures with MNRCs holding 49 per cent of the equity. The plants operated efficiently and at full capacity, though the larger of the two experienced a 50 per cent cost overrun and technical problems because the reconditioned plant had not depended on seawater as a coolant at its previous locale. NEC completed two wholly state-owned enterprises during the second oil boom to produce urea and methanol. For managerial purposes the urea plant was closely linked to one of the joint-venture fertilizer units. The NEC made liberal use of expatriate management in its wholly owned plants and opted for informal vertical integration by securing long-term marketing agreements with MNRCs for the bulk of plant output. NEC learned from its major error in steel and became an effective launch vehicle for small RBI projects within less than a decade. As with Saudi Arabia's SABIC, the wholly state-owned subsidiaries of diversified state firms like NEC benefit from the spillover of operating standards from the parent company's MNRC joint-ventures.

HICOM was established in 1980 as a state holding company to spearhead Malaysian diversification into heavy industry as part of its autocratic prime minister's 'look east' policy. The holding company was organized on a functional basis with seven divisions (internal audit, finance, legal affairs, training, corporate planning, project development, and project implementation). HICOM was responsible for five subsidiary companies in which it held 51–100 per cent of the equity and four associated companies in which its holding was 30–35 per cent (HICOM 1985). The subsidiaries included three in property development (mostly associated with the management of industrial estates for which HICOM projects were the lead industry) and one subsidiary each in steel and automobile production. The associated plants comprised one for cement production and three for the manufacture of motorcycle engines. Entry into the production of seamless steel pipe, rolled steel, steel sections, die casts, forged goods, tractor undercarriages, and ethylene was either being implemented or under study.

The HICOM board comprised ten officers with a non-executive chairman appointed by the country's prime minister. Other board members were the president and vice-president of HICOM, one representative each from the Ministries of Finance, Industry, and Planning and four private sector representatives. Major policy issues were determined by the prime minister who intervened on steel and automobile pricing policy. However, experienced MNRC partners were secured for all projects involving technology transfer and—the initial ambitious scale and product mix of the strategy aside—commercial criteria were pre-eminent. In addition, a strong preference was shown for managers drawn from the private sector, though civil servants could be seconded for four years at remuneration levels above those in the government. Manning levels were modest and HICOM's total employment in 1985 was 2,500.

The HICOM plants involved $1.4 billion in direct investment (and $1.5 billion in linked infrastructure) and experienced relatively modest cost overruns. However, they did encounter severe marketing difficulties. The projects were initially targeted at the small domestic market, but the mid-1980s recession halved demand for the key products (cement, steel, and automobiles) while the appreciation of the yen (in which the bulk of the capital was denominated) severely weakened their cost structure. The Japanese equity partners eased these problems significantly. Nippon Steel closed the unprofitable DRI unit which was experiencing both technical and cost problems, with full compensation to HICOM. Freed from its dependence on relatively high-cost DRI, the HICOM steel plant raised viability by importing low-cost billet and restructuring its capital. In the case of automobiles, Mitsubishi stepped in to integrate the car plant into its own export markets. Malaysia's steel and automobile projects illustrate how joint-venture partners help to share risk.

Low autonomy conglomerates: CVG, SGI, and SNI

Three other RBI conglomerates suffered from low levels of autonomy and were far less successful than the high autonomy conglomerates. The largest was the Corporación Venezolana de Guayana (CVG), established in 1960. CVG was intended to reduce the dominance of Caracas and Maracaibo in the Venezuelan economy by creating a growth pole in the empty eastern region. The growth pole was based on heavy industry at the confluence of the Orinoco and Caroni Rivers. It would use hydroelectricity and gas to process domestic iron ore into steel for the domestic market and to smelt imported bauxite into aluminium for export. CVG failed to generate an adequate internal cash flow and a sizeable fraction of the oil windfall was used to accelerate its mandate. Unfortunately, CVG scaled down its use of joint-ventures and experienced considerable political (and overtly nationalistic) intervention as its operations expanded.

CVG was organized as a holding company which oversaw eleven subsidiaries by the early 1980s. CVG's largest subsidiary (43 per cent of the total equity) produced electricity, the second largest (37 per cent) produced steel, while four separate companies (just under 15 per cent) were active in various stages of aluminium production. The remaining five subsidiaries were engaged in mining, forestry, international sales, and procurement (CVG 1985). The Caracas-based holding company co-ordinated the activity of the subsidiaries, monitored their financial, technical, and logistical performance, and developed overall strategy. However, both broad policy decisions and smaller ones concerning implementation were made by the cabinet. The Fondo Inversiones do Venezuela (FIV) became CVG's major shareholder as a result of large cost overruns, and exercised varying degrees of control depending on the political party in power.

The holding company organizational structure failed to strike a satisfactory balance between the government and the subsidiary enterprises. Paradoxically, costly errors resulted from both over-centralized control of investment and inadequate monitoring of field unit performance. Overcentralization resulted in the setting of over-ambitious targets and design changes were made during RBI imple-mentation. Advice from managerial personnel, both MNRC and local, was ignored. The existing MNRC smelter partner halved its equity share to 15 per cent while new MNRC partners in smelting and alumina refining confined their holdings to only 20 and 5 per cent of the equity in highly levered ventures. The steel plant proceeded as a wholly state-owned enterprise.

Field unit performance suffered from failure to adopt a uniform accounting system. Manning rates were two to three times those of industrial countries, despite similar (pre-1983) wage levels. A further source of inefficiency arose from the limited freedom of CVG subsidiaries to seek competitive suppliers: they acted as captive markets for other CVG enterprises. Input pricing was severely distorted. For example, prior to the 1983 devaluation, the price of the smelters' hydroelectricity was below EDELCA's costs of production. Alumina prices reflected a severe cost overrun in the refinery and were 50 per cent more than import prices. It required a large devaluation in 1983 to secure net profits for the smelters (though at the expense of the key input suppliers, EDELCA and Interalumina). The steel company recorded its first operating profits in 1986, six years after planned completion. Elsewhere, the Ferrominera iron mining subsidiary was neglected after its nationalization in 1975 and experienced a remarkable decline in its efficiency and profitability (Radetzki 1985).

Although vertical integration was the rationale for steel from the outset, and for aluminium following bauxite discoveries in the late 1970s, neither industry functioned as an integrated concern. CVG claimed that the holding company structure removed the need for formal vertical integration but the evidence does not support this. Venezuela's relatively small and volatile markets for metals make a strong case for either direct vertical integration into fabrication plants at export markets or indirect links via committed MNRC joint-venture partners. The aluminium smelters were belatedly permitted to emulate PDVSA's lead and invest in captive fabrication plants at the market in the mid-1980s. However, the state steel plant continued to focus exclusively on domestic linkage, irrespective of the return. This reflected the fundamental flaw in Venezuela's RBI strategy: a nationalistic preoccupation with large projects at the expense of commercial efficiency. In a country that is remarkably free with financial data, the crucial performance index (total real return on investment) is unmeasured.

The two smaller RBI conglomerates also performed poorly. The Malaysian state of Sabah invested $1 billion through state-owned Sabah Gas-Based Industries (SGI) in plants producing methanol, hot briquetted iron, and power. The Sabah head of state intervened strongly with serious consequences for plant location (on a cramped site which he owned) and staffing (an important source of political patronage). Hastily conceived and built without MNRC skills, the SGI projects became a massive drain on state government resources. Heavy losses are projected into the 1990s (Auty 1987*b*).

Heavy losses were also experienced by the Cameroon conglomerate, Société Nationale d'Invêtissement (SNI), which was established in 1964. SNI was organized as a holding company under the direction of the Ministry of Industry and Commerce with a functional structure based on project planning, project management, finance, and administration (SNI 1985). By the early 1980s SNI held equity in 62 companies employing 54,000 workers which included service sector activities as well as manufacturing (although manufacturing, dominated by a pulp plant, accounted for more than three-quarters). Many appointments were political and SNI lacked qualified staff to evaluate and manage such diverse businesses.

SNI investments were biased towards larger, capital-intensive, resource-processing industries (notably wood, agro-industries, and building materials) which relied heavily on tariff protection. SNI secured its funds through low-interest long-term bonds which domestic banks were compelled to purchase with part of their profits. Despite SNI's favourable costs of capital, its performance has been dismal, even when measured on the broader socio-political basis of training and employing

Cameroonians. Some of the most heavily protected projects, such as the large sophisticated pulp and fertilizer factories, failed to operate profitably. The largest RBI project, a pulp and paper plant, was mothballed. By 1986 SNI prepared to privatize its holdings and concentrate on launching smaller, less import-dependent commercial enterprises (Financial Times 1986*b*).

RBI in the Middle East was spearheaded by high autonomy related diversified firms, usually partnered by experienced MNRCs in prudently financed ventures. Such firms came closest to reflecting the assumptions used in the base case model in Chapter 3. The high autonomy conglomerates tended to make greater use of MNRC partners than their low autonomy counterparts and they experienced fewer problems. An MNRC equity interest above 25 per cent appears a valuable (though not unassailable) bulwark against political corrosion. Yet SOEs can effectively launch RBI in soundly managed economies if they adopt high initial standards from experienced MNRC firms. The performance of Indonesia's horizontally integrated single product SOE, PT Pusri, supports this conclusion.

DOMINANT AND SINGLE PRODUCT FIRMS

The single product strategy is appropriate for new entrants in dynamic markets with modest barriers to entry at an early stage in the product cycle, such as fertilizer in Indonesia or Nigeria. The strategy proved less apposite for more scale-sensitive metals markets, where single product firms faced strong pressures for further investment in forward integration to enhance market flexibility. However, few were able to do so. Consequently, the main distinction among the undiversified enterprises— autonomy aside—is not between dominant and single product ones, but between firms that were horizontally integrated and those that were not.

Horizontally integrated single product firms

PT Pusri, the Indonesian fertilizer company is a successful example of horizontal integration whereas Nigeria's Steel Development Department (SDD) is not. The success of PT Pusri hinged on the efficient execution of the first of a series of correctly scaled plants. Although MNRC equity participation was eschewed, liberal use was made of foreign personnel while domestic workers were sent for training in plant design and operation to the headquarters of the firm supplying equipment. The relatively high initial plant costs that resulted from recourse to overseas consultants and to generous design capacity were quickly recouped through the foreign exchange savings emanating from the rapid execution of the project and its subsequent high capacity utilization.

Although major investment decisions by PT Pusri were subject to approval by the government, the management retained considerable autonomy in setting production plans and in funding on-line improvements. This yielded an efficient and motivated staff which was further encouraged by social pressures to maintain the initial high operating standards as well as by profit-sharing. Horizontal integration entailed the constructon of new plants at the original site so that infrastructure, overhead, and inventory costs could be shared. The construction of new plants was carefully phased so as to build a pool of experienced local personnel (rather than overstretch it, as in CVG) familiar with all stages of plant design, erection, and operation.

At the start of the second oil boom, PT Pusri operated four plants in two locations with indigenous staff as well as its own consultancy business and a joint-venture engineering firm with its MNRC equipment supplier (World Bank 1986c). Unfortunately, there is evidence that the expansion of Indonesia's fertilizer industry by new SOEs at other locations during the second oil boom failed to replicate PT Pusri's fine launch. It also poached its management with unfavourable consequences for PT Pusri itself (Auty 1987c). Such a trend is consistent with the Caribbean SOE model (Auty 1986c) and Venezuelan experience of an initially favourable start by SOEs being slowly undermined.

Although Nigeria's long-term steel plans called for full integration from iron ore to semi-finished products, inadequate feasibility studies precluded backward integration to domestic ore and coal while the products of the steel plants were mismatched to the domestic market. Not only were the benefits from vertical integration missed, the potential advantages from horizontal integration were squandered also. Although the two principal steel projects were under the control of a single enterprise, SDD, they were commenced simultaneously, with different technologies at different sites and neither exhibited high standards of performance. The political attraction to a weak political regime of maximizing the dispersal of the steel industry led to the simultaneous launch of two large plants. It also brought the wasteful subdivision of Delta Steel milling facilities into four units, three of which were operated by separate companies scattered across the country.

As an offshoot of the Ministry of Mines, Power, and Steel, the SDD had all the failings of the deteriorating Nigerian civil service. It lacked both the autonomy and administrative ability to discharge its duties but had ample scope for graft. The ten-man board, with one representative from the Ministry for Steel, one each from Planning and Finance, and the remainder appointed by the Executive Committee, had a very low ceiling for investment authorization. This was reflected in the corporations responsible for each plant, the Delta Steel Corporation and Ajaokuta Steel. The separation of responsibility for finance from that for production severely eroded accountability and, therefore, efficiency. In the case of Ajaokuta Steel, no accounts at all were kept from its inception in 1979 while a review of Delta Steel concluded in 1984 that 'the magnitude of financial mismanagement, fraud and maladministration discovered was so great that it could only have happened in Nigeria and at the time that it happened' (Daily Sketch 1984).

The Nigerian steel corporations had little co-ordination and appeared to use whatever discretion their limited autonomy gave them over hiring and capital spending to maximize patronage rather than efficiency. The steel corporations became a classic public sector sink (Gelb *et al.* 1986) and provide the clearest example of inefficiency at the micro level compounding that at the macro level in the eight oil-exporting countries (Chapter 9).

SINGLE PRODUCT FIRMS

The principal distinction among SOEs pursuing an unintegrated single product strategy is between those engaged in joint-ventures with MNRCs and those functioning as wholly state-owned firms. Few petrochemicals plants were undertaken by single product firms while in the metals sector, single product steel ventures soon required vertical integration in order to diversify markets. State aluminium ventures secured *de facto* vertical integration through essential technical links with MNRCs.

PT Krakatau Steel, the large wholly state-owned Indonesian steel producer, pursued a single product strategy when it was spun off from Pertamina in 1976. However, by that time its chances of efficient operation were irrevocably eclipsed and the debt-burdened plant struggled to compensate for low capacity utilization and high operating costs by controlling imports, monopolizing key segments of the domestic market, and diversifying its product mix. The firm published no accounts, shrouded its operations in secrecy, and appeared set to function indefinitely as a public sector fiefdom until the mid-1980s oil price collapse brought pressure from the macro-economic technocrats for improvement (Auty 1987*c*).

The Inalum aluminium smelter in Indonesia also operated as a single product enterprise, but with majority Japanese equity participation. Its efficient construction contrasts with that of PT Krakatau Steel. However, although private Japanese equity participation provided safeguards for technical efficiency and managerial autonomy and secured *de facto* vertical integration to Japanese fabricators, severe marketing problems still occurred. This resulted in large measure from the consortial nature of the Japanese participation: the individual Japanese partners had low equity exposure because of high government-backed debt financing and the large number of equity participants. In consequence, when ingot prices fell in the mid-1980s the Japanese investors took their profits at the fabrication stage by buying ingot cheap, rather than sharing them at the smelter stage with their Inalum partners. Inalum shows that marketing gains may not accompany the implementation benefits of joint-ventures if a consortial partnership is used.

A second disadvantage of small individual MNRC equity participation is illustrated by Nafcom, the Nigerian fertilizer plant launched in the mid-1980s with 30 per cent equity held by Kellogg, the equipment supplier. Kellogg agreed to train Nigerian staff to operate the sophisticated plant within four years. By that time Kellogg would be permitted to liquidate its equity. The risk is clearly that the equipment supplier may secure sufficient profit on plant sales before (and after) commissioning to compensate for any operating losses. Experience elsewhere suggests Nafcom is unlikely to avoid the corrosion of start-up efficiency as the equity partner's stake is liquidated.

CONCLUSIONS

SOEs played a prominent role in RBI project launch because nationalistic objectives frequently overrode caution to discourage heavy reliance on MNRC partnerships. The SOEs differed considerably in their size, product strategy, organizational structure, autonomy, and degree of commercial orientation. Ten categories of SOE may be recognized based on high and low autonomy subclasses of the five basic types. They are:

- single product firms with horizontal integration;
- single product firms without horizontal integration;
- vertically integrated dominant product firms;
- related diversified firms;
- unrelated diversified firms (conglomerates).

Although the performance of wholly state-owned enterprises was generally disappointing it was not inevitably so. Successful examples are provided by PT Pusri and the later unambitious NEC projects which all relied on MNRC assistance to establish initial high performance standards. However, such initially successful wholly state-owned ventures risked performance decline in the absence of MNRC equity unless they were operated by a holding company which also had joint-ventures.

None of the organizational structures adopted for RBI project launch was totally effective in blocking corrosive government interference. The critical minimum requirement for sustained operational efficiency was 25 per cent non-consortial MNRC equity in a prudently levered venture. Even then, the desired enterprise autonomy was not automatic, as the contrasting experiences of Saudi Arabia's Petromin oil refineries and SABIC petrochemicals demonstrate. MNRC participation is therefore a necessary, though not sufficient, condition for satisfactory RBI enterprise performance.

Few of the SOEs which launched RBI projects adopted an appropriate product strategy. This compounded their problems of inadequate autonomy. When RBI product prices fell below the universally overoptimistic projections, highly autonomous export-orientated joint-ventures encountered least adjustment problems. The MNRC partners (consortia excepted) provided access to overseas markets and spurred efficiency. The wholly state-owned single product firms functioning in shrinking national markets experienced the most severe adjustment problems. Strongly nationalistic RBI strategies such as those of Nigeria and Venezuela were therefore particularly disadvantaged. Elsewhere, the single product wholly state-owned enterprises which were originally targeted at, or subsequently turned to, export markets found relief only through informal links with MNRCs. Nigeria's domestically orientated steel firm performed particularly poorly, but even Indonesia's more favourable macro-economic environment could not redeem PT Krakatau Steel.

Although the SOE performance did broadly reflect, and therefore amplify, macro-efficiency, this was by no means inevitable. At the extremes, the dominance of Saudi Arabia's RBI strategy by SABIC, a high autonomy-related diversified firm, meant the technical implementation of RBI complemented that country's solid macro-economic achievements, whereas Nigeria's low autonomy SOEs clearly compounded that country's very severe problems. Bahrain's experience reflected that of Saudi Arabia while Venezuela's RBI strategy, like that of Nigeria, compounded the country's macro-economic ills because it was dominated by the low autonomy, nationalistic conglomerate CVG rather than the high autonomy related diversified state oil firm PDVSA. Elsewhere, the results were mixed: the low autonomy Cameroon SOEs performed poorly and failed to reflect the country's reputation for sound macro-economic management. Trinidad and Tobago's unusually autonomous NEC improved after a disastrous start. The South-east Asian SOEs performed well when foreign participation was substantial (Chapter 9). It seems clear that MNRC participation was conditional on a reasonable expectation of commercial success. MNRC participation was therefore less likely to be forthcoming where macro-economic management was unsound and socio-political considerations dominated RBI launch. In this way MNRC participation completed a virtuous circle of macro- and micro-economic efficiency.

9
Micro-Efficiency: RBI Sectoral Performance

DEPARTURES FROM PROJECTED RBI PERFORMANCE

Chapter 8 showed that countries characterized by imprudent macro-economic policy also tended to give insufficient autonomy to their RBI firms. This implies that, all else being equal, the performance of the RBI projects of Saudi Arabia and Bahrain should be superior to that of Venezuela or Nigeria. Between these extremes of macro- and micro-efficiency, RBI projects in the South-east Asian countries should be more effective than those in Cameroon (poor micro-efficiency) and Trinidad and Tobago (deteriorating macro-economic effectiveness). However, such conclusions lack the strength of deterministic laws and must be qualified in the light of two other important factors affecting RBI project performance, namely product sector and project size.

There are clear sectoral differences in RBI project performance, though the actual ranking differs both from that found by Stauffer (1975) for the Persian/Arabian Gulf in the mid-1970s as well as from that projected for the mid-1980s base case (Chapter 3). Measuring RBI performance in terms of construction efficiency, operating efficiency, and competitiveness, petrochemicals outperformed metals, with steel the weakest subsector. However, Murphy's contention, based on a survey of Third World macro-projects 1970–9, that project size is inversely correlated with implementation difficulties and viability (Murphy 1983) receives only very qualified support. Specifically, such size-related difficulties tended to affect the very specific subset of RBI projects that were launched by wholly state-owned enterprises.

The systematic performance variations with product sector and project size reflect the country macro- and micro-efficiency differences. At the extremes, joint-venture petrochemicals projects were most important in the Saudi and Indonesian RBI strategies (Table 9.1), whereas metals (mainly wholly state-owned steel projects) dominated the weaker RBI strategies of Nigeria and Venezuela. The remarkably successful parallel expansion of the South Korean steel industry (after extensive initial Japanese assistance) indicates steel projects, even when wholly state-owned, need not perform poorly (Amsden 1987).

TABLE 9.1. *Principal RBI investments, by country and product ($ billion)*[a]

Country	Total investment ($ billion)	Average project size ($ billion)	Sectoral share (%) Metals	Petrochemicals
Indonesia	13.466	1.035	29.6	70.4
Saudi Arabia	11.735	1.303	6.8	93.2
Nigeria	6.739	1.685	84.3	15.7
Venezuela	6.401	1.600	100.0	—
Malaysia	3.034	0.506	23.6	76.4
Trinidad and Tobago	1.304	0.326	38.9	61.1
Bahrain	0.830	0.277	50.6	49.4
Cameroon	0.595	0.198	10.9	89.1[b]

[a] Excludes major infrastructure.
[b] Includes Cellucam pulp plant.
Sources: Industry sources.

This chapter is structured in six şections. Two sections compare the performance of large and small petrochemical projects. Thereafter, three sections examine metals, contrasting the large aluminium projects first with the very unsuccessful large state-owned steel projects and then with the smaller steel projects. However, the five sector reviews are preceded by an examination of the capital structure of the RBI projects. This is because the almost universal departure from prudent debt/equity financing for RBI seriously weakened competitiveness under depressed market conditions. This had especially serious consequences for the large steel projects.

THE INFLEXIBILITY OF HIGH DEBT/
EQUITY RATIOS

High initial capital costs and RBI project overruns

Capital charges dominated RBI costs, comprising between one-quarter and one-half of average costs upon start-up. Whereas the newly industrializing countries of East Asia had transformed their cheap labour into plant construction costs which undercut even the Japanese, this was far from the case in the oil-exporting countries. There, as noted in Chapter 4, the projected capital costs of greenfield plant were significantly higher than those in the industrialized countries. Specifically, the capital costs of new RBI projects in the oil-exporting countries were likely to be from 25 to more than 100 per cent above those of the base case or similar units built in the industrial countries. For example, UNIDO (1981) estimated that US Gulf capital costs were half West African costs. Capital costs for Japan were 90 per cent of US Gulf levels while those for South Korea and Taiwan were 85 per cent of US Gulf levels. The oil-exporters' high construction costs resulted from skill shortages, lack of infrastructure, distance from equipment producers, overelaborate plant, and graft. Although the latter element is difficult to quantify, for obvious reasons, industry sources suggest it typically added 30 per cent to the cost of greenfield plant construction in West Africa during the oil booms.

Since capital charges dominated average costs, RBI was especially vulnerable to cost overruns. Unfortunately, the period during the two oil booms when most of the RBI plants were built was characterized by particularly rapid inflation in factory equipment prices. Data for a major Japanese supplier of hydrocarbon equipment show a sharp rise in the real cost of equipment at the outset of each oil boom. The costs of such plants were boosted 30 per cent above the underlying rapid rate of inflation 1974–5 and 15 per cent above the underlying rate 1979–80 (Tanaka 1985). The feasibility studies typically assumed a 10 per cent contingency figure for cost overruns, but unforeseen delays in plant erection could boost construction costs by much more than this.

Murphy (1983: 18–28) suggests large projects were more prone to construction cost overruns than small ones. The average overrun on projects of $250 million or less in her sample of Third World macro-projects 1970–9 was 30 per cent compared with just over 100 per cent for plants of more than $1 billion. However, these figures overstate the advantage of small projects for two reasons: first, projects in the smaller size category which experienced severe cost overruns would automatically be pushed into the higher groupings. Second, and more important, Murphy's figures include cost escalations *before* construction, which would automatically be greater on large complex projects during the high-inflation 1970s. This is because such projects took longer to clear feasibility, tender, and finance stages. A more meaningful measure of cost overrun (and efficiency of project implementation) is provided by unbudgeted increases, i.e. those occuring *after* the implementation decision. That measure weakens the inverse correlation between RBI project size and cost escalation with the important exception of the steel sector, which was dominated by wholly state-owned enterprises.

RBI plants with high initial capital costs that experienced severe cost overruns were especially vulnerable to the unexpected price/cost squeeze which followed the abrupt termination of the second oil boom. As their expected cheap energy advantage waned with declining real energy prices, such plants were increasingly at a disadvantage *vis-à-vis* established industrial country producers. The latter benefited from proximity to major markets and heavily depreciated plant which yielded very low capital service charges. Most new RBI entrants in the oil-exporting countries lacked the flexible financial adjustment which prudent capital gearing provided. Almost without exception, the RBI projects relied heavily on loan finance and had heavily front-loaded financial structures. Moreover, many RBI projects which encountered cost overruns further diminished their flexibility by resorting to short and medium-term loan finance with floating and relatively high interest charges.

Additional inflexibility arose from the presence of a very high foreign currency component in the financing, the repayment of which was normally guaranteed by the oil-exporting country governments. The net effect was not only debt/equity ratios in excess of 4 and high capital service charges. Devaluation might actually erode the competitiveness of such RBI projects, while financial restructuring was greatly complicated when the guarantor governments already held large debts which they found difficult to service.

Imprudent financing

The base case assumes a debt/equity ratio of unity, with half the loan capital and 30 per cent of the equity emanating from abroad (Chapter 3). The Saudi projects came closest to achieving these conditions. SABIC normally split equity ownership 50/50 with a reputable MNRC partner and although loan capital comprised 70 per cent of total finance, six-sevenths of this was domestic capital with nominal interest charges. In contrast, many projects in the 'high-absorbing' oil-exporting countries involved more than 70 per cent state equity and relied on hard currency suppliers' credits for the bulk (more than 70 per cent) of the total financial resources.

Concessional financing in the form of suppliers' credits combined with sustained international inflation to encourage premature entry by developing countries into the steel, aluminium, and petrochemical industries. Suppliers' credits were very attractive under sustained inflation. They bore interest rates of 7 to 8 per cent which were significantly below commercial rates and became low or even negative in real terms in the late 1970s. Since suppliers' credits usually had an initial grace period of two to three years, high inflation meant the size of the principal repayments shrank sharply in relation to the inflating income stream expected from the RBI project. Under such conditions, the commitment to repay the depreciating principle in sixteen equal instalments over an eight-year period appeared to have little risk. Expectations of continuing inflation also reduced the perceived risk of covering cost overruns with additional loans, rather than equity. Such loans were frequently drawn from foreign banks and were repayable over the short and medium term at floating commercial rates.

New RBI entrants sought to accelerate the feasibility stages in order to complete, and thereby inflation-proof, projects whose capital-servicing charges were one-quarter to one-half of average production costs. Inflation also encouraged the belief that—in the absence of inflation accounting—ongoing inflation would inevitably result in the capital cost of new capacity exceeding that of even an expensively constructed plant of older vintage. Consequently, the penalty for an ill-judged entry decision appeared to be one of several years of poor profitability rather than permanent non-viability. Moreover, as noted in Chapter 4, incautious governments justified the unattractive initial high capital cost hump of RBI in terms of the expected (but unquantified) benefits from the capture of dynamic economies of scale and the proliferation of linked economic activity.

This combination of dynamic scale economies, concessional loan finance, and inflation encouraged the imprudent financing of over-ambitious RBI strategies (Chapter 10). The resulting risks were especially high in countries where macro-economic management was inadequate.

MNRC PARTNERS SCREEN LARGE PETROCHEMICAL PROJECTS

In contrast to the steel sector, large petrochemical projects (LNG, olefins, and export oil refineries) proceeded with MNRC partners. They were subject to high cancellation rates, but those large petrochemical plants which did proceed were effectively implemented. Joint-ventures were less evident in smaller petrochemical plants, the reverse of the case in steel, and the performance was more mixed.

LNG: successful MNRC risk screening

The LNG (Liquefied Natural Gas) projects were not only among the largest RBI projects executed, they were also the most resilient in face of declining prices. By the mid-1970s the minimum efficient scale for an LNG project required access to gas reserves sufficient to deliver 6 million tonnes annually for twenty years. Yet the youthfulness of the industry precluded multi-sourcing of LNG regassification terminals at the market. Consequently, LNG projects had to be financed as a complete vertical chain from liquefaction plant, through specialized ships, to regassification terminal. Moreover, this vertically integrated distribution chain was anchored at either end to very large investments. The gas was frequently purchased by electric utilities operating large capital-intensive power plants while suppliers needed to prove up reserves in excess of 4 trillion cubic feet and install an adequate gas gathering system.

Such large sums of capital dependent on a single transportation project involved risks that dictated a strong commitment. This was required not only from the gas supply and gas consuming companies, but also from their respective governments (Office of Technology Assessment 1980). The resulting stringent financial and technical safeguards made it highly unlikely that an ill-conceived and poorly implemented LNG project would proceed.

Only three of the six LNG projects planned in the eight oil-exporting countries were built. All three were constructed as joint-ventures on schedule and close to budget. This was so in spite of rapid inflation. A single LNG train which cost $125 million in the early 1970s cost two-and-a-half times as much five years later and more than four times as much in the early 1980s (Far Eastern Economic Review 1982*b*). The three-train Malaysian LNG plant built in the early 1980s cost $1.6 billion, with a further $800 million for five ships and around $500 million for a regassification terminal. The gas gathering system added a further $1.46 billion to push the total commitment to almost $5 billion, a figure which still excluded the distribution system and consuming plants. By the time the Malaysian plant came on stream, the two earlier Indonesian projects (in remote parts of northern Sumatra and Kalimantan) were already in a position to capture dynamic scale economies through low-cost brownfield expansions.

Indonesia split the equity in the LNG terminals between the state oil firm Pertamina (55 per cent) and foreign partners (45 per cent). Jilco, a thirty-one-member consortium of Japanese consumers, trading firms, and banks held 15 per cent of the equity while the two MNRC partners each held 15 per cent. The MNRCs were Mobil at Arun (North Sumatra) and Huffco—an Ultramar subsidiary—at Badek (East Kalimantan). Japanese loans, mainly in the form of suppliers' credits, comprised the bulk of the $1.7 billion first stage finances, with a public agency (OECF) playing a prominent role. Returns were high, buoyed by the price increase from the second oil shock and the real return to the MNRC partners was estimated in excess of 50 per cent. In the boom year of 1981 the revenue-sharing formula gave Pertamina $1.2 billion, Mobil $400 million, and Huffco $300 million.

The Indonesian LNG plants ran at 20 to 45 per cent above rated capacity. Their flexibility was further enhanced by the addition of new trains which doubled capacity. Even though the new trains came on stream as prices softened 1983–4, the netbacks still exceeded $1.50/ MCF (Table 9.2). By 1986, Badek took advantage of this flexibility to make short-term sales to markets as distant as Boston for $3.99/MCF. The Arun plant was even more competitive than Badek since its gas gathering costs (50 cents/MCF) were less than half those of its sister plant. Indonesian LNG was the only RBI investment in the eight oil-exporting countries to make a significant contribution to export and revenue diversification (Table 9.2). The Malaysian LNG project, constructed later and without the efficiency gains from brownfield expansion, was less competitive.

Two of the three planned LNG projects (those in Cameroon and Trinidad and Tobago) were quickly marginalized by the termination of the second oil boom. The Cameroon gas reserves were sufficient only for a two-train unit whose return was one-third lower than a three-train system. It required a FOB gas price three times that for Badek. The prospective investors in the Trinidad and Tobago LNG project displayed considerable ingenuity in minimizing its capital costs. They proposed to use an LNG terminal and ships idled by the failure of an Algerian gas agreement and to construct the liquefaction plant in pre-shipped modules in North America to minimize inflation risks. However, relatively high gas gathering costs, reported in excess of $2/ MCF, made the Trinidad and Tobago LNG project especially vulnerable to the falling gas prices of the mid-1980s (Auty and Gelb 1986).

In contrast the planned Nigerian Bonny LNG project was much larger and came very close to implementation. With a total investment projected at $16 billion it was second only to the Master Gas Scheme in Saudi Arabia in size. The second oil boom created particularly favourable marketing opportunities as West European countries sought to diversify their gas supplies away from the USSR and Algeria ahead of declining Dutch production. However, Nigerian hesitation caused delays and faltering markets and shrinking financial resources rendered later scaled-down versions marginal. The Nigerian LNG project

TABLE 9.2. *Indonesian LNG production costs and export earnings, 1977–8 and 1984–5*

	1977–8	1978–9	1979–80	1980–1	1981–2	1982–3	1983–4	1984–5
Production costs ($/MCF)								
CIF price	2.63	2.79	4.03	4.98	5.12	5.15	4.37	4.33
Freight	0.42	0.43	0.45	0.49	0.54	0.48	0.50	0.51
Recovery costs	1.01	1.58	2.04	2.02	2.10	2.27	1.90	1.80
Capital servicing	1.15	0.79	1.01	0.35	0.45	0.35	0.41	0.66
Residual	0.05	0.00	0.55	2.12	2.06	2.05	1.56	1.36
Total exports FOB ($ b.)								
LNG	0.162	0.516	1.345	2.111	2.343	2.461	2.398	3.482
Oil	7.192	6.358	10.995	15.187	16.482	12.283	12.050	10.623
Non-hydrocarbon exports	3.506	3.996	6.171	5.587	4.170	3.928	5.367	5.907

Source: Industry sources.

remained under review through the late 1980s as the MNRC joint-venture project filter continued to work.

Domestic and export olefins complexes

Olefins projects were central objectives in the RBI strategies of four of the eight oil-exporting countries. As with LNG, the perceived necessity of a joint-venture partnership caused the MNRC filtering mechanism to work. The three olefins plants which were orientated to domestic markets (in Indonesia, Nigeria, and Malaysia) did not get beyond the feasibility stage, but three export projects were built in Saudi Arabia. The olefins complexes show the problems of adding lumpy new capacity in a volatile market. Lengthy RBI project lead-times mean that even well-executed projects may come on stream long after the favourable market conditions upon which they were predicated have evaporated.

Pre-feasibility projections of global ethylene in the mid-1970s, when Saudi Arabia's Al Jubail and Yanbu RBI growth poles were planned, forecast annual growth in global demand of almost 10 per cent. Such growth would require the construction of 63 greenfield worldscale units over a decade. The Saudi feasibility studies were undertaken 1977–8. Actual global demand expanded at one-third the projected rate. Saudi Arabia proceeded with three units instead of the five originally planned: plant construction commenced 1980–1 and the plants came on stream in 1985. SABIC secured experienced equity partners (Shell and Mobil) for two of the projects and they were implemented as fully vertically integrated units. The withdrawal of Dow from the third project prompted SABIC to proceed on its own with a scaled-down version. However, SABIC contracted construction and initial operation to experienced firms and marketed the bulk of its ethylene through joint-venture downstream subsidiaries.

SABIC's three greenfield olefins plants represented an investment of $5.7 billion and came smoothly on-stream ahead of schedule and under budget in 1985. Their combined rate capacity of 1.61 million tonnes added almost 9 per cent to the market economies' output and contributed to weak mid-1980s prices. Even at 110 per cent of design capacity, the Yanpet plant had difficulty in covering its costs. Effective implementation was not enough to ensure satisfactory profits in the face of the unexpectedly sharp decline in oil prices of 1986 which had eroded the low-cost energy advantage on which the export olefins complexes were predicated.

Production costs are particularly difficult to estimate for integrated olefins complexes like the Saudi joint-ventures because of the diversity of the product slate and the importance of plant-specific features. However, data are available for the simple SABIC ethylene cracker (Table 9.3) which illustrate the olefins plant's sensitivity to changes in key parameters. With effective implementation and full capacity operation, the plant was capable of generating a sizeable return on the equity at 1985 prices. However, falling feedstock prices in 1986 significantly improved the competitiveness of established industrial country producers since feedstocks comprised 11 per cent of cash costs for the Saudi unit compared with two-thirds for an amortized OECD unit. Even with prudent financing and effective implementation, a developing country greenfield unit has little cost-cutting reserve because of fixed capital service charges, labour costs, tariffs, and freight rates. SABIC planned to trim its 1400 olefins workforce by one-third over a five-year period but it required the price recovery of the late 1980s to secure reasonable profits for the highly efficient export-orientated olefins complexes.

The three domestically orientated olefins complexes planned by Indonesia, Nigeria,. and Malaysia were prudently postponed. The Nigerian olefins complex was originally planned in the late 1960s but was unable to secure an MNRC equity partner. The only offers made were for the supply of technology and management in lieu of investment. Nigeria pursued a smaller first phase petrochemical scheme which, like its steel projects, was divided into three geographically dispersed units. Each unit was linked to a regional oil refinery. The scheme experienced a threefold cost overrun and chronic excess capacity. Despite such an inauspicious experience, NNPC scaled up the planned ethylene complex from 300,000 to 400,000 tonnes. The required investment rose from N1.15 billion in 1980 to N2.5 billion ($3.75 billion) four years later. Such a high cost plant would be uncompetitive and, even assuming no cost overrun and 5 per cent growth in domestic demand (as opposed to stagnant or declining demand), Nigeria's domestic market would absorb barely half the output.

Malaysia also persisted with plans for a domestically orientated olefins complex until the mid-1980s. It was intended to be a joint-venture between Petronas and HICOM and was suboptimal in size, having only one-third the capacity of the Nigerian project and one-fifth that of the Saudi ones. The dominance of nationalistic goals over commercial ones is shown by the absence of an experienced MNRC partner and Malaysian reluctance to tap surplus cheap ethylene from the neighbouring worldscale ethylene cracker in Singapore.

A potentially more viable Indonesian project was planned as a joint-

TABLE 9.3. *Comparative polyethylene cash costs, Saudi Arabia and major competitors ($1985/tonne)*

Product/input	EEC	EEC	Saudi	Saudi
Ethylene				
Capacity (thousand tonnes)	500	500	500	500
Capacity utilization (%)	71[a]	85[b]	85[b]	120[c]
Feedstock (net of by-products)	210	210	30	30
Other variable costs	9	9	10	10
Non-financial fixed costs	130	110	130	92
Fixed financial charges	—	—	27	19
Total cash cost	350	330	200	150
Polyethylene				
Ethylene (1.04 tonnes/tonne)	365	345	208	157
Other non-financial fixed costs	123	123	133	111
Financial charges	—	—	24	20
Total cash cost	490	470	360	290
Freight	—	—	40	40
Marketing cost and tariffs	20	20	100	85
Total cash cost CIF	510	490	500	410

Memo item: SRI ranking of most competitive producers for South Korean market in LLDPE ($/tonne)

Plant	Capacity (TPA)	Vari-able	Fixed	Total FOB	Trans-port	Cash Cost
SABIC/Exxon (Jubail)	312,000	423	149	572	35	607
SABIC/Mobil (Yanbu)	346,000	440	145	585	35	620
SABIC/Mitsubishi (Jubail)	156,000	443	175	618	35	653
Lucky (South Korea)	130,000	821	86	907	—	907
Exxon (USA)	327,000	589	89	672	64	736

Note: Capacity utilization:
  [a] 1981–3 average.
  [b] mid-1980s average.
  [c] actual Saudi level in 1986.

Sources: Banque Indosuez (1985: 11–12) and industry sources. Memo item: SRI International.

venture with Exxon, but cancelled in 1983. Instead, the Arun gas stream was diverted to LPG exports to Japan. This decision simultaneously cut $1.5 billion from development expenditure and promised an earlier (positive) cash flow from the gas to ease mounting foreign exchange and revenue constraints. It also allowed downstream plants in Indonesia to take advantage of softening prices by integrating backwards into their Japanese joint-venture partners' olefins complexes in Saudi Arabia. However, the prospect of firming prices and discounts from equipment makers like Chyoda revived plans for the Indonesian olefins complex in 1987.

Export oil refineries' sharply diminished viability

Three types of oil refinery may be recognized in the eight oil-exporting countries, namely:

- resource-based export refineries;
- export refineries based on imported crude;
- locally sourced domestic refineries.

The export refineries were the most adversely affected of the large petrochemical projects by the oil price decline. Their marketing problems were exacerbated by uncharacteristically sluggish responses by the joint-venture partners. The domestic refineries recorded a more mixed performance and although several involved investments in excess of $500 million, their analysis is more conveniently examined below in the section on small petrochemical projects.

Prior to the first oil shock, export refineries overcame the disadvantageously high shipping costs of oil products relative to crude oil, provided they were located close to large markets. With relatively unsophisticated configurations they could sell light products to surrounding developing countries (whose modest demand, which could not support a viable domestic refinery, they dominated) and dispose of the heavy products, notably fuel oil, in industrial countries (Resources Systems Institute 1985). The oil shocks appeared to enhance export prospects for sophisticated refineries by reducing the relative cost of product freight charges and boosting demand for lighter products relative to fuel oil.

Plans for upgrading the existing large export refineries in Venezuela, Trinidad, and Bahrain were drafted and five new worldscale export refineries were started, two in the Venezuelan heavy oils region and three in Saudi Arabia. The unforeseen slowdown in global consumption during the early 1980s caused by conservation and recession created excess capacity which marginalized not only the experimental heavy oil projects in Venezuela and the simple Saudi export refinery at Rabigh, but also the sophisticated Yanbu and Al Jubail export refineries. The unexpected 1986 oil price decline brought losses to the Saudi plants.

The established simple export refineries in Bahrain and Trinidad were most adversely impacted by change in the oil products market. Since oil refining dominated the existing manufacturing sector of each tiny country, the prospect of refinery closure created serious problems. The joint-venture Bahrain refinery lost $28 million in 1985 while annual losses at the small Trinidad refinery averaged $29 million 1980–4. The large MNRC-owned Trinidad refinery incurred undisclosed sizeable losses as its capacity utilization tapered off to less than 15 per cent. In 1985 the total losses of the Trinidad refineries were estimated at $100 million as their combined throughput fell below 20 per cent of design capacity. Yet investment in product upgrading was extremely costly, estimates ranging from $450 million for the smallest Trinidad refinery to more than $1.5 billion for the Bahrain plant. In the absence of such measures, extreme cost-cutting was the only alternative to closure. Yet the existing large refineries were grossly overmanned: the Trinidad unit had over four thousand workers, four times the level required by efficient units. Significantly, the joint-venture Bahrain refinery pursued rationalization measures aimed at restoring profitability by the late 1980s, whereas the Trinidad and Tobago government bowed to militant union pressure and purchased the MNRC refinery for almost $200 million rather than permit it to close.

PDVSA, the large Venezuelan state oil firm, halved its capital expenditures 1982–4 and saved $3.5 billion by halting its refinery upgrading programme in midstream. Development of a prototype 100,000 bpd heavy oil refinery (costed at $8 billion) in the eastern part of the country was also stopped. Export capacity was redirected to the domestic market and, in the face of strong political opposition, outlets were secured for almost half the country's unprocessed hydrocarbon exports through equity purchases of North American and European refining companies. PDVSA thereby became the first state oil corporation in the eight oil-exporting countries studied to emulate its Kuwaiti counterpart and integrate directly into export markets.

The impact of slumping oil prices on the Saudi export refineries' competitiveness is illustrated in Table 9.4. An oil price of $28/bl. was required to break even since at that price the $2 per barrel saved by using gas as a fuel was sufficient to offset both the higher freight costs of oil products and higher capital service charges *vis-à-vis* OECD market-

TABLE 9.4. *Refinery competitiveness: Gulf export versus OECD import ($/ barrel)*

	Import refining			Gulf export refining	
	USA	EEC	Japan	Market loan	Saudi finance
Operating cost	1.56	1.26	1.26	1.26	1.26
Energy cost	1.57	1.47	1.87	0.15	0.15
Crude oil transport	0.75	1.05	0.83	—	—
Ex-refinery cost	3.88	3.78	3.96	1.41	1.41
Product transport	—	—	—	2.60	2.60
Delivered cost	3.88	3.78	3.96	4.01	4.01
Product value less crude cost	6.50	0.99	0.54	2.12	2.12[a]
Net cost (pre-capital charge)	(2.62)	2.79	3.42	1.89	1.89[b]
Scenario 1					
Capital charge	0.29	0.29	0.29	3.70	1.59
Relative cost	(2.33)	3.08	3.71	5.59	3.48[c]
Scenario 2					
Capital charge	1.45	0.98	0.70	3.70	1.59
Relative cost	(1.17)	3.27	4.12	5.72	3.61[d]

[a] The sophisticated US refineries yield the highest product value, while the simple hydroskimming EEC and Japanese refineries yield the lowest product value, with the Gulf refineries of intermediate sophistication.

[b] On a cash cost basis the Gulf export refinery is more competitive than the EEC or Japanese import refineries, but less competitive than the US refineries. The underlying Gulf refinery rationale was that its lower energy input costs would offset freight disadvantages *vis-à-vis* import refineries.

[c] Assuming amortized OECD refineries with modest maintenance charges, the Gulf export refineries become less competitive than those of the EEC, even allowing for Saudi financial advantages (and equity servicing).

[d] Assuming a 16% IRR on 50% of the value of existing plant as the OECD equity return restores the Saudi-financed Gulf export refinery edge in the EEC, but not in the USA. However a one-third decline in crude oil prices eliminates the Gulf refinery's edge over even Japanese domestic refineries.

Source: After Fesharaki and Isaak (1985: 106–9).

orientated oil refineries. Ample margins on light products were confidently predicted as late as mid-1982 when construction of the Saudi refineries was well advanced (Carter 1982). A mid-1983 estimate by Fesharaki indicated that to secure a full market return on capital the Saudi export refineries would need refining margins 70 per cent higher than those of an amortized plant in Western Europe and 40 per cent higher than such a plant in Japan (Browning 1984). Fesharaki expected the Saudi plants to break even but other consultants such as Trichem were more sceptical (Petroleum Economist 1983).

The two Saudi export projects partnered by Shell and Mobil were completed under budget and ahead of schedule in 1985. A third less-sophisticated unit, undertaken as a joint-venture with a Greek firm, was deliberately delayed. However, unlike SABIC's petrochemical plants neither of the completed refineries initially operated at more than two-thirds of capacity. This was so in spite of access to the distribution networks of Shell and Mobil. The low operating rate resulted from the failure of the bureaucratic SOE, Petromin, to dispose of its product share. Petromin's inflexible response was partly due to rapidly changing markets and partly to a conflict between Petromin's need to shore up crude prices and the joint-venture's need to maximize its cash flow. Even a 20 per cent departure from full capacity boosted pre-freight break-even costs by 25 per cent and required an average FOB-product processing margin of $3.60 per barrel over crude. Both Saudi refineries experienced initial losses: excess global capacity had eliminated post-operating cost margins for sophisticated refineries as well as simple ones by the mid-1980s (Shell 1985). The Saudi government responded by cancelling two domestic refineries and delaying the third export refinery in the expectation that by the late 1980s domestic demand would permit full capacity use.

Summarizing, MNRC partners successfully screened large petro-chemical projects: many were cancelled, but those which did proceed avoided large cost overruns and—with the notable exception of Petromin's joint-ventures—quickly reached or surpassed design capacity. The especial success of the very large LNG projects underpins the solid overall RBI performance of Malaysia and Indonesia (Chapter 10). However, the Saudi experience with large olefins plans and export oil refineries shows that even well-implemented projects in prudently managed economies might still struggle to break even with the depressed price levels prevailing in the mid-1980s. However, the long-term prospects of the large petrochemical plants are bright, unlike those for the large steel projects.

SMALLER PETROCHEMICAL PROJECTS

The smaller petrochemical projects were potentially less risky than the large ones because of their relatively modest plant size and simple technology. Fertilizer projects benefited most from access to buoyant domestic markets. The methanol plants had to be export-orientated so that freight and tariff charges squeezed their margins. Consequently, they were more sensitive to macro-efficiency. Domestic oil refineries

TABLE 9.5. *Comparative product profitability, SABIC RBI projects 1985–1986*

	Steel	Ethylene	Methanol	Ammonia
Total investment ($ b.)	0.800	0.837	0.247	0.357
Capacity utilization (%)	127	100	110	110
Cost per tonne ($/tonne)				
Energy inputs	15.04	31.59	21.30	16.95
Other variable costs	208.17	114.22	44.98	57.72
Depreciation	39.30	83.70	20.55	32.45
Debt service	31.44	46.87	11.10	17.52
Performance				
Profit/loss ($ tonne)	−14.56	—	17.12	31.32
Return on investment (%)	−1.8	—	4.2	4.8
Return on equity (%)	−6.2	—	13.9	24.6

Source: Auty (1986c).

were often pursued for nationalistic rather than commercial reasons, but the resulting cost penalties were modest compared with those from nationalistically motivated domestic steel projects.

The lower risks of methanol and fertilizers

Compared with LNG, olefins, and export oil refineries, the fertilizer and methanol projects were smaller and less likely to be cancelled. The lower risks meant that the returns were inferior only to LNG. This is most clearly demonstrated by reference to the Saudi petrochemical projects because the uniform macro-economic environment and efficient project execution facilitates product cross-comparison. Whereas the export oil refineries initially incurred losses and the olefins complexes barely broke even, ammonia and methanol projects quickly generated profits—even at depressed mid-1980s prices (Table 9.5).

Five methanol and thirteen fertilizer projects were initiated during the two oil booms in the eight oil-exporting countries. Both the projected and realized gas netbacks tended to be higher on fertilizer than methanol. For example, feasibility studies undertaken for Trinidad and Tobago in 1985 indicated a netback of $0.37/mcf for a greenfield methanol plant compared with $0.75/mcf for ammonia. A recent survey in Cameroon (Le Guern 1986) confirms this ranking. A large 900,000 tpa methanol plant which took full advantage of scale economies could not anticipate a netback above $0.65/mcf with prices at $150/tonne, less than even a small fertilizer plant could expect. However, actual project performance in the eight oil-exporting countries was not uniform. Although implementation was easier and risks were lower, the impact of macro-efficiency was not eliminated. The smaller projects were also more likely to be undertaken as wholly state-owned enterprises.

Both the new export-orientated joint-venture Gulf fertilizer projects came on stream ahead of schedule and under budget. They quickly exceeded design capacity and, with cheap gas, favourable finance, and capital costs some 50 per cent below those of plants of similar vintage in Indonesia, they generated profits within months of start-up. An earlier Saudi plant, which came on stream in 1970, also contributed to the region's profitable export of fertilizer. Preparations were advanced for a joint-venture between the original Saudi plant (60 per cent privately owned) and a new Taiwanese joint-venture.

The performance of the South-east Asian fertilizer plants was more mixed. The successful expansion of PT Pusri in southern Sumatra during the first oil boom illustrates that, provided high initial standards are set through liberal use of expatriate skills, wholly state-owned enterprises can effectively launch fertilizer plants (World Bank 1986c). However, Indonesia's later fertilizer plants in Northern Sumatra and Kalimantan had a more disappointing record, showing that performance can decline. The second generation of fertilizer plants started with relatively high budgeted capital costs which were further inflated by significant cost overruns. The production costs of the new Indonesian plants were double those of the older Pusri units and more than twice the subsidized domestic fertilizer price. Worse, Indonesian output outstripped demand by 20 per cent in the mid-1980s so that two newly commissioned ASEAN joint-ventures (Aceh in northern Sumatra and Malaysia's Bintulu) found themselves competing for exports. The Malaysian plant experienced a modest 10 per cent cost overrun and was relatively high-cost. Despite the importance of agriculture in the Malaysian economy, the plant produced more than twice the domestic nitrogenous fertilizer requirement.

Trinidad and Tobago also had mixed results with its two export fertilizer plants. The first project, a joint-venture between the government (with 51 per cent of the equity) and Grace, came on stream in 1977. It was sufficiently profitable to prompt a 1985 agreement to double output via a $250 million brownfield expansion. Although a second fertilizer project which came on stream in 1983 was also a joint-venture and larger, it was less satisfactory. Unlike Grace, the MNRC equity partner (Amoco) was the gas extractor and had no previous experience with fertilizer manufacture. The large plant was purchased secondhand and had a 30 per cent construction cost overrun, mainly because of problems in converting the cooling system from fresh to salt water. Cumulative losses exceeded $55 million 1983–6 before profitability was attained.

The two West African countries each planned one nitrogen plant but only the Nigerian project proceeded, and then in 1984 after lengthy delay. The Cameroon proposal, a joint-venture with Norsk Hydro, foundered over a requirement that gas be supplied at $0.65/MCF. This was probably fortunate since even a small plant would have produced fifteen times domestic demand, prompting heavy dependence on uncertain regional export markets. The Nigerian delay was caused by financial problems. Nigeria's poor implementation record with RBI projects made the estimated ERR of 10 per cent uncomfortably low. A 10 per cent cost overrun or a one-year delay in completion would each depress the ERR by more than 1 per cent. Although the constructor, Kellogg, held 40 per cent of the equity, it would liquidate its share within four years when its operating contract expired. Japanese suppliers' credits accounted for 70 per cent of the finance and equity for 30 per cent. The Nigerian government bore the entire risk.

All five export-orientated methanol plants constructed in the eight oil-exporting countries came on stream 1984–5, having been sanctioned on the basis of the optimistic projections made during the second oil boom (Rischard 1982). By the mid-1980s the deterioration in markets caused projects in Cameroon and Trinidad and Tobago to lapse. This was in spite of low plant price quotations from hard-pressed equipment suppliers that were less than two-thirds the cost of units just entering production. The Gulf methanol plants were constructed before the price decline and had minimal cost overruns, but the Trinidad and Tobago and Malaysian (Sabah) plants encountered more start-up problems.

Both the struggling plants had originally been conceived as joint-ventures with MNRCs, but proceeded instead as wholly state-owned enterprises with the MNRC responsible for half the sales under long-term contracts. Neither plant reached full capacity at a time when lower-than-expected methanol prices rendered such operation unprofitable. The financial performance of the Sabah methanol plant is combined with that of a sister metals plant. Losses were reported at more than $150 million in 1985, a level likely to continue through the decade and require $500 million in loans to avert collapse (Petroleum Economist 1986). While figures are not available for the Trinidad plant, serious consideration was given to mothballing it in the late 1980s. Both the struggling wholly state-owned units explored the possibility of investing further to transform methanol into MTBE (a gasoline additive) or into protein for animal feed.

In contrast, the three Gulf methanol plants quickly surpassed design capacity and operated 10 to 20 per cent above that level. The SABIC plants were undertaken as joint-ventures with Japanese firms and secured better market access than the Bahraini unit. When combined with their cheap gas and favourable financing, the joint-venture Saudi plants were able to generate profits even at prices of $135/tonne cif eastern Mediterranean. The Bahraini plant, built in tandem with an ammonia unit as a joint-venture between the Bahrain government and the Saudi and Kuwaiti petrochemical SOEs, was more dependent on Western markets than the joint-venture Japanese projects. Its returns were adversely affected by the mid-1986 imposition of a 13 per cent tariff by the EEC.

The performance of fertilizer and methanol projects is broadly consistent with macro-efficiency expectations. It also suggests joint-ventures were most effective but that state enterprises could be successful entrants and that inexperienced MNRC partners could err. Finally, although fertilizer projects were easier to implement than most RBI projects, the mixed returns from Indonesia and Trinidad and Tobago show that success was not guaranteed.

The domestic oil refineries

Domestic oil refineries attracted significant investment. The protection given to domestic refineries by price controls and high freight costs on product imports tempted state oil corporations to build ahead of demand. This contributed to excess global capacity in two ways: first, by closing potential markets to more efficient export refineries and second, by providing surplus products (usually heavy ones) for export as domestic requirements lagged overoptimistic forecasts (Wijetilleke and Ody 1984). Implementation was often poor, especially where wholly state-owned oil corporations dominated.

Pertamina ran into difficulties with an ambitious domestic refinery expansion programme designed to triple capacity through the construction of three new units for $4 billion. Rapid growth in domestic demand was the principal spur, but that demand was itself based on fuel subsidies estimated to have increased from 3 to 20 per cent of routine government expenditures 1977–81. When the new refineries came on stream the country had a potential refining surplus of 30 per cent. By the mid-1980s, financial constraints had curbed subsidies and the economic slowdown lowered demand compared with the forecasts. Serious teething problems in any case prevented rapid attainment of full capacity and caused Pertamina to hire BP to help rectify operational problems. Cost overruns caused financing problems so that Pertamina fell $100 million in arrears on loan repayments. The wholly state-owned projects executed by the low-autonomy state oil firm performed well below the level which Indonesia's sound macro-economic performance would predict.

Only one refinery operated in Nigeria prior to the first oil shock but, as with the downstream petrochemical plants, paper plants, and steel mills, the new capacity was split among three units rather than one out of political considerations for dispersing windfall spending. The Kaduna refinery was particularly unattractive: it required not only a pipeline to bring crude from the coast, but also facilities to transport refined products back to the main south-western market. The first two new refineries (Kaduna and Warri) were constructed in the early 1980s for $700 million (around $7,000 per barrel) and experienced severe teething problems. The NNPC was forced to call in the French firm, BEICIP and invest half as much again on debottlenecking. Nevertheless, a third refinery was sanctioned alongside the original 60,000 bpd Port Harcourt unit. Financial restrictions fortunately caused the indefinite postponement of a fourth plant in the south-east, where demand was inadequate.

As small countries, Cameroon and Malaysia had difficulty matching the refinery product slate to domestic demand. Both countries constructed refineries of suboptimal size (40,000 and 30,000 bpd respectively) largely for prestige reasons. Malaysia's wholly state-owned refinery was built for Petronas on schedule and under budget, but at a cost per tonne of capacity four times that of a worldscale unit. The refinery was intended to provide a boost to the East Coast economy and move Petronas towards becoming a vertically integrated firm. A second suboptimal refinery would have cost as much as a Saudi export refinery but with half the capacity. It was fortuitously cancelled owing to Malaysia's mounting macro-economic problems rather than to recognition of commercial error by Petronas.

The Cameroon refinery cost twice as much as the small Petronas unit but provided only one-third more capacity. Its remarkably high cost prompted speculation that its prime function was to accommodate rent-seeking behaviour. (In neighbouring Nigeria a 150,000 bpd unit had been costed at $1.3 billion by the NNPC during the second oil boom compared with $700 million estimated by the World Bank. Under post-boom conditions, the cost was estimated at $500 million). The

Cameroon refinery was completed as a joint-venture, but four partners (with a combined holding of 35 per cent of the equity) chose to share the risk (Willame 1985). The simple configuration produced barely sufficient light products to meet domestic demand but had a substantial surplus of heavy products requiring export. Domestic consumers bore the cost through higher prices.

ALUMINIUM: EXPANSIONARY PRESSURES AND MARKET RIGIDITY

The performance of the metals projects, especially steel, was generally inferior to that of petrochemicals. The aluminium projects illustrate both the importance of vertical integration and the difficulties of achieving it. They also reveal the benefits from brownfield expansion. Steel most starkly shows the link between macro- and micro-efficiency. It attracted large investments and dominated the RBI strategies of Venezuela and Nigeria (Table 9.1).

The greenfield aluminium projects

Aluminium technology, unlike that of steel, was widely considered to require an experienced MNRC partner. As with LNG and olefins, this increased the sensitivity of aluminium projects to market signals. Although all eight oil-exporting countries evaluated aluminium projects, only two greenfield smelters were constructed (in Indonesia and Venezuela) while five were prudently cancelled (in Saudi Arabia, Malaysia, Trinidad and Tobago, Cameroon, and Nigeria). The Venezuelan state conglomerate, CVG, ambitiously added an alumina refinery and bauxite mine to its plans. Three brownfield smelter expansions (in Bahrain, Cameroon, and Venezuela) show the attractions of that more cautious option.

The two largest projects were greenfield Japanese 'build for export' schemes involving $1.7 billion (including smelter-linked hydro) in Indonesia and $0.2 billion in Venezuela (including an alumina refinery but excuding the brownfield smelter expansion, bauxite mine, and hydro). Both greenfield smelters were planned with majority MNRC participation, but ambitious changes to the Venezuelan plan caused the MNRC partners to reduce their holdings. The Indonesian project closely followed the original plan. Consistent with macro- and micro-efficiency predictions the Indonesian smelter—once it had been sanctioned— proceeded on schedule and within budget. In contrast, design changes and bureaucratic delays almost doubled the planned Venezuelan investment (Auty 1986b).

The ambitious Venezuelan aluminium expansion occurred adjacent to, and simultaneously with, CVG's massive steel and hydro expansions (combined investment over $10 billion). It entailed two greenfield plants (a 280,000 tonne smelter and a 1 million tonne alumina refinery) and a 50,000-tonne brownfield smelter expansion. Overrapid indigenization of management marred the start-up of the greenfield smelter: the inexperienced Venezuelan president ignored warnings from MNRC personnel, and incurred $80 million damages in potline repairs and lost sales. Although the greenfield refinery started up with remarkable success under Alusuisse direction, the severe cost overrun made the recovery of its capital unlikely. Even the brownfield Venezuelan expansion encountered cost overruns, despite its smaller scale.

The joint-venture Indonesian scheme commenced in 1977 and was completed on time and within budget, in contrast to its Venezuelan sister smelter (Far Eastern Economic Review 1982*a*). However, its consortial financing brought severe marketing problems which led to losses of $47 million in the first two years of operation that almost certainly increased as ingot prices thereafter declined. The losses could not be remedied by devaluation since any benefits from lower domestic costs and rupiah debt service were overwhelmed by the plant's low domestic added value and high yen-dominated capital. The Indonesian smelter's problems were exacerbated by the 1986 yen appreciation so that, despite its effective implementation, it required the higher prices of the late 1980s to cover its capital service charges.

Successive large devaluations transformed the initially high-cost Venezuelan aluminium industry into one of the world's cheapest producers by the mid-1980s. CVG calculated the average return on the Bs 5.9 billion smelter investment at 33 per cent. However, these figures overstate the competitive advantage of Venezuelan aluminium since the returns on the alumina refinery and hydro scheme were only 6.2 per cent and 0.8 per cent respectively. The return on smelting is halved to 17 per cent if the investment incurred on the alumina refinery and the smelters' share of hydro is included. That figure remains an overstatement since it is expressed in nominal terms rather than real terms. Most importantly, the investments were made at an exchange rate of Bs 4.3/dollar while the mid-1980s revenue and returns are calculated at a rate of 14.50 and higher. The real return on Venezuelan aluminium smelter investment is probably less than one-fifth the official 33 per cent figure.

Indonesia wisely postponed plans for further aluminium expansion, including backward integration into an alumina refinery. The suboptimal size of the latter, dictated by the poor domestic ore quality, would have resulted in costs 50 per cent above those of imported alumina. Venezuela was less cautious. Undeterred by the inefficient execution of its first large-scale expansion, the post-devaluation Venezuelan government planned a further $2 billion of investment to boost smelter capacity by 70 per cent, push upstream into a bauxite mine (whose output will be high cost and, even at minimum viable size, will still exceed domestic requirements), and integrate downstream into a rolling mill (considered by Alcasa executives to be of a size two-thirds larger than projected sales).

The low opportunity costs of the Ciudad Guayana construction industry provided the principal rationale for the second major expansion, together with an (uncertain) projected price upturn. Such investment in vertical integration will only be beneficial if the linked projects have been carefully appraised and are effectively implemented. Even if poor implementation is avoided, the scale of the undertaking makes it high risk. However, the Venezuelan aluminium expansion illustrates the attraction of dynamic scale economies (agglomeration benefits, vertical integration, and brownfield expansion).

The attraction of brownfield expansion

The principal advantages of brownfield over greenfield expansion are that it involves smaller increments to capacity, raises the productivity of existing plant, and lowers the unit cost of capacity construction. Of the three brownfield expansions undertaken, that of Bahrain was most effective and that of Venezuela least effective. The Bahrain smelter was initially poorly constructed in the late 1960s through a combination of inexperienced contractors, workers, and investors. Losses persisted through the 1970s as technical improvements were made and labour productivity boosted. In 1979, SABIC took an equity stake which permitted a 55,000 tonne (45 per cent) capacity expansion at a cost of just over $2,000 per tonne compared with $3,000 for greenfield capacity built in industrial countries. No increase in the labour force was required while overhead costs fell: operating costs declined 10 per cent. A second (45,000-tonne) expansion was planned in the late 1980s at a cost of $3,500 per tonne (including backfitted energy conservation measures) which would further shrink overhead and labour costs while also raising energy efficiency. The brownfield expansion made the Bahrain smelter one of the most competitive in the world, despite power costs above those of Canada and Venezuela and relatively high labour costs (Table 9.6).

The Cameroon brownfield expansion also occurred in the late 1970s

TABLE 9.6. *Aluminium RBI: estimated production costs at full capacity and actual capacity use*

	Base case	Inalum	Venalum	Alcasa	Alucam	Alba
Project characteristics						
Location	—	Indonesia	Venezuela	Venezuela	Cameroon	Bahrain
Vintage	New	New	New	Brown	Brown	Brown
Scale (million tonnes)	0.200	0.225	0.280	0.120	0.085	0.175
Investment ($ billion)	0.660	1.230	0.770	0.550	0.132	0.185
Start-up date	1984	1982	1981	1965	1960	1971
Cost/tonne ($) at 100% *capacity*						
Alumina	412.45	331.30	429.90	429.90	468.00	315.24
Other materials	205.00	212.00	219.87	312.32	326.70	178.00
Electricity	135.00	135.00	73.11	74.42	180.00	73.74
Labour	48.00	78.40	155.51	150.75	103.70	219.66
Maintenance	30.00	106.00	203.05	182.90	23.60	144.34
Overhead	20.00	20.00	71.20	110.90	15.73	56.48
Depreciation	150.00	277.78	97.25	56.80	80.73	79.38
Interest	60.00	345.30	79.00	344.90	101.50	64.95
Return at $1250/tonne	189.55	(255.98)	(78.95)	(319.39)	(42.48)	118.20
Performance						
Investment overrun (% expected)	100	100	175	166	n/a	n/a
Debt/equity (%)	50	78	60	82	65	45
Manhours/tonne	12	25	28	47	30	26
Investment return (%)	6	−5	−2	−7	−3	7
Equity return (%)	13	−21	−5	−39	−8	13
Actual capacity use (%)	100	100	100	100	100	100
Performance predictors						
Macroeconomy	H	F	W	W	F	F
Micro:						
Product strategy	SP	SP	DP(VI)	DP(VI)	DP(VI)	SP
Autonomy	HA(JV)	HA(JV)	LA(JV)	LA(JV)	HA(JV)	HA(JV)

Note: Macroeconomy: H = high efficiency; F = fair; W = weak; L = low. Strategy: SP = single product; DP = dominant product; VI = vertical integration. Autonomy: LA = low autonomy; HA = high autonomy; SO = state ownership; JV = Joint-venture.

Source: Auty (1986*c*)

and boosted the capacity of the joint-venture smelter from 55,000 to 85,000 tonnes. Despite competitive charges for labour, electricity, and capital, the plant lost $43/tonne in 1984 when its break-even price was a modest $13,000/tonne. The losses resulted more from the high cost of imported inputs than low export prices. This suggests that Pechiney (the joint-venture MNRC) was earning profits in its vertically integrated system upstream from the smelter stage at the expense of Cameroon interests—including those of the government.

The brownfield Venezuelan expansion was directed at domestic demand and had fewer marketing problems than the greenfield units but it was still unsuccessful. Undertaken simultaneously with Venezuela's massive greenfield expansion, the benefits were lost by inefficient construction. The average capital cost of the new capacity was more than $8,000 per tonne—above that of a greenfield unit.

The performance of both greenfield and brownfield aluminium projects is broadly consistent with the macro- and micro-efficiency predictions. The greenfield Indonesian project was more effectively implemented than those in Venezuela, where the overambitious plan of CVG caused the MNRC partners to shrink their equity participation and the projects to be poorly implemented. However, greater Venezuelan reliance on domestic capital meant that massive devaluation did enhance competitiveness. Undeterred by the results of its earlier ambition, CVG embarked on a further round of hydro and smelter expansion intended to boost domestic production to one million tonnes. CVG expects to make more effective use of the alumina refinery and bauxite mine. Following the lead of PDVSA, CVG also invested in OECD fabrication capacity to improve market access. Yet, desirable as it is, vertical integration in aluminium demands an extremely large share of human and financial resources in a country the size of Venezuela so that broad-based industrial diversification is hampered (Chapter 10).

STEEL: SCALE-RELATED LOSSES IN AN SOE-DOMINATED SECTOR

The state steel sector spawned overambitious projects which were poorly implemented, operated well below capacity, and were uncompetitive. They sucked in more financial resources to cover losses, debt service, and 'market diversifying' new investments. The four largest oil-exporting countries all planned steel projects of two million tonnes (or greater), even though joint-venture partners were not forthcoming and the technology of DRI/steel permitted expansion in increments of

500,000 tonnes without severe diseconomies of scale. Elsewhere, steel plans were more modest, start-up problems milder, and losses less dramatic.

The overambitious steel complexes

Venezuela proposed to build three 5 million tonne units over fifteen years and Nigeria considered constructing three plants within a decade with a combined capacity of 6 million tonnes. Significantly, the more prudent countries (Saudi Arabia and Indonesia) re-evaluated their options. Indonesia confined its efforts to completion of the 2 million tonne plant commissioned by Petronas on a scale four times that sanctioned by the government. Saudi Arabia scaled its early plans down to one-quarter of the original intent and proceeded with an 800,000 tonne unit. The ambitious steel complexes were the largest RBI projects executed during the two oil booms, ranging from $2.25 billion in Indonesia to almost $5 billion in Venezuela and more than $6 billion in Nigeria. The cost of capacity ranged from $1,100 per tonne in Indonesia through $1,400 in Venezuela to more than $2,000 in Nigeria compared with 'best practice' estimates of less than $500 per tonne (Barnett and Schorsch 1983).

Although part of the higher cost resulted from the social and economic infrastructure demands of (often remote) greenfield sites, overambitious design was the central problem. The long-planned Nigerian integrated steel plant at the remote materials-orientated location of Ajaokuta was delayed until 1981 and commenced despite clear evidence that the local coal and iron ore deposits were of inferior quality and much poorer than pre-feasibility surveys suggested. The cash flow from the initial 1.3 million tonne unit was expected to finance the rapid quadrupling of capacity required to achieve economies of scale.

Successive Nigerian governments resisted cancellation and as the minimal completion time doubled to nine years, any prospect of securing a positive return was precluded. This was so even under the unlikely assumption that operating problems would not match those of Ajaokuta's sister plant at Warri. Although not subject to the same construction delays, the Warri DRI unit still had high capital costs (Table 9.7) even though its installed finishing facilities were only one-third of its liquid steel capacity. Three inefficiently dispersed satellite mills, costing more than $750 million, processed the rest.

CVG's fourfold expansion of steel production at the Sidor plant in Ciudad Guayana took twice as long as expected to complete and

TABLE 9.7. *Steel RBI projects: estimated full capacity costs and actual capacity use*

	Sidor	Delta	PTK	SABIC	HICOM	Iscott	Base case
Project characteristics							
Location	Venezuela	Nigeria	Indonesia	S. Arabia	Malaysia	Trinidad	—
Vintage	Brown	New	New	New	New	New	New
Scale (million tonnes)	4.8	0.95	2.0	0.80	0.56	0.70	0.70
Investment ($ billion)	4.81	1.70	2.25	0.80	0.44	0.51	0.25
Start-up date	1979	1981	1981	1983	1985	1981	1984
Cost/tonne ($) at 100% *capacity use*							
DRI materials and energy	46.46	43.50	63.00	39.75	67.45	45.50	58.20
Scrap	13.42	27.00	14.00	16.00	16.00	16.00	14.00
Energy	12.20	78.00	85.00	9.00	51.06	14.70	9.00
Other materials	42.31	121.60	81.08	70.26	59.46	64.86	52.70
Labour	96.15	53.05	54.23	63.41	26.80	16.50	8.00
Maintenance and overhead	29.70	51.30	43.30	24.79	19.72	18.10	5.35
Depreciation	74.60	89.45	56.25	39.90	29.43	36.20	17.85
Interest	114.30	33.15	10.12	31.45	20.70	39.10	7.14
Return at $280/tonne	(149.24)	(139.05)	(126.98)	(14.56)	(12.62)	29.04	107.76
Performance							
Investment overrun (% expected)	150	n/a	n/a	n/a	110	132	100
Debt/equity (%)	71	31	10	70	55	60	50
Manhours/tonne	13	15	28	5	5	4	4
Investment return (%)	−15	−8	−13	−2	−2	4	30
Equity return (%)	−34	−11	−113	−5	−4	10	60
Actual capacity use (%)	60	25	45	127	60	n/a	100
Performance predictors							
Macroeconomy	W	L	F	H	F	F/W	H
Micro:							
Product strategy	SP	SP(HI)	SP	SP	SP	SP	SP
Autonomy	LA(SO)	LA(SO)	LA(SO)	HA(SO)	HA(JV)	HA(SO)	HA(JV)

Note: Macroeconomy: H = high efficiency; F = fair; W = weak; L = low. Strategy: SP = single product; HI = horizontal integration. Autonomy: LA = low autonomy; HA = high autonomy; SO = state ownership; JV = joint-venture.

Source: Auty (1986c)

incurred a cost overrun of more than 50 per cent. It strained the country's resources of skilled technicians and managers so that production at the older steel plant declined as personnel were drafted to cope with mounting problems in the new plant. Two-thirds of the new capacity relied on HYSL reduction units of a scale never built before, which failed to achieve one-third rated capacity five years after scheduled completion. Like Ajaokuta, delays pushed up Sidor construction costs, postponed cash flow, and piled up debts to make nonsense of the feasibility studies.

In contrast, PT Krakatau Steel was rapidly completed 1979–83. However, the mid-1970s' three-year delay caused by re-examination of terms and reallocation of contracts following the Pertamina debt crisis sharply boosted, and muddied, the capital costs of the steel complex. The finances of PTK were restructured to ease the heavy debt burden. The final debt/equity ratio of 70/30 was transformed to a more flexible one of 10/90.

Even with financial restructuring the debt burden was onerous because all the large plants operated well below design capacity (Table 9.7). Capacity utilization rates in the mid-1980s ranged downwards from 50 per cent for Sidor to 45 per cent for PTK and 25 per cent for Delta. Inadequate input supplies were the prime cause of Delta's poor performance and unsatisfactory markets for that of PTK. Sidor suffered from both sagging domestic demand and technical problems. Such was the magnitude of error in domestic market projections that the effective available capacity of all three countries would have been more than twice domestic demand (assuming in Nigeria's case that Ajaokuta had been completed as expected). Even at full capacity utilization, the onerous capital and operating costs of the large state steel corporations pushed their estimated break-even costs (excluding a return on equity) some 30 per cent above those of an efficient producer in the cases of PTK and Sidor and 100 per cent for Delta (Table 9.7).

Measures to reduce operating costs were inadequate. Overmanning was acute: compared with best practice levels of 4 manhours per tonne, potential mid-1980s rates for Sidor were 13, for PTK 17, and for Delta 56. Adjaokuta achieved the dubious distinction of being grossly overmanned several years before its principal production units came on stream. Wage rates were high relative to national averages: estimated rates, including fringe benefits, averaged $1.80/manhour in Nigeria and Indonesia and $10 in Venezuela. The SOEs failed to slim their labour force in line with capacity utilization. For example, Sidor kept open its obsolete, labour-intensive, pre-expansion plant while the Warri manager failed to make payroll cuts stick when sacked workers protested angrily about tribal discrimination.

Costly stoppages arising from poor maintenance were a shared problem. In the case of the Nigerian DRI/steel unit logistical inefficiency and foreign exchange shortages reflected poor macro-economic management and amplified operating problems. Nor did favourable energy costs offset other disadvantages. While the unit cost of gas to PT Krakatau Steel and gas and electricity to Sidor were cheap by international levels, their power costs—like those of Nigerian plants—were high. Moreover, design defects in the Sidor HYSL DRI units pushed consumption rates 50 per cent above best practice levels.

PTK losses were reported at $400 million 1977–80 (Far Eastern Economic Review 1983*a*) and almost certainly continued after financial restructuring, albeit at lower levels. For 1979–83 the cumulative losses for Venezuela's Sidor were $1.8 billion and the first operating profits occurred only after the large 1986 devaluation. The Nigerian steel industry was estimated to entail annual loan costs of $641 million 1983–7 and annual subsidies of $167 million, even with favourable assumptions of speedy completion, start-up, and effective capacity utilization for Ajaokuta. Far from generating resource rents the large, overambitious, and inefficiently operated state-owned steel plants became sinks for increasingly scarce public financial resources—not merely on account of loss-covering subsidies—but also for additional large investments required to 'improve' total investment returns.

The smaller steel projects

The smaller steel plants were built by more efficient SOEs and incurred smaller cost overruns. Although they were unprofitable in the mid-1980s, they were much more competitive than the larger steel complexes (Table 9.7). DRI/steel units were constructed in Saudi Arabia, Trinidad and Tobago, and Malaysia, an iron ore pelletizer was built in Bahrain, and a hot briquetted iron (HBI) plant in Sabah.

SABIC's DRI/steel unit, built with 5 per cent Korf equity and operated under a foreign management contract, came closest to break-even. Scaled down from the original ambitious plans, it functioned well below local demand in a well-managed economy and quickly exceeded its design capacity. In 1985 it operated 25 per cent above capacity and was close to profitability, albeit with the advantage of very low real interest rates. The other small steel projects performed less well.

The HICOM steel plant, in which an eight-member Japanese

consortium (headed by Nippon Steel) held 30 per cent of the equity, experienced a modest cost overrun of around 15 per cent and technical problems with Nippon's new DRI process. Initial losses were high since the imperfectly working, energy-intensive DRI unit did not receive concessional energy rates and was undercut in the domestic market by scrap-based imported Taiwanese billet. Benefiting from heavily depreciated mills, HICOM's established domestic rivals retained their market share leaving HICOM to operate at less than two-thirds of capacity. Prospects deteriorated further with the sharp yen appreciation in 1986 since Japanese suppliers' credits accounted for much of the debt. However, these problems were eased when Nippon Steel, the joint-venture partner, wrote off the troubled DRI plant and provided compensation to HICOM equivalent to almost half the original total investment.

The Trinidad and Tobago SOE, NEC, had no such MNRC partner to fall back on when it ran into serious problems with its DRI/steel plant. NEC constructed an export-orientated DRI/steel unit following the failure of pre-construction negotiations with MNRC equity partners. Constructed 1977–81, the Iscott plant was wisely scaled down from earlier plans and 1979 proposals to double DRI capacity and integrate backwards into a 2 million tonne pelletizer were also shelved. However, a cost overrun of 30 per cent resulted from overextension of the domestic construction industry. This was due to the simultaneous erection of an ammonia plant and large infrastructure facilities— compounded by a snap decision to double DRI capacity (through fear of scrap shortages).

Although financial restructuring and managerial improvements could have offset the resulting cost penalty, exclusion from the US market following a successful anti-dumping suit brought by four US companies (including a subsidiary of Korf, the supplier of Iscott's plant) proved disastrous. That market had been targeted for two-thirds of plant output. Annual losses averaged $108 million 1982–5 and the option of mothballing the plant was rejected in favour of a managerial contract with two European steel companies. Technical efficiency, capacity utilization, and competitiveness all improved.

The two other small iron ore processing plants were also export-orientated. Sabah's 750,000 tonne HBI plant was wholly state-owned and one of three units in a $1 billion project to export the remote state's gas. It experienced a 60 per cent cost overrun, suffered acutely from depressed regional demand for steel inputs, and, with its sister methanol plant, incurred losses exceeding $100 million annually.

Like the Sabah unit, the Bahrain iron pelletizer also underperformed according to macro predictors—and according to enterprise type as well. The Bahrain pelletizer came on stream in 1985 as the only wholly private RBI venture in the eight oil-exporting countries. It was prudently financed with a debt equity ratio of 50/50 as a joint venture among private regional investors. It was efficiently implemented under budget. However, it encountered the most severe market problems. Designed to exploit the potential steel demand of the oil-rich region, the prolongation of the Iran/Iraq war effectively barred access to half the Bahraini plant's planned market. The pelletizer achieved less than one-fifth of its design capacity in its first full year of operation and quickly exhausted the financial reserves provided at its start-up. In such a context, the decision of Cameroon not to implement a DRI/steel project and instead to contemplate, but reject, a reconditioned 150,000 tonne scrap-based unit, was wise.

Summarizing, the performance of the large steel projects reflects enterprise type and is clearly consistent with the macro-efficiency ranking of the countries. The dominance of overambitious and poorly implemented steel projects in the RBI strategies of Venezuela and Nigeria accounts for much of the poor performance of those strategies. The more modest steel projects of the better-run economies also performed poorly, but their implementation was more effective (Sabah's HBI plant aside) and where their output was correctly matched to markets, their medium-term viability was much more favourable.

A common response to the steel plant troubles was to seek yet more investment to enhance market flexibility through diversification of the product range. In some instances, such as the Sabah HBI plant and AISCO pelletizer, the diversification envisaged adding steel-making plant whose cost exceeded the original investment.

CONCLUSION: DISAPPOINTING RBI PERFORMANCE

The attraction of suppliers' credits at low or negative rates of interest encouraged debt/equity ratios well above prudent levels. Before the sharp rise in real interest rates which accompanied the termination of the second oil boom, even commercial loans were preferred to equity infusions in meeting cost overruns. Overall debt/equity ratios were often in excess of 4 : 1 and hampered flexible adjustment to price declines. The heavy frontloading typical of RBI projects placed them at a severe competitive disadvantage compared with established producers operating amortized plants.

RBI performance in the eight oil-exporting countries is measured in terms of construction efficiency, operational efficiency, and competitiveness. Project size significantly depressed performance only where wholly state-owned enterprises were involved. The large wholly state-owned projects were prone to high cost overruns, technical problems, and marketing difficulties. Differences in sectoral performance were more significant than differences in project size.

Metals ventures (notably the large wholly state-owned steel projects) were most problematic. In contrast, large petrochemical projects achieved a better performance and invariably proceeded as joint-ventures. The huge LNG projects recorded the best performance. The more limited competitiveness of the large olefins complexes and export refineries was short-term and reflected unexpectedly low prices during the mid-1980s rather than deficient implementation and operation. Among the smaller petrochemical projects, fertilizer outperformed methanol while domestic oil refineries were more disappointing. The domestic refineries were usually motivated by nationalistic rather than commercial concerns.

RBI project performance tended to reflect macro-economic efficiency. Sustained growth of the domestic market and prudent price policy limited the risk of cost overruns and furnished a predictable home market for effectively implemented RBI. Access to export markets was facilitated by maintenance of a competitive exchange rate and assisted by (non-consortial) joint-venture partners. The overall RBI performance of the South-east Asian projects was superior to that of South America and Africa, but below that of the Gulf region, echoing macro-economic performance (Balassa 1982, Hasan 1984). Some qualification is in order: with the exception of Nigeria, each country shows a range of resilience in project performance, though the spread tends to be greater outside the Gulf region and especially so in South America.

Paradoxically, losses and low returns encouraged further expansion in pursuit of economies of scale. This took the form of either prudent brownfield expansion, forward integration to improve market flexibility, or backward integration. In many cases the size of the new investment matched or even surpassed that of the initial project. The sharp post-boom reduction in equipment costs (fuelled by suppliers' boom profits) encouraged such investments.

The performance of the RBI projects in the eight oil-exporting countries fell well below expectations. The negative spillover effects from the misallocation of capital to RBI included low growth, expanding debt, and retarded structural change. The weak overall RBI performance placed the main burden of post-boom adjustment on the non-hydrocarbons tradeables sector (Chapter 10).

PART 4

RBI Impact

10

The Impact of RBI on Economic Growth and Structural Change

This chapter analyses economic growth and structural change in the eight oil-exporting countries through the two oil booms and into the immediate post-boom period (1981–4). The oil windfalls were expected to accelerate growth of the non-oil economy and promote healthy structural change in preparation for the eventual demise of oil. All eight oil-exporting countries either assigned RBI a central role in this process or planned such a role for it. Yet RBI severely overtaxed implementation capacity in some countries and proved initially disappointing in most so that its contribution to both economic growth and structural change was at best minor and at worst negative. The decline in real oil prices through the mid-1980s provided a key test of how prudent the deployment of the oil windfalls for RBI had been.

The eight oil-exporting countries diverged significantly in their progress towards accelerated economic growth and healthy structural change. The paternalistic autocratic regimes in the 'low-absorbing' Arabian countries worked with a longer time horizon than the 'high-absorbers' and insulated their fragile non-oil tradeables sectors against unexpected downswing with sizeable overseas savings, once-for-all construction projects, and large guest workforces. The four lower-income West African and South-east Asian countries started with healthier non-oil tradeables sectors and relatively large resilient farm sectors, but Nigeria squandered its advantage here. The middle-income South American democracies proved vulnerable to populist pressures and lacked both large savings and a protective agricultural cushion.

Progress towards accelerated growth and healthy structural change is now analysed in four stages. First, trends in the growth rate and structure of the non-oil economy are monitored through the two booms and into the post-boom period. Following Gelb (1988), two counter-factuals are used namely:

● departures in economic growth from pre-shock trends and
● departures in structural change from the Chenery and Syrquin norms

for countries of similar size and level of development (Chenery and Syrquin 1975).

Second, the industrial policies of the eight oil-exporting countries are compared, paying particular attention to the role of RBI and to the resilience of non-resource-based manufacturing. Third, differences in the management and importance of the agricultural sector in the eight oil-exporting countries are examined. Finally, the efficacy of windfall absorption is tested by comparing the eight oil-exporting countries' response to the post-boom deterioration in oil prices.

GROWTH AND STRUCTURAL CHANGE IN THE NON-OIL ECONOMY

Pre-shock conditions

Table 10.1 measures the pre-shock oil dependence of the eight oil-exporting countries in terms of the commodity's contribution to their GDP, exports, and revenues. A single index of dependence is derived by assuming that each of the three measures is of equal importance and taking the mean. Excluding the late-starters whose oil booms did not commence until the late 1970s, three levels of pre-shock oil dependence emerge: high for the 'low-absorbing' Gulf states, relatively low for Indonesia and Trinidad and Tobago, and moderately high for Venezuela and Nigeria.

Variations in the pre-shock oil dependence of the oil-exporting countries are reflected in differences in the composition of absorption (Table 10.1). At the extremes, the rate of total absorption by both the late-starters (Cameroon and Malaysia) was very close to the Chenery and Syrquin norms for countries of similar size and level of development. However, for 'low-absorbing' Saudi Arabia the absorption rate was 30 per cent above its norm. That for Bahrain was higher still, but this reflected distortions arising from the dominance of that country's tiny economy by the oil sector. Nyrop (1977*b*) estimated that foreign investment in the Bahraini oil sector caused half its GDP to leak abroad (shrinking its per capita income below $700). The remaining four 'high-absorbers' occupied an intermediate position with absorption rates equivalent to some 10 to 15 per cent of non-mining GDP more their norms.

The two countries with the lowest per capita income, Nigeria and Indonesia, used their extra resources to boost pre-shock consumption well above the Chenery and Syrquin norms whereas the two wealthier

TABLE 10.1. *Pre-shock oil dependence and absorption, eight oil exporters*

	GNP/head ($ 1972)	Oil dependence 1972 (%)				Absorption 1970–2 (% non-mining GDP)			
		GDP	Exports	Revenues	Index	Private consump- tion	Public consump- tion	Invest- ment	Total
Bahrain	1,605[a]	66	100	60	75	257	57	7	321
Cameroon	201	—	—	—	0	72	13	16	101
Indonesia	90	12	51	31	31	84	10	17	111
Malaysia	520	—	—	—	0	63	17	21	101
Nigeria	146	15	80	67	54	80	9	22	111
Saudi Arabia	1,022	60	100	87	82	61	38	31	130
Trinidad and Tobago	1,163	9	78	25	37	81	n/a	31	112
Venezuela	1,308	21	86	65	57	63	16	37	116

[a] Reflects dominance of the large (then foreign-owned) oil refinery. Extraction of the latter reduces GNP/head by half (Nyrop 1977b)

Sources: Gelb (1986a); Kanovsky (1986); Young *et al.* (1980); World Bank.

South American 'high-absorbers' emphasized domestic investment. The late-starters showed a similar income-related difference: richer Malaysia invested 5 per cent more of its GDP than did Cameroon. Saudi Arabia, with much the highest level of absorption (Bahrain aside), enjoyed rates of consumption and investment that were both significantly above its norms (Table 10.1).

Table 10.2 summarizes the pre-shock structure of the eight oil-exporting countries' non-oil economies and compares it to the Chenery and Syrquin norms for countries of similar size and level of development. While Gelb (1988) furnishes standardized data on structural change for Indonesia, Nigeria, Trinidad and Tobago, and Venezuela the data for the other four countries are drawn from diverse sources and are less reliable.

There were substantial differences between the eight oil-exporting countries in the pre-shock structure of their economies (Table 10.2). Among the four countries with the lowest per capita income, the two late-starters and Indonesia diverged little from their predicted pre-shock economic structures. However, Nigeria's large agricultural sector was close to the norm, but its manufacturing sector was remarkably underdeveloped (one-third the norm). The four higher income countries all had agricultural sectors that were significantly smaller than predicted— a reflection of pre-shock 'Dutch disease' effects. Moreover, the manufacturing base of all four higher income countries was less diversified than the norms for non-oil producers of similar size and level of development. In the case of the two smallest countries, Trinidad and Tobago and Bahrain, Table 10.2 overstates their degree of industrial diversification because large export oil refineries dominated their tiny economies.

The promotion of healthy structural change was most pressing for the four higher income countries. However, whereas the two 'low-absorbers' were able to insulate their economies through the accumulation of overseas reserves, political pressures for rapid absorption made saving less practical for 'high-absorbing' Venezuela and Trinidad and Tobago (Gelb 1988). Yet neither of the South American countries possessed the sizeable and employment-intensive agricultural safety nets of the two large low-income countries (Nigeria and Indonesia). Consequently, Venezuela and Trinidad and Tobago were most vulnerable to falling oil prices and had the greatest need to develop competitive non-oil tradeables. They both assigned RBI the critical role in structural diversification (Auty 1986b).

Table 10.3 shows that prior to the first oil shock real growth in the

TABLE 10.2. *Pre-shock structure of eight oil exporters' non-mining GDP, actual 1972 and C–S norms (%)*

	Bahrain		Cameroon		Indonesia		Malaysia		Nigeria		S. Arabia		Trinidad & Tobago		Venezuela	
	A	N	A	N	A	N	A	N	A	N	A	N	A	N	A	N
Agriculture	3	29	31	31	45	46	31	32	39	38	9	23	6	16	8	14
Manufacturing	19	19	12	16	11	11	17	18	5	15	20	26	22	26	19	27
Construction	7	5	4	3	4	3	4	4	11	4	10	6	8	6	6	7
Services	71	47	53	50	40	40	47	46	45	43	60	43	64	52	67	52
(Mining)	66	7	—	6	12	6	7	5	15	5	60	3	9	2	21	2

Note: A = Actual; N = Norm.

Sources: Gelb (1986a); Kubursi (1984); Kanovsky (1986); Young *et al.* (1980); World Bank.

204   RBI Impact

TABLE 10.3. *Growth trends in oil exporters' non-mining GDP, 1967–1984*

	Percentage	Annual change (%)		Ratio to pre-shock rate	
	1967–72	1972–81	1981–4	1972–81	1981–4
Mid-income oil importers	5.8	5.1	1.9	0.88	0.33
Bahrain			7.4		
Cameroon	4.2	5.7	6.2	1.36	1.48
Indonesia	8.5	8.2	4.8	0.96	0.56
Malaysia	6.8	8.1	6.5	1.19	0.96
Nigeria	9.2	5.3	−1.2	0.58	−0.13
Saudi Arabia	8.6	12.7	4.8	1.48	0.56
Trinidad and Tobago	5.3	5.4	−5.0	1.02	−0.94
Venezuela	6.6	5.1	−1.3	0.78	−0.20

Sources: World Bank; Kanovsky (1986).

non-oil economy was quite fast in all seven countries for which data are available (i.e. excluding Bahrain). Compared with the middle-income oil-importing countries (MIOCs), the oil exporters had significantly higher rates of growth during the pre-shock period. The three largest economies grew especially rapidly: Nigeria and Indonesia were both recovering from disruptive domestic strife while Saudi Arabia was experiencing a large expansion in its crude oil production capacity. Venezuela and Trinidad and Tobago grew more slowly since both were experiencing temporary downswings in oil-based activity as the pre-shock period drew to a close.

Diverging rates of economic growth

Whereas economic growth decelerated slightly in the MIOCs through the two oil booms, it accelerated for the oil-exporters as a group, albeit by a modest amount. However, during the post-boom downturn 1981–4 the rate of economic growth decelerated in both groups of countries and by a similar order of magnitude. Relative to the pre-shock trend, the economic growth rate slowed by two-thirds in the MIOCs and by three-fifths for the oil-exporting countries. Yet the average deceleration for the oil-exporting countries masks significant differences between them.

Only three countries, Saudi Arabia and the two late-starters, experienced a significant improvement in the rate of growth of their non-oil economies during the boom periods. Indonesia and Trinidad and Tobago registered little change from the pre-shock trend while Venezuela and Nigeria, especially the latter, slowed significantly. The latter two countries had the most disappointing economic growth record and both were adversely affected by the inefficient implementation of an overambitious RBI strategy.

Significantly, it was the two late-starter countries which, initially at least, recorded the fastest economic growth in the post-boom period. This was partly because the decline in real oil prices was offset for them by expanding oil output, and partly because their remarkably resilient non-oil economies had been exposed to the boom effects from oil windfall deployment for a relatively brief period. Whereas the post-boom growth rate of the Cameroon non-oil economy maintained the steadily accelerating trend evident from the mid-1960s, that of Malaysia declined slightly from the pre-shock trend to one-fifth below the rate during the two oil booms.

All six countries which had been oil exporters before the first shock experienced post-boom slowdowns in their non-oil growth rates, though of markedly different severity. Least affected were Indonesia and Saudi Arabia though their growth rates halved from the pre-shock period. In the case of Saudi Arabia, that was to barely one-third the very high 13 per cent non-oil growth rate it had sustained during the two oil booms (Table 10.3). Although earlier economic growth figures are not available for Bahrain, it seems likely Saudi Arabia dragged that tiny country in its wake. Economic growth in Venezuela and Nigeria flagged during the second oil boom and turned negative thereafter. In per capita terms, economic growth contracted sharply in these two countries since the population growth was close to, or above, 3 per cent per annum.

However, it was Trinidad and Tobago which, despite its initial cautious efforts at prudent windfall deployment, registered the most precipitous decline in non-oil output. Like Nigeria and Venezuela, Trinidad and Tobago had staked its diversification effort on RBI and, in the process, neglected the remainder of its non-oil tradeables sector. Yet unlike Saudi Arabia, which also relied heavily on RBI to spearhead its diversification, the reserves which Trinidad and Tobago had accumulated (equivalent to half non-mining GPD in 1982 compared with twice non-mining GDP for Saudi Arabia) were insufficient to offset the downturn.

Trends in oil dependence and structural change

Tables 10.4–10.6 show the change in oil dependence 1972–81 of the eight oil-exporting countries and their economic structure in 1981. Only Bahrain appeared to reduce its oil dependence (albeit from a very high

TABLE 10.4. *Oil exporters' oil dependence 1981*

Country	Percentage share of oil			Dependence Index (Average)
	GDP	Exports	Revenue	
Bahrain	27	70	91	63
Cameroon	15	50E	70	48
Indonesia	22	60	74	52
Malaysia	15E	32	26	26
Nigeria	24	81	97	67
Saudi Arabia	66	92	99	86
Trinidad and Tobago	36	64	93	64
Venezuela	27	76	95	66

Note: E = estimate.
Sources: Gelb (1986a); World Bank.

TABLE 10.5. *Oil exporters' 1981 non-mining GDP structure (%)*

Country	Agriculture		Manufacturing		Construction		Services	
	A	N	A	N	A	N	A	N
Bahrain	2	14	17	33	14	7	67	46
Cameroon	26	30	12	22	5	4	56	44
Indonesia	30	33	19	14	6	4	45	49
Malaysia	24	23	19	26	5	5	52	46
Nigeria	20	31	10	14	16	4	54	51
Saudi Arabia	6	6	11	33	17	7	66	54
Trinidad and Tobago	3	11	12	28	12	7	74	54
Venezuela	7	11	19	28	6	7	68	54

Note: A = actual structure; N = Chenery and Syrquin norms.
Sources: Gelb (1986a); World Bank.

level). Saudi Arabia and Venezuela experienced increases in dependence, but by a small amount relative to the five remaining countries. However, Bahrain, Saudi Arabia, and Venezuela all still recorded high scores on the oil dependence index. The two late-starters and Indonesia were least dependent on oil in 1981, though all three underwent sizeable increases in their oil dependence during the two oil booms (Tables 10.1 and 10.4–10.6).

TABLE 10.6. *Oil exporters' structural change 1972–1981 (%/yr change in non-mining GDP*

Country	Agriculture		Manufacturing		Construction		Services	
	A	N	A	N	A	N	A	N
Bahrain	−0.11	−1.67	−0.28	1.56	0.82	0.22	−0.42	0.11
Cameroon	−0.47	−0.11	0.02	0.67	0.12	0.11	0.32	0.67
Indonesia	−1.50	−1.31	0.77	0.34	0.26	0.10	0.48	0.86
Malaysia	−0.72	−1.00	0.18	0.89	0.09	0.11	0.46	0.00
Nigeria	−1.90	−0.67	0.48	0.11	0.53	0.03	0.88	0.53
Saudi Arabia	−0.37	−1.89	−0.98	0.78	0.72	0.11	0.63	1.00
Trinidad and Tobago	−0.31	−0.49	−1.03	0.20	0.37	0.05	0.99	0.35
Venezuela	−0.10	−0.32	−0.04	0.06	0.02	0.03	0.13	0.24

Note: A = actual structural change; N = Chenery and Syrquin norms for structural change.
Sources: Gelb (1986a); World Bank.

In addition to promoting industrial development through RBI, the four higher-income countries sought to arrest (and, in the case of Saudi Arabia, reverse) the rate of contraction of their shrunken agricultural sectors. However, the non-oil tradeables sectors of the higher income countries were two-thirds or less of their Chenery and Syrquin norms. Yet the figures in Tables 10.4–10.6 still overstate the degree of diversification achieved because oil refining continued to account for one-quarter of manufacturing output in Venezuela and more than half in the other three countries, while agricultural production was heavily subsidized in all four countries (especially Saudi Arabia).

With the exception of Nigeria, manufacturing was 73 per cent or more the size predicted for countries of similar size and level of development in the four countries with the lowest incomes. Although Nigeria's manufacturing sector expanded faster than the norm, it did so from a relatively small initial base and it remained underdeveloped. Worse, Nigeria's agricultural sector experienced severe 'Dutch disease' effects (Pinto 1987). In constant prices, real output in Nigerian agriculture contracted almost three times as fast as its norm through the two oil booms (Gelb 1988), whereas the contraction of Indonesian agriculture was just 15 per cent faster than its norm. The agricultural sectors of both late-starters were larger than their norms.

Tables 10.1 to 10.6 provide a descriptive overview of the changing oil dependence and economic structure of the eight oil-exporting countries, but they reveal very little about the underlying competitiveness of the non-oil tradeables sectors. The eight oil-exporting countries' responses to post-boom conditions offer one test of their non-oil tradeables competitiveness. An evaluation of their industrial and agricultural policies provides another. Before turning to post-boom macro-economic adjustments, the non-oil tradeables sectors are first compared. The analysis of the manufacturing sector measures the disappointing contribution of RBI to value added and explains the difficulties experienced by the oil-exporting countries in establishing competitive non-RBI manufacturing sectors. Agriculture is then examined in order to determine and account for differences in the sector's capacity to cushion against the mid-1980s oil downturn.

PROGRESS TOWARDS A COMPETITIVE MANUFACTURING SECTOR

The post-1950s superiority of a (prudently executed) outward-orientated industrial strategy over an inward-orientated one is well documented (Balassa 1982, Chenery, Robinson, and Syrquin 1986). Yet only the two Arabian countries pursued outward-orientated industrialization strategies throughout the period studied. Although Venezuela maintained a relatively liberal import policy this was selective and designed to dampen inflationary pressures rather than to promote competitive manufacturing. Elsewhere, Malaysia switched from outward-orientation to import substitution as its oil revenues expanded through the second oil boom. The four other countries (Nigeria, Trinidad and Tobago, Indonesia, and Cameroon) adhered to strongly inward-orientated industrialization strategies, even when faced with evidence of its declining effectiveness (Auty 1987c). However, as will be shown, the more prudent macro-economic management of Indonesia and Cameroon muted the potential negative spillover effects on agriculture which such an industrial strategy risks.

Despite these differences in industrial policy, none of the eight oil-exporting countries successfully nurtured industrial diversification. Arabian industrialization was hampered by the disappointing performance of export RBI, relatively small domestic markets, and high labour costs. The preoccupation of both the Malaysian and Venezuelan governments with RBI (mostly orientated to import substitution) caused them to leave broader-based industrial diversification to an overregulated private sector which suffered increasingly from declining investor confidence and the crowding out of investment. Elsewhere, government intervention in the pursuit of import substitution created lucrative local monopolies, increased the opportunities for corruption, and enhanced the attractions of short-term investments in trade compared with the more long-term commitment which manufacturing required. Such policies proved expensive for taxpayers and domestic consumers and became insupportable when RBI proved incapable of compensating for declining oil revenues.

The disappointing RBI impact

Table 10.7 summarizes the RBI strategies of the eight oil-exporting countries and compares them in terms of an overall index of risk. The three principal subcomponents of that risk are:

● overambitious strategy design;
● poor implementation;
● market failure.

In summary, a high-risk RBI strategy is one in which:

● an overambitious slate of undiversified RBI projects dominates industrial policy;
● implementation is poorly synchronized and executed by low autonomy SOEs;
● sales are targeted either at domestic markets which depend on sustained growth to materialize or at export markets requiring very keen prices.

Table 10.7 shows that Nigeria and Venezuela pursued the riskiest strategies. In each case this involved a concentration on overambitious metals projects: the nationalistic accelerated implementation of the Ciudad Guayana metals complex in the case of Venezuela and the two steel complexes in Nigeria. Trinidad and Tobago also relied heavily on RBI but, despite its small size, it chose a more diversified mix of projects than Nigeria and Venezuela. Trinidad and Tobago also made greater use of experienced MNRCs, but its implementation was marred by the bunched construction of the steel and large fertilizer plants in the late 1970s. Saudi Arabia was the fourth country to rely heavily on specialized RBI, though it proved wiser to plump for petrochemicals rather than metals. Moreover, as the risk index suggests, Saudi implementation benefited from reliance on MNRCs and careful synchronization of infrastructure and process plant construction.

The remaining four countries pursued less ambitious RBI strategies and relied less on RBI for their economic diversification. They also tended to be more cautious in their implementation of RBI. Even so,

TABLE 10.7 *RBI strategy and risk*

Country[a]	Risk factor						Index[b]
	1	2	3	4	5	6	
Cameroon	1	3	1	1	1	5	0.40
Bahrain	3	3	1	1	3	1	0.40
Indonesia	3	1	1	3	3	3	0.46
Malaysia	3	1	3	3	3	3	0.53
Saudi Arabia	5	5	1	1	3	3	0.60
Trinidad and Tobago	5	3	3	3	3	3	0.67
Venezuela	5	5	5	5	3	3	0.87
Nigeria	5	5	5	5	5	5	1.00

Notes:
[a] The countries are assigned weighting from 1 (low risk) to 5 (high risk) on the following six risk factors:

Strategy	*Low risk*	*High risk*
1. Role of RBI in development policy	Minor	Dominant
2. Specialization within RBI	Low	High
Strategy Implementation		
3. RBI project sequencing	Phased	Bunched
4. Access to MNRC expertise	High	Low
Marketing		
5. Growth of domestic non-oil GDP	Sustained	Erratic
6. RBI export market access	High	Low

[b] 1.0 = high risk in all six factors.

Cameroon and Indonesia were somewhat fortunate that the abrupt puncturing of the oil boom prevented them from executing over-ambitious strategies while the relatively modest and yet diversified Malaysian RBI strategy was an important cause of the overextension of its public sector in the early 1980s.

Nigeria experienced the most acute marketing problems: its domestically orientated plants were predicated on sustained boom conditions yielding adequate domestic demand for full capacity utilization. The Ajaokuta integrated steel plant, which required rapid execution of successive units to generate an adequate cash flow, was most adversely impacted. Venezuelan steel also suffered from flagging domestic demand linked to weak macro-economic management. But exchange-rate corrections in the mid-1980s significantly improved Venezuelan aluminium export prospects, whereas the postponed Nigerian devaluation conspicuously failed to help its steel sector. Export markets created initial problems for Trinidad and Tobago steel as well as for the larger Saudi petrochemical projects, despite the prudent implementation of the latter (Part 3). The Saudi experience underscores the risks of RBI: the many critical phases of project implementation and operation must all go right so that there is little margin for error even in a well-conceived and implemented strategy.

The above briefly summarizes Table 10.7 with reference to the efficiency constraints on RBI examined in Part 3. The immediate concern of this chapter is with the consequences of disappointing RBI for economic growth and structural change. Table 10.8 measures for disappointing results from RBI. It compares the principal RBI projects' estimated value added in the mid-1980s with their output if they had achieved an ICOR of three. Taking all the RBI projects covered, the overall capital/value added ratio in the eight oil-exporting countries was eight. The investment in RBI generated less than half the added value assuming an ICOR of three and less than one third of the output projected by the feasibility studies.

The significance of the poor RBI performance can be illustrated by expressing the shortfall in terms of the oil-exporting countries' non-mining GDP. The unweighted mean RBI investment for the eight oil-exporting countries was equivalent to 15.3 per cent of their 1984 non-mining GDP. The estimates suggest that the added value generated by RBI averaged just over 2 per cent of non-mining GPD. Had the investments achieved an ICOR of three, the average boost to non-mining GPD would have been equivalent to 5.6 per cent. This was sufficient to boost manufacturing output in the typical oil-exporting country by one-third.

Table 10.8 shows that the average performance of the four smaller countries was superior to that of the four larger ones. This confirms the inversion of the expected positive relationship between country size and RBI benefits. It arises from the tendency of the larger countries to squander their potential scale benefits through overambitious RBI strategies while the smaller countries, more mindful of risk, were more cautious. Indonesia, recorded the best mid-1980s economic perform-ance of the larger countries and this, like the good Malaysian results, owes much to the dominance of the large and highly successful LNG projects. In the case of Bahrain, the solid performance of the well-executed brownfield aluminium expansion more than offset the poor performance of the iron pelletizer. In Trinidad and Tobago, the small petrochemical plants offset losses in steel.

The poorest results in the mid-1980s were achieved by Venezuela, Nigeria, and, surprisingly, Cameroon and Saudi Arabia. The Cameroon ICOR is heavily influenced by the mothballing of a $200 million pulp plant. However, the average ICOR of the well-implemented Saudi

TABLE 10.8. *Estimated RBI investment and mid-1980s ICOR*

Country	Total RBI Investment		Estimated Added Value				
			(Actual ICOR)			(ICOR = 3)	
	A	B	A	B	C	A	B
Indonesia	13.446	(19.0)	2.600	(3.2)	5.2	4.482	(6.3)
Nigeria	6.739	(13.7)	0.172	(0.4)	39.2	2.084	(4.2)
Saudi Arabia	11.735	(19.6)	1.097	(1.8)	10.7	3.912	(6.5)
Venezuela	6.401	(14.0)	0.756	(1.7)	8.5	2.134	(4.7)
4 Large countries	38.321		4.625		12.0		
Malaysia	3.034	(12.2)	0.928	(3.7)	3.3	1.011	(8.3)
Cameroon	0.595	(7.8)	0.077	(1.0)	7.7	0.198	(2.6)
Trinidad + Tobago	1.304	(17.2)	0.202	(2.7)	6.5	0.435	(5.8)
Bahrain	0.830	(18.9)	0.180	(4.1)	4.6	0.277	(6.3)
4 Small countries	5.763		1.387		4.2		

Note: A = billion dollars; B = % non-mining GDP; C = ICOR.

Source: Industry sources.

projects was below that of the poorly implemented Venezuelan ones. Part of the explanation lies in the method of calculating added value: it neglects viability since it leaves value added as a residual which may, or may not, cover capital service charges. Part also comes from the particularly poor returns on the Saudi export refineries and olefins plants. Those plants absorbed more than one-quarter and one-half, respectively, of the total Saudi RBI investment and came on stream just as prices slumped. Their performance is especially sensitive to price fluctuations and is considerably better with late 1980s prices.

The figures summarized in Table 10.8 measure the direct economic stimulus from RBI. Some indication of the opportunity cost of the strategy is furnished by subtracting the actual value added by the RBI investment from that which it would yield assuming an ICOR of three. The loss is equivalent to some 3.3 per cent of non-mining GDP. However, the disappointing launch of the RBI projects depressed the anticipated indirect stimulus from linked industries. The opportunities for investment in both cost-reducing brownfield expansion and more labour-intensive downstream activities were diminished by the uncertain future of many of the RBI projects. Still more important, the figures in Table 10.8 take no account of the output-depressing effect that high-cost domestic RBI products and subsidized losses imposed on domestic consumers and taxpayers. Nor do they quantify the neglect of the two other leading tradeables subsectors (non-resource-based manufacturing and agriculture) which government preoccupation with RBI entailed and to which attention now turns.

Non-resource-based industry

A rapid expansion in public ownership occurred within the manufacturing sector as a consequence of the combination of the governments' preoccupation with RBI, their insistence on SOE participation, and their readiness in the high-absorbing countries to take over large failing private firms. This was especially noticeable in the two South American countries. In Venezuela, for example, the government increased its share of manufacturing investment from 20 to 60 per cent during the 1970s and its share of manufacturing added value rose to 75 per cent (UNIDO 1983). Since many of the RBI projects were initially unprofitable (as were the numerous failing private enterprises taken over by the Trinidad and Tobago government (Auty and Gelb 1986)), the public manufacturing sectors of the two countries had acquired the character of large resource sinks by the second oil boom, which unproductively absorbed a sizeable fraction of government revenue.

The private sector in all eight oil-exporting countries was expected to expand non-resource-based manufacturing as well as to develop most of the linked industries downstream from RBI. The role of the government in regard to private sector manufacturing was that of regulator and overregulation became a barrier to the development of a robust diversifying manufacturing sector. The inward-orientated policies adopted by most 'high-absorbing' oil-exporters tended to discriminate strongly against activities such as agro-industry, which involved the labour-intensive processing of domestic inputs. It discriminated in favour of non-traditional, capital-intensive assembly industries (including capital goods in the larger countries) located in the largest cities. For example, one Nigerian estimate suggests that by the early 1980s, that country's manufacturing sector imported three-quarters of its inputs.

Overregulation allowed monopolies to emerge which penalized domestic consumers and created vested interests dependent on the maintenance of high tariffs and/or an overvalued exchange rate. In Indonesia, for example, many manufacturing subsectors in both the public and private spheres were basically economic fiefdoms. They extended political patronage into the manufacturing sector and impaired its crucial role as an engine of economic growth. Effective rates of protection in such industries were high: typically exceeding 60 per cent and ranging above 200 per cent. Not surprisingly, many Indonesian manufacturers viewed the stable Indonesian government as a beneficial source of long-run opportunities (Flatters and Jenkins 1986). A strong and highly visible urban lobby emerged in favour of exchange-rate overvaluation, high tariffs, and quotas. For a while, it blocked reforms that would yield a more dispersed, competitive, and employment-intensive manufacturing sector (Ropstorff 1985).

In the other high-absorbing countries, the net effect of government industrial policy was to create an uncertainty that encouraged rapid recoupment of capital and favoured investment in trade at the expense of production. For example, government regulation in Cameroon restricted manufacturing mark-ups to no more than 12 per cent compared with up to 70 per cent on imports, despite the lower risk of the latter business. Such activity became prevalent in extreme form in Nigeria, prompting Schatz (1984) to dub the system as one of pirate capitalism. That system encouraged entrepreneurs to use their ingenuity to seek ways of turning government regulations to short-run personal advantage rather to lay the basis for the long-term creation of national wealth.

Private manufacturing investment also disappointed in Venezuela.

There, squeezed profit margins arose as a consequence of an anti-inflation policy which combined relatively liberal imports with price controls and labour legislation (Auty 1986*b*). Exchange-rate policy undermined domestic non-oil competitiveness through the oil booms and thereafter devaluation lagged behind the needs of competitive manufacturing (Quintero *et al.* 1985). Even Malaysia, which had made more progress than the other 'high-absorbers' in the development of competitive industrialization by the early 1980s, experienced a downturn in manufacturing as the government's efforts to force the pace of change through state-owned import substitution industries strained public finances.

Unfortunately, those countries which followed open industrial policies also failed to establish a viable base for post-boom economic diversification. In Saudi Arabia, business ventures in the non-tradeables sector, notably real estate and trading, offered far higher returns with lower risk than domestic industry during the oil booms. Though industrial progress was made (Wells 1986), it was from a tiny base and, despite substantial government incentives, the mid-1980s' investment response to the new downstream RBI activities was muted. After the mid-1980s oil price decline, the Saudi government pursued infant industry protection more vigorously.

The preoccupation of governments with RBI and their snail-like progress in the creation of competitive non-resource-based manufacturing provided an inadequate industrial base from which to sustain economic growth and export diversification when the oil booms waned. Under such circumstances, the agricultural sector assumed great significance as a cushion against the severity of the oil-related slowdown.

THE RESILIENCE OF AGRICULTURE

The pre-shock share of agriculture in total production was small in the desert countries of Arabia, shrunken from the Chenery and Syrquin norms in the long-established mid-income oil-exporting countries of South America, but sizeable in the four other countries (Table 10.2). Three different agricultural strategies were followed:

- sizeable subsidies were given to high-cost producers in Saudi Arabia, Venezuela, and Trinidad and Tobago.
- discrimination in favour of large inefficient state farms was pursued in Nigeria;

- smaller producers were favoured in Cameroon, Malaysia, and Indonesia.

The latter policy proved the more enlightened, though it was followed less because of a far-sighted appreciation of the important role of agriculture in economic development (Johnston and Mellor 1961) than on account of the political importance which all three countries attached to their rural constituencies. Nor is it a coincidence that two of the three countries which maintained relatively robust agricultural sectors were late-starters as oil producers. The agricultural sectors of Cameroon and Malaysia benefited from shorter exposure to 'Dutch disease' effects.

Indonesia paid considerable attention to domestic food producers, especially the small Javanese rice growers but imposed mounting social burdens on the estate crop sector. Per caput agricultural production rose 33 per cent in Indonesia from the pre-shock level compared with a developing-country average rise of 6 per cent and a decline in Nigeria of 15 per cent (Gelb 1988). Mindful of the rural disturbances which had undermined its predecessor, the Soeharto regime combined green revolution techniques with favourable pricing policies to achieve food self-sufficiency by the mid-1980s.

Even so, continued agricultural resilience was by no means assured since crops other than rice had been neglected. Whereas rice production had increased by more than 4 per cent annually during the oil booms, non-rice food crops grew at half that rate and traditional 'estate' export crops by still less. The overemphasis on rice was exacerbated by the government's earlier preference for transmigration over labour-intensive rural industry as a solution to Javanese overpopulation. Consequently, just as the economic downturn deepened, the Soeharto regime needed to execute a politically delicate transition away from rice for which it was ill prepared (Auty 1987c). By comparison, Malaysia and Cameroon had greater flexibility than Indonesia in their rural sectors because, although both favoured small farmers, Cameroon did not target a single crop while Malaysia did not discriminate as strongly as Indonesia against efficient, privately owned, export-orientated plantations.

Whatever the cause, the maintenance of a robust agriculture provided Indonesia, Malaysia, and Cameroon with useful export, employment, and revenue cushions against economic downturn. Nigeria, which also possessed a large, robust agricultural sector on the eve of the first oil boom, experienced severe 'Dutch disease' effects. The share of Nigerian agriculture in non-mining GDP declined almost three times as fast as the Chenery and Syrquin norms predict (Gelb 1988). Although the Nigerian government allowed food prices to rise substantially (unlike many other countries in Africa) and channelled part of the windfall to rural investment throughout both oil booms the supply response was poor. Rural investment was primarily used to mute tribal divisions so that conspicuous dispersal held priority over efficiency. Overall, Nigerian rural investment was small relative to the size of the sector.

Nigerian agricultural investment was also deficient in quality. It concentrated largely on infrastructure (roads and education) with a long payback period and when it was directed at boosting supply it was channelled into the expansion of large inefficient state farms (Stevens 1984). Peasant agriculture, which employed nine-tenths of Nigerian farmers (and 60 per cent of the country's workforce) was neglected. Growth in per caput production lagged population increase, and food self-sufficiency gave way to high import dependence. The resulting low rural purchasing power deprived the domestic manufacturing sector of an important market while low farm output denied it a source of industrial inputs. Meanwhile, the rural exodus accelerated despite high urban unemployment and inadequate infrastructure (RAPID 1985). It is estimated that Nigeria can produce six times its mid-1980s food output by doubling its cropping area and tripling yields (Nelson 1982), yet its post-boom agriculture was severely constrained by an adequate input supply system and the drainage of manpower.

The agricultural sectors of the four richest oil-exporting countries also fared poorly. Dwindling land and water resources confined Bahraini agriculture to a small fringe along the north coast. Saudi Arabia did achieve a massive expansion of grain production but this was through highly subsidized prices. While small farms in the south-west remained an important source of employment, most of the agricultural subsidies encouraged dairy and wheat production on large, capital-intensive farms for the big northern cities. The generosity of Saudi wheat subsidies diverted land from fodder crops to wheat and within five years transformed a deficit into an embarrassing surplus which proved hard to restrain. Worse, demands for irrigation water mined underground reserves and increased long-term dependence on costly desalinated supplies. Such agricultural production was a drain rather than an asset during economic downturn.

Agriculture was also an important source of rent seeking opportunities in Trinidad and Tobago and Venezuela. Programmes to expand domestic food production and shrink the plantation sector in Trinidad and Tobago were poorly conceived. Although, unlike Bahrain, supplies of land were adequate the planners chose inappropriate sites and inexperienced farmers for the new farming schemes. Meanwhile, nationalization of the erstwhile dominant sugar industry was accompanied by sharply rising wage costs and declining production as unions tested the financial resources of the government. Production costs accelerated to ten times those of a competitive producer as the government subsidies were used to postpone rationalization (Auty and Gelb 1986).

Government assistance to agriculture in Venezuela was similarly abused as cheap loans were frequently used by larger farmers for non-agricultural purposes. Although per caput food production kept pace with increasing population, subsidies were required to boost grain production (in which the country held little comparative advantage) while the largely unsubsidized livestock sector expanded even faster (Auty 1986b). However, whereas Venezuelan agriculture was stimulated in the post-boom period by the 1983 devaluation, the reluctance of the Trinidad and Tobago government to devalue postponed necessary adjustment there.

A TEST OF DIVERSIFICATION: POST-BOOM ECONOMIC RESILIENCE

The eight oil-exporting countries' response to the post-boom downturn provides a test of their progress in sowing the oil for economic diversification. Although all eight countries remained overdependent on oil, they differed in their capacity both to cushion the downturn and to make appropriate policy adjustments. Bahrain, Venezuela, Indonesia, and—to a lesser degree—Malaysia, responded most positively. Costly delays were experienced by the four remaining countries, especially Nigeria and Trinidad and Tobago.

The cushioned low-absorbers' responses

The real decline in oil revenues called for timely exchange-rate and fiscal adjustments (including expenditure cuts and revenue diversification measures). Saudi adjustment was tardy and relied heavily on the sizeable cushion of overseas reserves estimated in excess of $140 billion at its peak. Government expenditures peaked at around $86 billion in fiscal year 1981–2 and were almost halved to an estimated $48 billion, including defence spending, by 1985–6 (Economist 1986, Ministry of Planning 1986). Developing expenditures bore the brunt of the cuts: public spending on construction shrank from $50 billion in 1981 to $19 billion in 1985 while the rate at which new public contracts were awarded declined even faster from $20 to $4 billion over the same period (Financial Times 1986*a*). One-third of the large immigrant workforce was estimated to have departed as the cushioning effect of the infrastructure investment cuts worked through the economy.

However, recurrent expenditures proved more difficult to restrain. The annual cost of operating and maintaining the 'once-for-all' infrastructure system built during the two oil booms was estimated at $6 billion, one-eighth of total mid-1980s' public expenditure. Transfers and subsidies comprised one-fifth of total government expenditure and one-third of recurrent expenditure. Subsidies on electricity and water, hitherto supplied at less than one-sixth of their cost, were trimmed but along with food subsidies and cheap construction loans they continued to account for $4 billion annually. Public sector wages were cut 30 per cent in 1985 and the more efficient state corporations trimmed their workforce as the burgeoning cost of government emerged as the largest single consumer of revenues.

Although public expenditures almost halved 1982–6, revenues fell even faster to around $35 billion, of which oil comprised just under $20 billion (Financial Times 1986*a*). This left a deficit estimated at $12 billion. Oil revenue was expected to lie between $10 and $18 billion 1986–7, assuming oil prices of $10 and $16/barrel, respectively. Although non-oil revenues expanded absolutely as well as relative to oil, they remained smaller than oil and, reflecting the structure of the economy, dependent on injections of oil revenues. A slowdown in government payments as well as reductions in the reserves of major public corporations, Aramco and Petromin (estimated at $5.5 billion in 1985), postponed reserve withdrawals but alarmed foreign and domestic investors. Moreover, IMF estimates suggest the foreign reserves declined from $141 billion in 1982 to $109 billion in February 1986. The latter figure understates the rate of drawdown since it includes asset revaluations as well as more than $35 billion in illiquid assets such as loans to Iraq and non-performing loans elsewhere in the Gulf region.

From a surplus on current account equivalent to 25 per cent of GDP in 1980 (around $41 billion), Saudi Arabia slipped into a deficit of similar relative size (but $23 billion of a shrunken GDP) by 1985. Although the RBI projects came on stream with extraordinary speed, their expected contribution to export earnings was depressed by low prices. Import capacity was reduced by the sharp fall in the dollar (to which the riyal is tied) relative to the Japanese and EEC currencies and was projected to decline from 70 to 50 per cent of non-oil GDP 1985–90. However, further devaluation was needed to reduce imports and increase the domestic value of government oil revenues (Barclays Bank 1987).

Bahrain also possessed sizeable overseas reserves and it responded confidently to the mid-1980s' downturn. The dominance of foreign workers at all levels provided considerable scope for increasing the indigenization of the economy during the transition, despite some doubts over Bahraini diligence. Capital spending allocations were spread over two additional years, effectively reducing annual expenditures by one-third. An initial 5 per cent cut was made in recurrent spending, with similar reductions targeted for succeeding years. Subsidies, used with modest success to restrain inflation from the mid-1970s, offered further scope for cuts. The reserves (estimated at $2 to $4 billion) were considered sufficient to underpin several years of non-oil revenue expansion which the more diversified Bahraini economy was better placed than its larger neighbour to achieve.

Misdirected Venezuelan action and Trinidad and Tobago's inaction

Both the middle-income South American countries had sought to accumulate a cushion of reserves against economic downturn. Venezuelan failure in this regard forced it to adjust earlier than Trinidad and Tobago. However, Trinidad and Tobago's indecisiveness quickly voided its sizeable reserve cushion. The new Acción Democrática government in Venezuela rescheduled Venezuela's $26 billion public sector debt late in 1984 but full agreement embracing private sector debt was delayed. Although the substantial 1983 devaluation opened export opportunities for agriculture, some private manufacturing (such as textiles) and the aluminium RBI projects, oil still accounted for more than 93 per cent of exports in the mid-1980s.

The case for economic liberalization in Venezuela had been tarnished by the disappointing performance of the COPEI government which briefly embraced it during its first year in office. The Acción Democrática government of the mid-1980s committed further resources to large-scale aluminium expansion by CVG while PDVSA also planned a major expansion in petrochemicals. A second large devaluation in 1986 increased the competitiveness of such projects, but failed to attract repatriation of the estimated $20 billion held by Venezuelans abroad. The 1986 devaluation effectively shifted resources from the public to the private sector which, in the absence of a more positive policy towards the private sector, seemed likely to intensify recession (Fontiveros and Palma 1987).

Trinidad and Tobago gambled unsuccessfully on the resumption of real energy price rises. The government short-sightedly resisted devaluation and strengthened protective tariffs for manufacturing when the second oil boom ended. Although public spending cuts reduced the budget deficit from 13.9 to 6.9 per cent of GDP 1982–4, the RBI projects could not compensate for falling oil revenues so that the prudently accumulated reserves fell from just over $3 billion (equivalent to 50 per cent of non-oil GDP) to $500 million 1982–6. Repeated failure over two decades to revitalize the non-resource tradeables sector of its economy left Trinidad and Tobago without a safety net when its reserves ran out.

Timely Indonesian and tardy Nigerian downswing adjustments

Indonesia's incremental technocrats responded to the initial oil downturn by making adjustments which were timely (Gillis 1984) and therefore smaller and less painful than those that Nigeria was subsequently forced to make (Pinto 1987). Deteriorating economic prospects were signalled by the widening of Indonesia's current account deficit from 3 per cent of GNP in 1981–2 to 8 per cent by 1982–3, compared with a sustainable rate estimated by the World Bank at 2 per cent. By 1983 the country's foreign debt had reached $23 billion and the debt/service ratio had risen to 21 per cent. Although Indonesia's resource gap problem was nowhere near the same magnitude as that of Nigeria the government reacted boldly and promptly. Plans for large-scale, capital-intensive industry were quickly shelved and domestic tax reforms were introduced in order to increase non-oil revenue. Although tax thresholds had been adjusted during the oil booms they had increasingly trailed oil revenue expansion.

A 30 per cent devaluation in March 1983 was supported by measures to restrain domestic inflation and retain the competitive advantage. Plans were drafted for structural change which recognized the dominant role of diversified competitive industrialization. The new strategy was intended to boost growth from the 2.5 per cent rate of 1981–3 towards 6 per cent, still some 2 per cent below the pre-1980s level. The country needed to generate 1.8 million new jobs annually in order simply to hold the combined level of unemployed and underemployed labour at 25 per cent. Since agriculture was projected to expand at only 3 per cent through the 1980s, a 10 per cent growth target was required of the manufacturing sector. However, although the bias towards import substitution was to be offset by streamlining export incentives and by establishing more Export Processing Zones, such measures were too modest. The rigidities inherent in the industrial fiefdoms which had slowed healthy structural change in Indonesian industry persisted into the late 1980s.

The abrupt 1986 oil price decline was the catalyst for reform. Although Indonesia had $10 billion in foreign reserves in the mid-1980s and depended less on hydrocarbons for exports (70 per cent of the total) and revenues (55 per cent) than other oil exporters, the sharp decline in oil prices threatened it with debt rescheduling. Its current account deficit tripled to 8.5 per cent of GDP and the debt-service ratio approached 40 per cent. A 30 per cent devaluation and further cuts in recurrent and development spending were implemented as the resilience of Indonesia's non-oil tradeables sector was put to the test.

In contrast to Indonesia, Nigeria repeatedly postponed exchange-rate adjustment until just before the 1986 price collapse. Stop-gap measures to curb expenditure and ration foreign exchange merely triggered inflation and overloaded an already ineffective and abused bureaucracy. Declining demand and shortages of imported inputs caused a sharp contraction in manufacturing output without any compensating surge from other tradeables subsectors. Export earnings (still totally dependent on oil in 1986) were estimated at $6 billion, less than one-third their value at the end of the second boom. Without rescheduling, debt service alone on Nigeria's $26 billion foreign debt amounted to $4 billion leaving little foreign exchange to cover the requirements of its highly import-dependent economy. When the exchange rate was finally adjusted in 1986 the naira declined precipitously to one-fifth of its former value.

A measure of the cost of Nigeria's policy errors is provided by a study (World Bank 1974) completed on the eve of the first oil shock. The study projected that by the mid-1980s oil would account for 12 per cent of Nigerian GDP and generate 90 per cent of exports, permitting investment to rise to one-fifth of GDP and per caput GNP to grow by 80 per cent. Although the actual financial impact of oil was larger than the study anticipated, Nigeria's oil windfall deployment not only failed to raise per caput incomes, it saw them fall. As oil revenues collapsed and Nigerian import capacity dwindled, the protected and relatively small manufacturing sector contracted. Yet the severely weakened agricultural sector was in no position to provide an alternative to oil as a generator of growth, at least through the medium term.

Costly delays in Cameroon and Malaysia

By 1984 the Malaysian dependence on hydrocarbons for its revenues had reached one-third compared with only 7 per cent in 1980 while hydrocarbons had increased their share of exports to 22 per cent. Having successfully diversified the economy away from dependence on rubber and tin since the 1950s, Malaysia was rapidly becoming dependent on hydrocarbons just as prices collapsed. In 1986 the current account deficit doubled to 5 per cent of GNP while the budget deficit jumped to 19 per cent of GNP and revenues failed to cover operating expenditures.

The redeeming view of the Malaysian drive into heavy industry—that it was a bold effort to eliminate a critical bottleneck in line with Hirschman's prescription of unbalanced growth—becomes less valid the higher the proportion of the country's limited capital, managerial, and administrative resources allocated to it. Total Malaysian investment climbed to nearly 36 per cent of GNP in 1982. Although the share of private investment rose by 3 per cent to 21 per cent of GNP, public sector investment jumped by 5 per cent to 15 per cent. These figures overstate the underlying trend in private capital formation since the 3 per cent rise is more than accounted for by investment in hydrocarbons and the expansion of quasi-public corporations. They also understate the scale of public sector investment expansion and the sharp rise in the public investment deflator points to reduced investment efficiency. The Malaysian budget deficit became so severe that even the highly diversified tradeables sector could not prevent a sharp deceleration in economic growth in the mid-1980s.

While Malaysia moved tardily to rectify fiscal imbalances, the Cameroon government made little long-term adjustment at all to the downturn. Its policy of secrecy over its windfall backfired since estimates had to be made in the absence of official figures and these proved easier to formulate for revenues than for expenditures. The size of the foreign reserve cushion was widely overestimated so that Cameroon was less buffered against the 1986 downturn than most observers thought (Devarajan *et al.* 1986). Although growth in the non-oil economy (dominated by small-scale agriculture) remained remarkably buoyant, the Cameroon government in early 1987 still lacked a coherent response to the lost foreign exchange and tax revenues. Worse, the sharp real appreciation of the French franc (to which the Cameroon currency had hitherto been generally beneficially linked) exacerbated the adjustment problem.

CONCLUSION

Efforts to speed economic growth and accelerate diversification through the two oil booms were unsatisfactory. The main RBI projects absorbed the equivalent of 15 per cent of non-oil GDP on average, but their contribution to added value was less than half that expected while the stimulation of linked industries also disappointed (Chapter 11). In addition, there were negative spillover effects from the RBI projects which included subsidies to the loss-making RBI ventures, high domestic prices, and the opportunity costs of allocating scarce human (as well as financial) resources to projects with poor returns.

In particular, preoccupation with RBI encouraged complacency over the non-resource manufacturing sector and blunted reforms required to improve its competitiveness. Indeed, the oil windfalls tended to encourage or reinforce a shift towards protected inward-orientated policies which favoured large, capital-intensive plants at the expense of smaller, more labour-intensive, export-orientated units. While the two late-starters and Indonesia preserved their agricultural sectors as resilient cushions against economic downturn through attention to small farmers, Nigeria undermined its initially large and dynamic rural sector. The four higher-income countries sought to arrest the decline of their small agricultural sectors, but this was achieved largely through subsidies. Consequently, only Cameroon, Malaysia, and Indonesia faced the mid-1980s' downturn with relatively dynamic non-oil tradeables sectors. Nigeria and Trinidad and Tobago were especially ill prepared and exacerbated their problem by postponing necessary downturn adjustments.

The large financial reserves of the Arabian countries permitted an orderly adjustment to the post-1981 decline in real oil prices. However, Bahrain's more diversified economy and sterner leadership gave it greater capacity to absorb the 1986 oil price decline than its larger neighbour. Saudi Arabia resisted domestic tax increases, ducked devaluation, and twice postponed its budget as it sought to restore oil market share and prices. The smaller reserve cushions of Cameroon and Trinidad and Tobago (fictitious and real respectively) also encouraged drift rather than decisive action with particularly severe consequences for the weak Trinidad and Tobago economy. Nigeria paid the heaviest price for poor initial deployment and subsequent delayed adjustment: real per capita income, which grew 30 per cent during the first oil boom, fell well below even pre-shock levels.

Only Bahrain and Indonesia emerged from both the deployment and post-boom adjustment periods with a laudable record. Yet, closer inspection reveals that Indonesia owed much to the rather fortuitous direction of resources to foodgrains expansion and delay of an overambitious RBI strategy. Moreover, sectoral policies towards over-population, non-rice crops, and industrial diversification lacked the incremental macro-economists' prudence, leaving even Indonesia vulnerable to the 1986 price collapse (Auty 1987c). But the disappointing RBI performance meant that those countries which pursued the most ambitious RBI strategies (Nigeria, Trinidad and Tobago, Venezuela, and reserve-cushioned Saudi Arabia to a lesser extent) remained most heavily oil-dependent, and so most vulnerable.

11

RBI's Spatial Impact: The Lagged Economic Stimulus

RBI GROWTH POLES AND THE SPACE ECONOMY

RBI locational options

In addition to accelerating economic growth and speeding healthy structural change, RBI was intended to hasten the spatial decentralization of economic activity. Drawing upon the concept of growth poles advanced by Perroux (1950), RBI was expected to propel the regional economy in which it was sited through brownfield expansion and linkage proliferation. The impact was assumed to be large enough radically to alter the spatial distribution of national economic activity.

The options for deploying RBI for spatial decentralization may be classified according to the initial size of the growth pole and its proximity to existing industrial activity (Table 11.1). The options range from the single isolated plant through the secondary growth pole (small clusters of RBI plants in remote or central locations) to large multi-plant industrial complexes adjacent to existing economic core regions. Promixity to large cores permits rapid capture of agglomeration economies while remoteness confers spatial monopoly advantages (von Boventer 1970). Differences in RBI proximity to the core region imply differing decentralization objectives. Close proximity of RBI to the core can relieve congestion by creating a multicentric spatial structure in place of an existing high density unicentric one. It extends the agglomeration economies over a wider area within the restructured region. Such a strategy was successfully used by South Korea around the established large southern city of Pusan. It was also used by the two smallest oil-exporting countries, Bahrain and Trinidad and Tobago.

Table 11.1 indicates that the core restructuring strategy was uncommon in the larger oil-exporting countries. They tended to locate RBI in lagging regions remote from the main concentrations of economic activity. The size of the growth pole is the critical factor differentiating between country policies. Alonso (1971) notes that small growth poles which are also remote tend to be unsuccessful. Richardson and

TABLE 11.1. *RBI growth pole options*

| | Core region proximity | |
	Remote	Adjacent
Isolated plant	Asahan (I) Ajaokuta (N)	Limbe (C) Cilagon (I)
Secondary pole	Bontang (I) Balikpapan (I) Lhokseumawe (I) Labuan (M) Bintulu (M) Kerteh (M) Kaduna (N) Warri (N)	Sitrah (B) Edea (C) Shah Alaam (M) Point Lisas (T&T)
Large pole	Abuja (N) Al Jubail (SA) Yanbu (SA) Ciudad Guayana (V)	

Note: Country location: (B) = Bahrain; (N) = Nigeria; (C) = Cameroon; (SA) = Saudi Arabia; (I) = Indonesia; (T&T) = Trinidad and Tobago; (M) = Malaysia; (V) = Venezuela

Richardson (1975) concur: they conclude that numerous small growth poles, unless located close to the existing economic core, dissipate the potential regional stimulus and so are far less effective than large growth poles. This is especially significant for RBI. Growth poles based on RBI benefit strongly from clustering because of their large lumpy infrastructure and their expectation of triggering linked industries that benefit from agglomeration and localization economies. Friedmann (1966) adds strong socio-political arguments to the economic ones in favour of large counter-poles. He considers that lagging regions result from political imbalances which require the creation of a large urban complex to guarantee sufficient lobbying power to challenge core region interest groups.

However, large remote RBI growth poles have their own problems since the immediate capture of agglomeration benefits implies a big push strategy. As the ambitious RBI strategies of Nigeria and Venezuela indicate, RBI can degenerate into a nightmarish Hirschmanian chain of *unvirtuous* unbalanced growth as additional investments are made to 'improve' poor initial RBI returns (Chapter 10). The required capital infusion is large and calls for careful synchronization if its initial productivity is not to be depressed (Hamer *et al.* 1986). Data for the eight oil-exporting countries indicate that basic infrastructure requirements in unserviced locations may boost RBI capital costs (already higher than in the industrial countries) by a further 30 to 100 per cent (Chapter 4). In the case of the two Saudi Arabian growth poles, the sophisticated infrastructure cost three times the direct plant investment.

The financing of such economic and social infrastructure costs is controversial. Barnett and Meunier (1985) urge that large RBI projects should be undertaken only if they can fully recoup their infrastructure costs. Yet some developing country planners object that this confers an unfair advantage on established industrial country producers and poses a near-insuperable obstacle to developing-country entry into heavy industry. They argue that government intervention is justified, even if initial returns are poor, in order to create long-term competitive advantage. The critical question then becomes how much investment should be sacrificed for this goal. This chapter suggests that RBI has a distinctly muted and lagged economic stimulus which makes the return poor. Capital-intensive RBI appears ill suited to regional decentralization, even for capital-surplus countries like Saudi Arabia.

Hydrocarbon location and spatial structure

The spatial diffusion of economic development is rarely even. A common pattern is for an economic core to emerge, dominated by a primate city in which political and economic activity is disproportionately concentrated. However, the urbanization indices in Table 11.2 show that among the six largest oil-exporting countries only Venezuela (dominated by the greater Caracas conurbation) and, to a lesser extent Saudi Arabia (with Jeddah prominent), displayed a strongly polarized pre-shock spatial structure. Yet the indices understate core-region dominance. For example, Lagos accounts for two-fifths of Nigeria's modern industry and Douala for two-thirds that of Cameroon. In Southeast Asia, the Kuala Lumpur–Port Klang axis holds a disproportionately high share of Malaysian manufacturing as does Western Java (with Jakarta as its hub) for Indonesia.

The political tensions associated with such concentrations of economic activity and political power may threaten the cohesion of individual countries. Table 11.2 identifies the principal core and periphery regions in the oil-exporting countries and summarizes both the pre-shock risk of political fragmentation and the potential of RBI to alter that risk. The initial risk is assumed low for the two tiny countries, high for the linguistically and tribally divided newly independent West African

TABLE 11.2. *Indices of spatial structure and the impact of hydrocarbon exploitation*

Country	Urbanization (%)		Spatial Structure				Spatial Cohesion	
	Pop. urban	Pop. in capital	Urban pop. in capital	Primate city	Core region	Periphery	Fragmentation risk	Hydrocarbon impact on risk
Bahrain	70	69	69	Manama	North-west	—	low	—
Cameroon	41	9	21	Douala	South-west	North-east	high	reinforce
Indonesia	25	6	23	Jakarta	West Java	Outer Isle	high	offset
Malaysia	31	8	27	Kuala Lumpur	West coast	East coast Borneo	moderate	offset
Nigeria	30	5	17	Lagos	South-west	North and East	high	reinforce
Saudi Arabia	72	13	18	Jeddah	South-west	North and East	moderate	offset
Trinidad and Tobago	n/a	22	n/a	Port of Spain	West coast	East coast	moderate	—
Venezuela	85	22	26	Caracas	North centre	South and East	low	offset

Sources: World Bank (1986*b*) except Bahrain, which is Nyrop (1977).

nations and the archipelago of Indonesia, and moderate for Malaysia, Saudi Arabia, and Venezuela.

RBI had the potential to exacerbate or ameliorate such tensions, depending on the proximity of the hydrocarbon resource to the economic core. Where distant core regions drained fiscal linkage from peripheral resource regions, as in the case of Caracas, the rapid expansion of RBI at a peripheral resource site could mute peripheral resentment. Conversely, where hydrocarbon resources were located adjacent to the cores, as in Cameroon, RBI could reinforce peripheral resentment. Table 11.2 suggests that RBI would offset regional tensions in Indonesia, Malaysia, Saudi Arabia, and Venezuela. RBI would have a neutral regional effect in the two smallest countries (though the prospect of secession by tiny Tobago and frictions between Bahrain's ruling Sunni Moslems and majority Shiites suggest spatial fragmentation is possible in even the smallest states). However, RBI would reinforce concentration in West Africa.

As Table 11.1 indicates, the actual responses of the eight oil-exporting countries to the RBI decentralization option ranged from the extreme dispersal of individual RBI projects in Nigeria to heavy concentration at a remote large growth pole in Venezuela. Saudi Arabia opted for two large remote industrial growth poles. Malaysia, Indonesia, and (to a lesser degree) Cameroon favoured secondary RBI growth poles. As already noted, the two tiny countries used RBI to ease urban congestion by creating a multiple nuclei structure in the most densely settled area. This chapter explores the RBI size/location continuum through a comparison of the efficacy of the RBI regional stimulus from isolated plants, secondary growth poles, and large growth poles (administrative as well as industrial).

ISOLATED RBI PLANTS: HIGH LEAKAGE

Contrasting proximity of Indonesian metals plants

Indonesia invested $4 billion in two metals plants (steel at Cilagon and aluminium at Asahan) at initially unserviced locations. The construction cost of both plants was high compared with OECD conditions: it was four times as high for the poorly implemented steel plant and twice as high (excluding the hydro) for the aluminium smelter. Cilagon was chosen for Indonesia's first major steel complex by Sukarno. The decision was taken partly on strategic grounds (100 km. west of Jakarta) and partly to assist a particularly poor farming region. The aluminium smelter site at Tanjung in North-east Sumatra is also a farming region, but it is much more remote. Its location was dictated by proximity to the Asahan River hydro-electricity system.

The aluminium project functioned as an enclave transmitting most of its economic stimulus outside the local region and overseas. It generated few local linkages since firms in such regions are not equipped to interact productively with a large capital-intensive plant. The vast majority of Indonesia's 1.3 million registered manufacturing firms (more than 99.4 per cent) are essentially cottage industries and fewer than 1.5 per cent use any machinery whatsoever. Most of the larger firms (which accounted for around 88 per cent of sectoral added value) are located in the established industrial centres. The gap between inexperienced local managers (and their unskilled workers) and the large modern industries is difficult to bridge. Outsiders dominate whatever links do emerge and their higher incomes and different life-styles add a cultural barrier to the technical and economic ones (Far Eastern Economic Review 1983*b* and 1985*b*). Even peripheral regions in advanced economies, such as the US Pacific Northwest or Queensland, Australia, have high rates of revenue leakage from aluminium (Auty 1983*a*).

The bulk of the Asahan expenditure during construction went on imported machinery or domestic equipment from the two largest cities (Jakarta and Surabaya). The extra-regional ownership of most construction companies meant that the leakage of profits and wages was also high. In the operating mode, regional revenue retention from the hydro-smelter was less than 10 per cent. Of this, some leaked out as remittances from the highly paid one-tenth of the 2,300 smelter workforce that was Japanese. A significant fraction of the local workers' wages also leaked out on non-basic consumption goods. The modest benefits of the smelter to North Aceh include one-ninth (50 MW) of the firm hydro power, the dam access roads, a small docking facility and three-quarters of the company's installed telecommunication lines. Yet even these modest local gains are offset by the overloading of local infrastructure and government services (Far Eastern Economic Review 1983*b*).

In the mid-1980s, some 44 per cent of operating revenue flowed directly out of the region to purchase inputs (including maintenance materials) while more than 46 per cent went to service capital (including the hydro). A combination of low domestic equity, initial losses, and the need to import the chief input (alumina) meant that few other Indonesian regions benefited from smelter linkages. Domestic aluminium consumption was scarcely one-tenth plant output and special requirements meant some of that was imported. Whatever processing (forward linkage) did occur in Indonesia took place at the main markets rather than at Aceh. Consequently, although national benefits will increase as debt is retired, domestic ownership rises, and domestic aluminium consumption expands, the smelter region will profit little because of its remoteness from national markets.

Steel provided a much larger regional stimulus, albeit at the expense of the national economy. High regional revenue retention reflected the steel plant's low capital service charges (on account of its restructured low debt–equity ratio), its more labour-intensive production function and its proximity to the relatively large domestic market. For a similar order of investment to the aluminium smelter, the steel plant generated twice as many direct jobs (5,000) and a further 10,000 indirect local jobs in steel-using industries such as ship-building and rig construction. Cilagon's population exceeded 100,000 in the mid-1980s (personal communication, Ministry of Industry). The steel plant's direct added value was expected to double with forward linkage into an $800 million cold rolling mill and a $300 million seamless pipe plant. Yet these local benefits from high revenue retention and linkages were at the expense of Indonesian taxpayers and consumers elsewhere. This is because steel users paid 20 per cent more than the imported steel price even after the 1986 devaluation. Even then, the return on the $2.25 billion investment was low.

Indonesia's metals projects confirm that the local stimulus from remote, highly capital-intensive plants like aluminium is small and the national economic stimulus is lagged. Less remote and more labour-intensive plants like steel have a greater local impact. Aluminium's principal advantage comes from the inflow of much cheap capital along with increased net foreign exchange as debt is retired and as domestic demand grows.

Wasteful Nigerian decentralization

African countries have a strongly primate spatial structure (Mabogunje 1972). By the mid-1970s Lagos accounted for more than two-fifths of Nigeria's modern manufacturing while Douala yielded two-thirds of Cameroon's industrial output. Although the Nigerian states of Kaduna, Kano, Cross River, Bendel, and Anambra each contained more than 5 per cent of national industrial production, their location quotients (which measure the extent to which share of national output reflects share of national population) were close to unity whereas that of Lagos was 13 (Onyemeluke 1984).

Nigeria's inward-orientated industrialization policy was at odds with government efforts to disperse the oil windfall because it biased industrial location towards the largest cities. The gap between rural and urban incomes in Nigeria widened steadily: from the early 1960s to the early 1970s the ratio of urban to rural per caput income increased from 3 to 6. The first oil boom boosted the index to 10 (Bienen 1983). The population of the capital city continued to expand at about three times the national rate and grew from four to six million between 1979 and 1985 (RAPID 1985). This was so even though combined unemployment and underemployment exceeded 30 per cent in Lagos by the late 1970s and the majority of those with jobs worked outside the formal sector. The first oil windfall did nothing to stem the drift to the cities because it failed to raise farm incomes. Only remittances from relatives in urban areas averted substantial declines in rural incomes during the 1970s (Nelson 1982).

In this context, the dispersal of the large RBI projects and the designation of Abuja as the new federal capital were intended to promote decentralization and spread the windfall through the federation. However, the cost was high in terms of the opportunity cost of capital, expensive (and unreliable) products, and ongoing subsidies. The local regions in which the plants were located secured double-edged benefits from the protracted plant start-up and the successful rent-seeking behaviour of the plant workforces. The inefficient units gave greater immediate local revenues than efficient ones would, but their diminished viability will stunt the proliferation of linked industries through the long term.

The Nigerian government invested $5.7 billion in five steel projects which employed 21,000 workers. The isolated Ajaokuta steel mill accounted for three-fifths of the investment and just under half the jobs, but required still further large unprofitable investment merely to complete its (suboptimal) first stage. Additional investments in brown-field expansion and downstream processing would boost local linkages only at high national cost. The $1.7 billion invested in the Delta DRI plant and its three dispersed satellite mills appears less inefficient. However, dispersal of the steel mills is partly responsible for capital costs four times those of an efficiently constructed single plant.

The mistake of fragmentation was repeated in the Nigerian pulp and paper sector. A Finnish study recommended construction of a single pulp plant but three were sanctioned despite projected low returns. At least one-third of the paper plants' high cost escalation reflected additions to infrastructure while timber shortages will require further outlays. Similarly, in the petrochemicals sector, three plants were implemented and although they used the infrastructure of existing refineries (at Warri and Kaduna), capital costs were still cripplingly high.

The pursuit of geographical decentralization led to the extreme dispersal of Nigerian RBI. It further depressed the efficiency of capital by boosting infrastructure requirements, raising the costs of transport and reducing the economies of scale. Nor did the relocation of the administrative capital to Abuja prove a more effective regional policy as a later section demonstrates and the experience of Brasilia forewarned (Katzman 1977).

Cameroon's aborted decentralization

Unlike their Nigerian counterparts, planners in Cameroon attempted to use RBI as more than simply a conspicuous way to spread the oil windfall throughout the country. RBI formed part of an integrated regional development strategy intended to halt the drift to Douala and Yaounde, which between them accounted for more than 90 per cent of industrial activity. Remote mineral resources like Dschang bauxite and Kribi iron ore were viewed as potential sites for industrial towns which would justify the construction of transport routes from the expanding coastal cities of Douala, Limbe, and Kribi. Those routes would improve access to rural areas and create intervening opportunities for agricultural production between regions of rural outmigration (such as the lower slopes of Mount Cameroon) and the existing major cities. Such areas of intervening opportunity would take diversified economic activity to the homelands of important tribal groups and curb resentment of, and migration to, the burgeoning industrial centres of Douala, Yaounde, and Limbe.

The strategy was flawed by overtly political considerations and never implemented. For example, Limbe (35,000 population) is the natural growth pole for oil-based and gas-based industry but its situation in the English-speaking region makes the government favour Kribi. Kribi is a French-speaking coastal resort centre of 20,000 population. Kribi was planned to be the country's (redundant) third deep-water port with a population of 235,000 by 2000. It would serve a planned LNG plant and inland iron and steel complex. When these RBI projects were postponed, serious consideration was still given to investing more than $250 million for port and road connections. Yet, in addition to duplicating investment and drawing gas-based RBI from Limbe, Kribi's poor agricultural hinterland further disadvantaged it as a growth pole.

Postonement of the RBI growth poles undermined Cameroon's bold regional strategy but the three RBI projects which were executed (the Edea pulp plant and aluminium expansion and the small Kribi oil refinery) suggest that initial benefits would have been few. The Cellucam pulp plant lost $85 million during the year ending June 1984 and was mothballed. The adjacent aluminium smelter's expanded output was exported at a loss while employment and added value in fabrication did not increase (SNI 1985). Although the Kribi oil refinery generated twice the added value of the smelter it did little to stimulate the chemical sector. The sixteen factories with over twenty employees which dominated chemicals employed less than 2,000. They made simple products like cosmetics, inks, and candles with few domestic backward or forward linkages (Le Guern 1986). Like Asahan aluminium, Cameroon's RBI generated few regional linkages and was unprofitable in the mid-1980s.

SECONDARY GROWTH POLES' LAGGED REGIONAL STIMULUS

The Indonesian steel and aluminium plants aside, the RBI projects of the two South-east Asian countries were grouped in clusters at remote locations. These secondary growth poles might lower the cost of shared infrastructure but they still triggered few linkages. Malaysia created three secondary RBI poles (one each for the east coast, Sabah and Sarawak) in line with its policy of seeding industrial estates in peripheral regions (Alden and Awang 1985). The Indonesian government recognizes five secondary poles (Far Eastern Economic Review 1983*b*) but only the three at major hydrocarbon extraction sites are significant. They are Arun (North Sumatra), Palembang (South Sumatra), and Balikpapen (East Kalimantan). Links between the secondary poles and adjacent transmigration settlements (the principal Indonesian regional policy tool) are negligible.

Indonesia's remote dualistic enclaves

The mainspring of Indonesian regional policy (and much else besides) was population pressure in Java where 60 per cent of the population resided in 7 per cent of the land area. Here too, the sprawling city of Jakarta with seven million people experienced serious congestion problems. Indonesia favoured transmigration over rural industry as a long-term solution to regional problems. Its inward-orientated industrial

TABLE 11.3. *Indonesian hydrocarbon regions: structural share in GDRP* (%)

| | Aceh | | East Kalimantan | | Riau | | Three regions |
	A	H	A	H	A	H	(% GDP)
1969	61.0	—	62.9	4.4	8.9	75.7	9.2
1976	48.9	24.0	12.1	62.3	3.4	87.4	18.6
1980	15.9	74.3	11.5	70.3	3.2	87.0	23.4

Note: A = Agriculture; H = Hydrocarbons.
Source: Sansui (1985: 44).

policy discriminated strongly against the growth of small labour-intensive rural businesses (Auty 1987c). Yet small rural enterprises had the potential to boost rural incomes (Ranis and Stewart 1987) with lower infrastructure costs than either city-based manufacturing (Richardson 1987) or transmigration. By the mid-1980s transmigration costs had risen to around $10,000 per family, excluding environmental costs and the social costs associated with the income reduction which most transmigrant families experienced (Economist 1984b).

The links between transmigrant schemes and the capital-intensive secondary poles were negligible. Yet it is clear that the secondary poles rely heavily on their local regional matrix to function effectively. Table 11.3 shows the extent to which hydrocarbons (the nucleus of Indonesia's three secondary poles) dominated their respective regions. In the long-established Southern Sumatra oil province, hydrocarbon extraction and processing increased its share of regional output from 76 to 87 per cent 1969–80 (Sansui 1985). The newer hydrocarbon provinces of Aceh and East Kalimantan underwent more dramatic changes, with the share of hydrocarbons in their regional product jumping from negligible levels to more than 70 per cent.

The three regions increased their combined share of Indonesian GDP from 9 to 23 per cent over the same period. However, very little of the economic stimulus spilled directly into their hinterlands. The flow of revenue to the national government dwarfed the return flow which, in any case, went mainly into capital-intensive activities that left most local inhabitants little better off.

East Kalimantan with 30 per cent of the national land area, but only 4 per cent of the population generated one-third of the country's foreign exchange and one-quarter of its hydrocarbon revenues (Financial Times 1986d). Much of the development was concentrated in two urban areas 150 km. apart, the Balikpapan oil refinery complex and the Bontang LNG complex. Balikpapen refined one-fifth of national crude output while Bontang produced just under half Indonesia's LNG. Even after large-scale LNG expansion, the Bontang labour force rose by just 50 per cent to 1,200 (8,000 during the construction stage) and supported a community of only 6,200. The $3 billion invested was equivalent to $2.5 million per direct job.

The spillover from the oil-based activities further south at Balikpapan was more significant, spawning a city of more than 300,000, of whom around 80 per cent were dependent on the oil industry. However, when oil prices faltered in the mid-1980s, unemployment mounted and population growth decelerated and then declined. The planners sought diversification into palm oil, shrimp production, and cattle breeding, activities with few links to hydrocarbons. Similarly, a planned engineering works at Medan, south of the Aceh complex, was orientated to agro-industry rather than to the hydrocarbons sector. All three of Indonesia's hydrocarbon poles functioned as economic enclaves.

Simple 'rule of thumb' multipliers for the prospective linkages from the Lhokseumawe complex in Aceh (Transcentury 1982) are consistent with the enclave nature of small remote secondary growth poles. Without active measures to promote spillover effects via productive linkages from the hydrocarbons projects and/or expansion of other export products, Lhokseumawe (based on the Aceh LNG and fertilizer plants and the deferred olefins complex) would boost local employment by 1.7 per cent and GDRP by 16 per cent (Table 11.4). This outcome (Scenario One) implies the region will fall further behind other parts of Indonesia in terms of both per capita income and manufacturing.

Two additional scenarios (Table 11.4) assume, respectively, active measures to enhance Lhokseumawe linkages (Scenario Two) and additional export promotion (Scenario Three). Relative to the persistent enclave (Scenario One), the improved Lhokseumawe linkages of Scenario Two would boost GDRP by a tenth (excluding income from oil and gas accruing to the national government) by the year 2000. The broader export promotion scenario (Three) would raise GDRP by a half. Even so, for the larger region of Aceh, Scenario Three would boost GDRP by less than 10 per cent and raise the annual rate of per capita growth in non-mining GDRP to 3.4 per cent compared with 2.6 per cent under Scenario One.

However, by projecting the model into the year 2025, the compounding of long-term benefits from the early promotion of fuller regional integration becomes clear. The annual per caput growth rate of non-

TABLE 11.4. *Three scenarios for Aceh and Lhokseumawe regional growth, 1978–2000 and 2025*

	Base 1978	Scenario One		Scenario Two		Scenario Three	
		2000	2025	2000	2025	2000	2025
North Central Aceh (Lhokseumawe)							
Population (millions)	0.732	1.251		1.267		1.324	
Net employment increase (millions)	—	0.202		0.207		0.226	
Increase in GDRP (Rp 1978 billion)	—	0.197		0.230		0.353	
Total GDRP (Rp 1978 billion)		0.438		0.486		0.683	
Per caput GDRP (US$ 1978)	172	350		387		516	
Aceh							
Population (millions)	2.441	4.290	8.140	4.305	8.200	4.360	8.385
Non-mining GDRP (Rp 1978 billion)	0.266	0.823	3.715	0.856	4.073	0.979	5.656
Manufacturing share of non-mining GDRP (%)	4	8	14	9	17	12	28
Per caput non-mining GDRP (US$ 1978)	172	304	722	315	787	355	1067
Growth in per caput non-mining GDRP (%)	—	2.6	3.5	2.8	3.7	3.4	4.5

Source: Transcentury (1982: 22–4, 29, 30).

mining GDRP under Scenario Three now rises to 4.5 per cent (compared with 3.5 per cent). Manufacturing's share of non-mining GDRP rises to 28 per cent by 2025 compared with 14 per cent by that date under Scenario One and 4 per cent in the late 1970s. The analysis assumes that as incomes rise the local multiplier declines in the absence of countervailing measures since spending patterns shift away from wage goods to more diverse and sophisticated products. Under Scenario Two, the fraction of consumed goods produced locally rises to 10 per cent while under Scenario Three it reaches 25 per cent.

Remote secondary RBI poles function as enclaves with a lagged and muted local economic stimulus. Accelerated growth in peripheral regional income requires broad-based diversification: the remote RBI secondary growth pole is inadequate on its own.

Malaysian contrasts in secondary pole remoteness

The three Malaysian RBI secondary poles suggest that increasing remoteness is positively associated with stunted and delayed linkages, echoing Indonesian experience with its metals plants and hydrocarbon centres. The Malaysian big push into heavy industry included vehicle manufacture in the Klang Valley core region as well as the three RBI poles. Listed in decreasing order of remoteness and increasing local linkages, the poles are: Labuan (Sabah), Bintulu (Sarawak), Kerteh/Chukai (Terengganu), and Shah Alaam (Klang Valley).

The Labuan iron/methanol pole was the least successful. Its remoteness is intensified by the choice of a cramped island site. Everything must be shipped and space is at an increasing premium. The RBI plants compound the poor record of earlier industrial ventures at Labuan, including shipbuilding and flour milling. Few local productive linkages exist and the dominant linkage is fiscal, decidedly negative, and unlikely to improve before the early 1990s if then (Far Eastern Economic Review 1983c). The Bintulu secondary pole is only slightly less remote but has a superior site with space reserved for iron ore, steel, and aluminium plants (the latter drawing on either gas or interior hydro-electricity) as well as secondary industries. However, although the large LNG unit and urea plant generate positive fiscal linkage there is little prospect of the early proliferation of productive linkages.

More scope for linkage generation resides in the East Coast steel and refinery plants, although they started poorly and would capture more linkages at a market location. The nationalist lobby within the Ministry of Industry favoured the east coast over the Klang Valley, Johore Bharu, or Bintulu for an olefins complex (Auty 1987b). Half the population of

Terengganu region is estimated to live below the official poverty line compared with the national average of one-third. The region generates less than 7 per cent of its GDRP from manufacturing compared with the national average of more than one-fifth. Yet the remote location of the ethylene cracker will weaken its competitiveness and the downstream activities which it supplies. Regional decentralization via such RBI will be slow and carry high national cost (Beyer 1985).

Malaysia's fourth large industrial project is a market-orientated automobile plant whose growth potential contrasts sharply with that of RBI. The $240 million plant in the Klang Valley, promises larger productive and final demand linkages than the RBI plants—and much sooner. It provides 1,350 direct jobs at start-up using one-third rated capacity, approximately twice as many jobs per unit of investment as the steel plant and thirty times that of the Bintulu LNG unit. A move to two-thirds of capacity use doubles the number of direct jobs without further investment and offsets expected losses at the existing inefficient car assembly plants. The indirect employment in components and marketing at the start-up is estimated at 10,000 jobs, an employment multiplier of 7. This figure is expected to expand considerably as domestic components sourcing rises from an initial two-fifths to more than 85 per cent (Journal of Japanese Trade and Industry 1986).

The more labour-intensive nature of both vehicle manufacture and component supply contrasts with that of RBI and implies a much larger total multiplier from final demand linkage. Such linkage would largely accrue to the Klang Valley as agglomeration economies (including modern transportation, nascent supplier firms, and a sizeable skilled labour pool) are tapped. Ironically, the location of the steel plant close to the main market instead of at the gas source would have lowered its construction and distribution costs.

The automobile plant and RBI units share initial low/negative capital returns. But the very high initial construction costs and small lagged multipliers of the RBI secondary poles (not to mention the isolated RBI plant) contrast with those of the market-orientated Malaysian car plant. Several conclusions emerge from the analysis thus far. First, remote locations intensify the very heavy demands which RBI makes on scarce capital resources even if RBI is clustered in a secondary pole. Second, RBI's enclave character yields minimal final demand and productive linkages which do little to speed regional diversification. Third, RBI is more likely to trigger competitive productive linkages if it is located near core regions in which more sophisticated enterprises are already established. Fourth, extensive regional investment in non-RBI activity is required to enhance RBI's long-term contribution to economic growth in remote regions.

These four conclusions suggest a further one: that the need to capture agglomeration advantages makes the large RBI pole a superior option to both the isolated plant and the remote secondary pole. However, the country which pursues such a regional policy must be both large enough and resilient enough to absorb the implied risk. The experience of Saudi Arabia, Venezuela, and Nigeria permits the exploration of this conclusion.

THE THREE LARGE RBI GROWTH POLES

Al Jubail's lagged stimulus

Saudi Arabia's two industrial growth poles (at Al Jubail and Yanbu) were intended simultaneously to diversify the non-oil economy and extend economic activity into the northern part of the country. Al Jubail reinforced the pull away from Jeddah which started with the rapid growth of Riyadh as the hub of public oil windfall spending. The West region (mainly Jeddah) received two-fifths of the investment during the 1975–85 construction boom (Aramco 1982, 1984) compared with almost one-third for the centre (mainly Riyadh) and just under 30 per cent in the eastern region (Dammam and Jubail). The national dominance of Jeddah and the more populous south-west (where over one-third of the population lived) correspondingly declined.

As noted in Chapter 10, the first generation of RBI proceeded as planned and came on stream slightly ahead of schedule and under budget. However, the expected proliferation of linked industries was notably muted. By March 1986, some sixty-three support industries, mostly small in scale, were operational at Al Jubail with only seven more under construction and eleven in the design stage. Construction-related industries and services dominated the secondary activities, followed by automotive repairs and cooling systems. Two important reasons why backward linkages were not greater are: first, the large RBI plants were designed to be as self-contained as possible and to minimize dependence on local maintenance. For example, although four-fifths of the maintenance materials used by the $2.7 billion Sadaf olefins plant were locally sourced, that represented less than 1 per cent of the original investment cost and half the normal rate. Second, much activity leaked out of the immediate Al Jubail area to established enterprises spawned by Aramco in centres like Dammam.

Forward linkages were also disappointing and reflected export market and scale-related domestic market problems. Even with pre-1986 energy prices the efficient Saudi plants were only marginally more competitive than efficient market-located EEC producers though their edge in Asian and East African markets was stronger (Table 9.3). However, the Saudi advantage waned moving downstream as large-scale market-located plants undercut the production costs of the planned Middle East intermediate-sized export units. The sharp 1986 decline in feedstock prices eliminated it entirely. Nor did the Gulf regional market offer a significant alternative. Exports typically comprised more than three-quarters of the output of the large olefins complexes. In most cases local regional demand would only sustain plants with an annual capacity of several thousand tonnes. Local requests for supplies were too small for the large export-orientated primary plants which were geared to large sales volume.

Plans for second-stage processing units, including MTBE (motor additive) and PVC, proceeded slowly. Even then, such activity might leak from the immediate region: one of the PVC plants located at the Riyadh market. As of mid-1986 firm plans existed for only three small secondary industries including 3,000 tpa polyols, 50,000 tpa wire products, and 12,000 tpa of fibre glass. Consequently, although employment in the primary industries was close to the planned levels and should exceed 10,000 by 1990, the multipliers from secondary industries and community services strongly lag the projections. In the mid-1980s the ratio of RBI employment to that in secondary industry, municipal services, and commerce combined was revised to 2.3, about half the original figure. The population to employment ratio was also scaled down so that Al Jubail might house 120,000 by 1995 and be well below the 350,000 envisaged by Buchanan for 2010.

Yet most of Al Jubail's economic infrastructure was built under the assumption that the plan targets would be tightly adhered to. The infrastructure invested 1975–85 for Al Jubail and Yanbu (including $22 billion for the Master Gas Scheme and $14 billion in industrial and urban support facilities) exceeded that for the actual plants (around $10 billion at Al Jubail and $4 billion at Yanbu) by a ratio of three to one. Saudi Arabia's relatively small high-income Gulf regional market precluded reorientation there. The infrastructure is likely to remain significantly underutilized into the foreseeable future. As with the smaller remote RBI poles, the economic stimulus from Al Jubail is distinctly muted and lagged. However, the longer-established Venezuelan industrial growth pole exceeded its employment targets despite market constraints similar to those of Al Jubail.

Unsoundly attained targets in Ciudad Guayana

Table 11.5 compares the actual size and structure of the Guayana region labour force in the early 1980s with the planners' mid-1960s projections. Consistent with experience in the other oil-exporting countries, Blanco and Ganz (1969: 71, 77) note that Venezuelan RBI showed a distinct early tendency for achievements to lag behind targets. An effort was made to overcome this by allocating a substantial fraction of the oil windfalls to speed up the faltering steel programme and boost the aluminium capacity target. At first sight, the Ciudad Guayana RBI growth pole's employment–population multiplier suggests that it succeeded remarkably well where the other oil-exporting countries failed. The actual mid-1980s Guayana labour force in heavy industry was one-eighth less than the planners' target of twenty years earlier, but total employment and population were both around twice the projected levels.

Three explanations suggest themselves. First, steel dominated the Ciudad Guayana complex and domestic demand in the larger oil-exporting countries makes steel's downstream linkages easier to capture than those from aluminium or petrochemicals. Second, the Guayana region embarked upon RBI earlier than Al Jubail (iron ore mining commenced in the early 1950s and downstream processing started in the mid-1960s): Venezuela's windfall unlocked the typically lagged RBI economic stimulus. Third, the employment figures are misleading and owe more to subsidies than to healthy linkage proliferation. There are elements of all three explanations in the Guayana performance so that their relative weight is the critical factor.

Like Indonesia, Venezuela's steel plant, generated more direct employment per unit of investment (50 per cent more) than its aluminium sector. However, the secondary industry multiplier was much lower in Venezuela (Table 11.5). This partly results from Sidor's internalization of steel finishing and partly from the depressing impact on local linkage proliferation of remoteness from the major Caracas market. Nor were backward linkages to iron ore initially positive. Steel expansion was associated with deteriorating output, profits, and capital stock as CVG neglected its iron ore mining subsidiary (Radetzki 1985). Neither did aluminium linkages compensate: even though there was strong backward linkage into alumina refining and eventually bauxite, it occurred at very high cost (Auty 1986b). Meanwhile, aluminium's forward linkage was much smaller than that from steel. Downstream aluminium fabrication absorbed less than one-quarter of total ingot

TABLE 11.5. *Early 1980s Guayana region employment structure, 1965 projection and 1984 outturn*

Sector	Projection (1965) (1)	Outturn (1984) (2)	Actual/ projection
Heavy industry			
Mining	6,900	4,542	0.66
Energy (and utilities, 1984)	900	4,171	4.63
Heavy manufacturing	26,000	22,658	0.87
TOTAL	33,800	31,371	0.93
Agriculture	5,500	5,010	0.91
Secondary industry	14,000	5,144	0.37
Construction	7,600	17,893	2.35
Services	29,100	117,957	4.05
TOTAL EMPLOYMENT	100,000	177,375	1.77
TOTAL POPULATION	357,000	753,172	2.11

Notes: Ratio of heavy manufacturing to secondary manufacturing: (1965) 1.86; (1984) 4.40. Ratio of heavy manufacturing to total employment: (1965) 0.26; (1984) 0.13; and to total population: (1965) 0.07; (1984) 0.03.

Sources: (1) Blanco and Ganz (1969); (2) CVG (1986: III–44 and IV–4–4).

production to feed 180 companies employing 5,500 (many outside the Guayana region) generating an added value of Bs 400 million in the early 1980s.

The Guayana region's economic structure in the early 1980s is consistent with the delayed RBI stimulus noted in other oil-exporting countries. Manufacturing dominated regional investment but its disappointing linkages and problematic implementation meant that activities associated with the creation—rather than the operation—of the Guayana growth pole were still large in the mid-1980s. Table 11.5 shows that construction employment was much higher than targeted while service jobs (including public administration) exceeded four times the level projected in the mid-1960s. Construction remained the driving force into the early 1980s. Whereas the mid-1960s plan called for the region's construction industry to generate 7 per cent of employment by 1980 as the heavy industry programme ended, that sector still accounted for one-sixth of regional employment in 1981, albeit down from almost one-quarter in 1978.

The delays in RBI project completion which accompanied the mid-1970s windfall boosted-acceleration simultaneously saddled the RBI projects with onerous debt and prolonged the construction boom beyond its anticipated 1980 termination. The Guayana region's burgeoning population was heavily dependent on the informal sector for employment. Planners expected to absorb three-quarters of Ciudad Guayana's population in modern facilities west of the Caroni leaving informal settlements on the east to absorb the rest. The actual ratios were almost exactly reversed. The high RBI/population ratio in Guayana owes more to continued heavy construction spending on relatively unprofitable projects than it does to favourable steel linkages or an early start.

The mid-1960s targets called for the Guayana region to earn a real return of 15 per cent on invested capital by 1980 so that it could be self-financing and contribute to diversification elsewhere in the country. Severe cost overruns and start-up problems absorbed additional financial resources so that direct investment in steel and aluminium was Bs 30 billion ($7.0 billion) while the hydro scheme accounted for a similar amount. Additional infrastructure spending boosted the total further, almost certainly by more than the one-tenth of direct investment cited by CVG.

Sidor incurred an average annual loss of Bs 1.15 billion (equivalent to 6 per cent of total investment) 1980–5 while the modest operating profit in 1986 owed much to unusual exchange-rate manipulation. Steel was not projected to earn more than a 5 per cent return, even with high domestic prices, unless costly new finishing facilities were efficiently installed (Mendoza 1987). The overall nominal return on the capital invested in aluminium is better (CVG personal communication 1987), but it is too small in relation to both the steel and hydro investments to push the overall return on RBI in Guayana towards the expected levels. Sidor accounts for two-thirds of the direct metals investment and one-third of the combined metals/hydro investment.

Gelb's (1988) observation that capital won the struggle with labour over the windfall by effectively capturing it abroad may be true at the national level, but it is less so within the Guayana region. Overmanning was a striking characteristic of the CVG operations. The aluminium plants employed twice the required levels. Sidor employed 17,200 directly, three times the level of similar sized plants in Western Europe. This was so even when Sidor renumeration levels ($23,000 per man) exceeded those before the 1983 devaluation. Capacity utilization struggled to 60 per cent some six years after start-up, but domestic demand was so low (less than one-quarter projected levels) that CVG found it necessary to export two-fifths of its production at prices significantly lower than those paid by captive domestic consumers.

Labour appropriated a sizeable fraction of the oil rents in the Guayana region through prolonged heavy construction expenditures, overmanning, and the trickledown from the highly paid RBI workforce. If sizeable devaluation prices the region's population into sustainable employment (and makes the majority of poorer people better off than they were) then the delayed RBI spillover may yet be effectively captured. But only low linkage aluminium production (responsible for less than 3 per cent of total direct employment) appeared capable in the mid-1980s of being self-financing—provided devaluation gains were retained. The attainment of RBI employment targets and the larger than planned multipliers in the mid-1980s reflected the fact that for much of the first two decades of its existence the Guayana region metals complex functioned as a large public sector sink.

Abuja: Nigeria's weak administrative growth pole

Nigeria's large administrative growth pole at Abuja proved no more successful. The 1978 master plan for the federal capital called for completion of the new city with a population of just over three million by the turn of the century. Administrative inefficiency and increasingly severe financial constraints retarded progress so that the population had only struggled to around 30,000 in 1987 even though $2 billion had been expended. Biennial funding then ran at N1 billion, intended to cover the construction of the two office complexes, ten thousand housing units, and associated infrastructure needed to relocate four ministries. The Ministries of National Planning, Information, Interior, and Trade had already moved, with the key portfolios of Industry and Finance to follow shortly. The revised targets called for the conclusion of Phase One with 110,000 people by 1991 (Financial Times 1987), an expansion rate well above that achieved, but still less than one-third the expansion rate originally envisaged.

The scale, remoteness, and specialized administrative function of the federal capital evoke comparison with Brasilia. Katzman (1977) concluded that by the mid-1970s Brasilia had moved about 600,000 consumers closer to a remote farming region. Brasilia raised returns to regional food producers by bringing a significant part of their market closer and improving access to the industrial centres of the south-east. However, the same improvements in communications enhanced the competitiveness of large city manufacturers over those in the region, hitherto protected by distance. Just as competition from São Paulo slows the economic diversification of the southern Mato Groso, so Lagos,

Ibadan, and Kaduna stunt Abuja's economic diversification. While long-term political benefits may accompany government relocation and the congestion diseconomies in Lagos may be reduced, the medium-term cost to the national economy is high.

CONCLUSION

The Richardsons' thesis that growth poles should be either small and close to existing concentrations (effectively creating multiple nuclei agglomerations) or large and remote receives qualified support from the oil-exporting countries' experience with RBI.

The Nigerian strategy of dispersing individual RBI projects reduced their viability and generated immediate local gains at the cost of long-term and national benefits. Cameroon failed to operationalize its more structured plans to use RBI plants to open up areas of intervening opportunity. The West African countries may better accelerate spatial diversification through a sharp reorientation away from large RBI projects and import substitution towards rural-based agro-industry.

The remote secondary growth poles in Indonesia and Malaysia show little early prospect of triggering local development. Complementary investments are required to reduce revenue leakage and reach the threshold for significant regional diversification. The secondary poles located closer to the industrial cores of West Java and West Malaysia show that market proximity enhances linkage proliferation.

The RBI stimulus from the large growth poles of Saudi Arabia and Ciudad Guayana is muted and lagged. It is also costly. The two countries yield a paradoxical result: efficient petrochemical enterprises in Saudi Arabia had a more muted regional impact than the poorly implemented Venezuelan metals projects. One reason is that the lagged stimulus from RBI is more strongly reflected in the performance of Saudi Arabia which embarked later than Venezuela on RBI. A second reason is that steel linkages appear easier for mid-sized economies to capture than petrochemical linkages. However, the third factor, successful rent-seeking behaviour in the Guayana region, appears most important.

Moscovitch (1969) calculated for Venezuela that small unirrigated farms would create five times as much employment and one-third more added value than steel over a fifteen-year period. The main attraction of steel was, ironically, that it would generate a higher capital return (about one-quarter more). Wadsted (1984) estimated that if the employment generated by CVG investment had matched the national manufacturing average, the total number of direct industrial jobs generated in the region would have been 286,000, some sixteen times the actual outcome. The massive capital investments, high risks, and slow creation of viable employment of RBI render it an inappropriate tool for regional development even for capital-surplus countries like Saudi Arabia.

PART 5

Conclusion and Policy Implications

12
A Model of RBI and some Policy Implications

With few exceptions, RBI made a disappointing contribution to the oil-exporting countries' economic growth, structural change, and geographical decentralization. The increasing volatility of the international economy made the 1970s and 1980s a particularly difficult time for entry into RBI. Factors external to the oil-exporting countries, notably sharply increased energy prices and negative real interest rates, initially encouraged entry. However, they turned abruptly unfavourable in the early 1980s, just as many of the new RBI plants were starting up or nearing completion. This poses the interesting question of whether the disappointing RBI performance was entirely due to the erratic performance of the global economy or whether it reflected factors inherent to RBI.

Developing countries are at a disadvantage in establishing large capital-intensive industries like RBI because of high construction costs (South Korea and Taiwan are notable exceptions in this regard) and remoteness from major markets. The oil windfalls improved RBI prospects for the oil-exporting countries by simultaneously raising resource rents on cheap energy inputs and shrinking the entry barrier which high capital costs presented to most developing countries. The projected rents on cheap energy inputs appeared large enough to offset the oil-exporting countries' disadvantageously high plant construction costs and remoteness from major markets.

Forecasts of rising real energy prices and continuing high inflation encouraged premature entry as new producers discounted risk and opted for early construction which they expected would help contain nominal RBI investment costs. Such forecasts tempted the larger oil-exporting countries to implement ambitious RBI strategies. The prospect of concessional capital (via suppliers' credits) at low or negative interest rates reinforced RBI's attractions, especially for the high-absorbing oil-exporting countries. It encouraged them to adopt imprudently high debt/equity ratios.

Having first worked to reduce the perceived RBI risk, external factors abruptly turned unfavourable and penalized new RBI entrants. Through the mid-1980s, prices were set by the cash costs of established amortized producers located close to major markets. Such prices failed to cover the average costs (including capital service) of efficient new entrants in the industrial countries, let alone those in the oil-exporting countries. Many new RBI plants were squeezed by a vicious circle of falling prices, shrinking capacity utilization, and rising fixed costs (including sizeable capital service charges).

Those RBI projects which had been poorly implemented by SOEs and/or financed largely through foreign loans were especially adversely affected. Loan service payments proved particularly burdensome for new developing country RBI projects when prices and capacity utilization rates both fell sharply below expectations. The financial restructuring of such debt-burdened RBI enterprises was hampered where the government guaranteed the debt and was already struggling with mounting national debt service. This delayed the adjustment of excess RBI capacity to global demand, aggravated RBI market rigidity, and made the period of depressed prices very protracted.

These unfavourable RBI launch conditions imparted a distinct time trajectory to the oil-exporters' economic stimulus from RBI. Measured in terms of direct added value and linked activities, the RBI economic stimulus was muted and lagged after an initial construction-related blip. Following start-up, domestic added value was meagre and even negative, being squeezed between unexpectedly low revenues and onerous fixed debt service payments to foreign banks. The resulting uncertain viability of the basic RBI project discouraged investment in linked activities. However, those new RBI projects which strove to pursue commercial objectives possessed strong rebound potential when excess global RBI capacity was eliminated and the construction debt was amortized (typically within ten years of start-up). Such RBI projects were then in a position to capture the dynamic economies of scale by using their vastly increased cash flow to invest in brownfield expansion, vertical integration, and the realization of agglomeration economies.

A MODEL OF RBI

The post-1960s volatility of the international economy made for an especially difficult RBI launch. However, the experience of an earlier generation of RBI plants in the eight oil-exporting countries suggests that the economic stimulus from RBI may be inherently muted and lagged. This is grounded in the developing countries' twin RBI penalties of high plant construction costs and remoteness from major markets. These penalties tend to be exacerbated by technical and/or marketing problems. This is because RBI demands the tight synchronization of many complex factors which most developing countries have found difficult to achieve. A theory of RBI based on these premisses is explored at length elsewhere (Auty 1988*c*) and a model of RBI is sketched below.

The persistence of both internal and external economies of scale beyond those secured by a single RBI plant of minimum viable size exerts constant pressure for further expansion. Internal economies of scale may be augmented by brownfield (*in situ*) expansion which lowers infrastructure costs (and therefore average capital costs) and generates pecuniary economies, and by vertical integration which reduces transaction costs and lowers investment risk. The external economies are the agglomeration and localization economies which result from the expansion of aggregate demand for goods and services. Such linked activities tend to be more employment-intensive and less scale-sensitive than RBI. They can be expanded more flexibly than RBI and are therefore less risky.

The initial RBI investment assumes the character of a 'hurdle' which must be overcome: additional investment will unlock the ungoing scale and linkage proliferation benefits. Developing country governments frequently use such benefits to justify the initial 'sinking' of capital in the relatively unattractive first stage RBI plant. The dynamic scale economies impart a Verdoorn effect (a virtuous cycle of growth-related efficiency gains) which is especially strong where rapid market penetration causes the growth rate of RBI demand to exceed that of GDP. The combination of initial entry hurdle and prospective Verdoorn effect yields the characteristic muted and lagged RBI economic stimulus.

The static and dynamic economies of scale make RBI a risky strategy for developing countries, especially the smaller ones. This is because the smaller the country, then:

- the lower the domestic revenue retention (because the limited geographical area reduces backward linkage opportunities);
- the smaller the forward linkage (because the small local market limits scope for domestic sales of higher margin downstream products) and the greater the dependence on export sales (where margins are trimmed by freight charges, tariffs, and discrimination against offshore suppliers);
- the more damaging the negative spillover effects from a poor RBI investment (because diversified non-RBI investment is a smaller part of GDP);

- the less the scope for avoiding politically sensitive dependence on MNCs for investment, technology, and marketing.

Figure 12.1 plots country size against scale returns (which shows rising total capital productivity with investment scale). It suggests that:

- the single RBI plant is likely to be non-viable in very small countries;
- only the largest countries can execute a 'big push' strategy;
- dynamic scale benefits exert pressure for a leftward shift in the option vector.

The energy price increases triggered by the oil shocks pushed the country size/RBI attraction vector to the left and encouraged premature entry by the smaller countries and the pursuit of dynamic scale economies by the large ones. The subsequent energy price decline pushed the vector to the right so that the new debt-burdened developing-country RBI plants were marginalized as RBI prices were set by the cash costs of established industrial country producers benefiting from market proximity and low capital service charges on their amortized plant.

In terms of the time trajectory of the RBI economic stimulus, whereas the increase in oil prices had afforded rents to the oil-exporting countries which promised to boost the immediate direct added value and advance linkage proliferation, the abrupt RBI price decline reversed this. As a result the initial RBI stimulus was further muted and linked investment

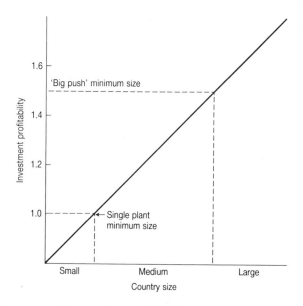

FIG. 12.1. Country size and RBI investment productivity

was further discouraged. Yet the trajectory also promises a strong rebound for commercially orientated RBI firms when their debt is amortized and global RBI demand and supply reach better balance.

The conclusions about country size and RBI advantage are subject to two important qualifications. First, increasing per capita income boosts aggregate GDP and offsets the small country constraints of low population and limited geographical area. Second, there is a tendency for an X-efficiency factor to work in scale economies whereby larger countries/firms squander their scale advantage. Specifically, the dynamic scale economies tempt many of the larger developing countries to pursue overambitious RBI strategies.

The pursuit of the dynamic scale advantages can unleash a risky Hirschmanian chain of unbalanced growth in which an initial large, lumpy, and unattractive RBI investment calls forth waves of complementary investment to 'improve' the average return. Taken to their logical conclusion such scale pressures result in a 'big push' RBI strategy such as that at the Ciudad Guayana metals complex or the Al Jubail petrochemicals complex. The RBI plants at Al Jubail (excluding infrastructure) cost 50 per cent more than similar facilities in industrial countries. Their infrastructure costs were massive: totalling three times the directly productive investment. The initial value added generated by RBI in Al Jubail and Ciudad Guayana has been disappointingly small.

POLICY FOR RBI RISK-REDUCTION

Prudent RBI strategy

The commitment of large sums of capital over long periods of time which RBI entails, makes a sound macro-economic environment an important prerequisite for RBI investment. The key requirements of such macro-economic policy are prudent fiscal policy and maintenance of a competitive exchange rate. Such policies help minimize domestic inflation during the lengthy RBI construction phase, provide sustained growth in domestic demand, and maintain the option for competitive exports. Countries with weak governments and/or inefficient bureaucracies are better advised to pursue a development strategy based on smaller, more flexible investments than RBI. Indeed, so demanding are the overall requirements for RBI, most developing countries might be well advised to eschew such a strategy, especially during periods of heightened volatility in the international economy.

The major risks associated with RBI are summarized in Table 10.7. Where appropriate macro-economic conditions permit, it is clear that the design of a risk-reducing RBI strategy requires that it is large enough to allow diversification into several RBI product lines and to capture the agglomeration economies without becoming so large as to dominate development strategy. This gives the larger and more developed countries a further advantage over the smaller countries. The initially muted stimulus from RBI and the lagged proliferation of linked activities effects mean that non-RBI investment must play the major role in sustaining economic growth and promoting healthy structural change. Such non-RBI investment enhances the prospect that RBI's linked activities will be captured domestically and accelerate through the long term, as the regional forecasts for North Sumatra demonstrate. The internalization of the potential RBI stimulus will be higher if RBI investment is clustered near existing established centres rather than dispersed at remote sites.

The Achilles' heel of RBI as a development strategy is that it is an insufficient departure from reliance on hydrocarbons. RBI's muted and lagged economic stimulus also diminishes its utility through the medium term for accelerating economic growth, healthy structural change, and geographical decentralization.

Reducing implementation risks

RBI carries substantial implementation risks. The fact that the larger oil-exporting countries were mainly unsuccessful in realizing their potential size advantage testifies to this. RBI can seriously overstretch domestic implementation capacity and thereby boost its already onerous capital costs even more. The eight oil-exporting countries suggest that the most effective RBI launch vehicle is a joint-venture with at least 25 per cent MNRC equity. This will enhance the primacy of economic over socio-political considerations, improve the chance of poor projects being postponed, and increase the likelihood of sound projects reaching capacity on time and under budget.

MNRCs have an important role to play in screening RBI projects by weeding out the weaker ones. Based on experience gained from the two oil booms, a leading multinational chemical company has summarized the criteria for evaluating specific RBI projects (Wilson 1985). It argues that developing country RBI projects should be evaluated in terms of the after-tax discounted cash flow rate of return over a fifteen-year period and under the initial assumption that the project carries 100 per cent equity finance. A return of 15 to 20 per cent (similar to that sought for new technologies in industrial countries) is commensurate with the higher risk associated with plants being set up in the developing countries. This compares with a real DCF return on equity of 5 to 10 per cent for experienced firms using tried technology in established industrial country petrochemical markets.

Even then, added guarantees may be required against the risk of project failure. These include a government guarantee to maintain tariffs at a rate capable of sustaining realistic prices (defined as those which justify reinvestment by efficient producers) and an adequate market at least until the end of the payback period. Further state assistance such as the provision of subsidized feedstocks and infrastructure might also be legitimate requests from state or private firms seeking to establish themselves in the face of uncertain global prices.

Provided the downside risks are minimized and the estimated returns are favourable under the 100 per cent equity assumption, the actual gearing should involve at least 30 to 40 per cent equity finance. This ensures the seriousness of the investors' commitment to the project. As a rule of thumb, the debt portion of the finance should not be so great as to push the ratio between the annual pre-interest operating cash flow and the sum of the interest and principal payments below a figure of 2. Such guidelines improve the likelihood that poor projects will be postponed and reduce the risk of excess global capacity depressing RBI prices below the replacement cost of an efficient new entrant.

MNRC participation needs to form part of a broader policy that makes prudent use of foreign goods and factors of production to fill gaps in domestic capacity. Saudi Arabia provides the clearest example of the benefits from strong MNRC links: once sanctioned, its ambitious 'big push' strategy proceeded as scheduled and within budget. The plants reached or exceeded design capacity remarkably quickly. The Saudi strategy illustrates the importance for effective implementation of the careful synchronization of infrastructure with RBI projects, as well as between the RBI projects themselves. The Al Jubail industrial growth pole was one of the largest construction projects ever undertaken anywhere.

Marketing risk

The importance to RBI of access to cheap natural resource inputs was overestimated and the market proved the most critical determinant of RBI performance. Low prices triggered a vicious spiral in many instances in which inadequate capacity utilization played a central part. Low prices were associated with depressed demand which lowered capacity utilization and raised average costs so that debt service became even more burdensome. The construction of large RBI projects with long lead times well ahead of demand may have been appropriate for the pre-1970s period of sustained high growth. But it proved a fundamental flaw in the oil-exporting countries' RBI strategies. Even South Korea experienced serious problems from building ahead of demand during that country's late-1970s heavy industry drive.

Vertical integration into markets provides an important safeguard for new RBI ventures with relatively high fixed costs. New RBI entrants that are vertically integrated into domestic markets are significantly advantaged—provided adroit macro-economic management minimizes the risk of a slump. The domestic advantage comes from the natural protection afforded by the absence of import duties, lower freight charges, and the absence of discrimination against offshore suppliers. In addition, the domestic market can be protected by government intervention in the event that short-run global prices fall below the costs of an efficient new producer.

However, the large country domestic market advantage is easily abused. During the oil booms, optimistic projections were made of domestic growth in order to justify construction of RBI plants where existing demand would not support a worldscale unit of minimum optimum size. Overoptimistic demand projections helped encourage premature entry. Even if macro-economic management is sound, it seems prudent to build for existing demand rather than ahead of demand. In all too many markets in the oil-exporting countries, domestic consumers paid for high-cost surplus domestic production through high prices. The 'security' of a captive domestic market was an important factor which encouraged the larger countries to discount risk and thereby squander their potential size advantage. Developing country governments need to set clearly defined limits on the degree to which inefficient local production will be tolerated, as South Korea has.

In the absence of a sizeable captive domestic market, vertical integration can still reduce the risk of dependence on export markets (where margins are both slimmer and more volatile). New developing country entrants can achieve vertical integration either directly through investment in fabrication at the market or indirectly through MNRC partners. Since most developing country governments are understandably reluctant to invest scarce capital resources abroad, the latter solution is advantageous—provided the MNRC partner is a reputable one with a sufficiently high individual equity share. Japanese consortia-style equity partners may help to ensure effective project implementation but they are less reliable in providing sustained market access, as the Inalum smelter shows.

The larger countries held a clear marketing advantage over the smaller ones under the depressed conditions of the mid-1980s. They could exploit glutted global markets to import cheap RBI inputs for domestic downstream users and thereby spur the expansion of the latter. This would strengthen such countries' future prospects of building an RBI plant. The rapid growth of domestic demand will facilitate backward integration into RBI when RBI prices justify it. By contrast, domestic downstream consumers would be seriously disadvantaged and domestic market growth correspondingly slowed if premature entry saddles large countries with high-cost domestic material.

Further advantages would accrue to all new entrants from a strategy of restrained backward integration into RBI—providing it was widely adopted. They include the more rapid recovery of global markets and prices and the reduced displacement effect on high-rent crude oil exports (Auty 1988*b*). The displacement effect on oil exports may have been small for individual countries, Saudi Arabia aside. However, in aggregate terms it appears to have been considerable as a result of the targeting of RBI by the oil-exporting countries.

This discussion of policy implications has so far focused on reducing the risk associated with an RBI strategy, an issue orientated towards the future. Much investment has already occurred and a more immediately pressing question in the eight oil-exporting countries—and others besides—concerns the appropriate policies for existing investments. This issue is now addressed.

POLICY FOR EXISTING RBI PLANTS

The model of RBI outlined earlier suggests that there is considerable rebound potential in new RBI projects. Through the medium term this arises from the price upswings associated with the cyclical volatility of rigid RBI markets. Through the long term, the rebound potential increases with the sharp rise in cash flow that follows debt amortization. Consequently, even poorly executed projects may yet bring significant benefits, provided they are reformed.

Plant closure

Closure is the starkest solution for ailing RBI plants. Many factors militate against such a decision. The size of the investment already made in most unfinished projects relative to that required for completion is large, so that only a modest outlay appears necessary to generate a positive cash flow. Moreover, the same debt-loaded capital structure which so compounds cash flow problems also militates against as drastic a measure as closure. All but the most poorly executed projects tend to yield a positive economic rate of return on a sunk cost basis (i.e. with existing investment written off). The government-guaranteed debt still has to be serviced, so any contribution might seem welcome.

These considerations, in combination with the loss of face associated with cancellation and intense political opposition from those with a direct interest in completion and operation, make closure virtually unthinkable. Hence, although the closure option was under active consideration for steel projects in Trinidad and Tobago, Venezuela, and Nigeria by 1983, it was not pursued. Even in Nigeria, the principal recommendation of a comprehensive review of that country's RBI programme was reported to be one of delay (in order to remove an anticipated hump in public debt service) rather than one of closure. Yet failure to close marginal projects has clearly been an important reason for the tendency of SOEs, noted earlier, to contribute to RBI market rigidity.

The rebound potential identified by the RBI model suggests a further reason why closure may be ruled out. The RBI projects have considerable potential for a rebound as technical problems are resolved, markets are secured, and debt is retired. Those plants which have used the depressed conditions of the mid-1980s to adopt commercial criteria are best placed to capture the rebound potential from improving markets. The major risk is that past lessons will not have been learned and that improved financial performance will trigger added investment to capture the dynamic scale economies. Such moves risk perpetuating the condition of excess global RBI capacity. Prudent incremental expansion, as the Bahraini aluminium smelter shows, involves modest cost-reducing investments that reduce competitiveness at low risk.

Financial restructuring

Without major changes in finance, enterprise structure, and product strategy there is no guarantee that reprieved projects will achieve the often modest ERRs projected for them on a post-sunk cost basis. In some cases revenues have failed to cover operating costs, as in the case of Venezuelan steel in the early 1980s. In such circumstances, a major devaluation (usually required of post-boom oil exporters) is a prerequisite for continued operation. Thereafter, financial restructuring can boost the firm's nominal cash flow. Calculation of net present value provides a basis for such financial restructuring. Enterprise flexibility is improved by formalizing government guarantees of debt and transferring the debt to central institutions.

However, while it is important to create conditions under which reorganized enterprises can pursue efficiency-maximizing criteria, it is also necessary to record the real return on investment in order to lower the risk of repeating past errors. Financial restructuring tends to mask the real cost of the investment and, given the momentum from the dynamic economies of scale for production expansion, may thereby trigger further imprudent investment. For example, Venezuela's aluminium industry recorded a high current return after capital restructuring and a devaluation (which pushed the exchange rate to one-third of its earlier level) while the country's steel industry generated operating profits. The Venezuelan government used the aluminium industry's performance in the mid-1980s to justify further massive investment in RBI. It favoured the same high risk overly specialized public sector route which caused the late 1970s' difficulties. It also blunted initiatives for more broad-based and flexible private sector diversification (Quintero *et al.* 1985).

Financial restructuring is clearly inadequate on its own: it must be part of a package which includes improved macro-economic performance, recognition of the RBI's limitations for rapid diversification, and the promotion of commercially sensitive RBI enterprises.

Enterprise structure and product strategy

There appears to be no enterprise structure which can guarantee the commercial autonomy of SOEs. However, some of the organizational structures which made SOEs indistinguishable from the bureaucracy (as with Nigerian steel) or an extension of the leader's office (as with Cameroon's SNH) are singularly inappropriate. As already noted, a relatively robust solution to the problem of political corrosion is provided through MNRC equity participation. As with new ventures, this means a prudently levered joint-venture with an experienced MNRC holding at least 25 per cent of the equity. If Venezuela moved towards such a policy, it could simultaneously ease its large public sector debt and improve the commercial autonomy of both CVG and PDVSA with fairly modest privatization.

However, it may be difficult to secure public acceptance for an MNRC to acquire significant equity in a restructured company for which the state has absorbed the costs of debt service. Such a situation is open to the criticism that after the state has borne most of the adjustment costs, private foreign firms stand to benefit disproportionately from the expected gains. Consequently, nationalistic pressures may constrain the adoption of joint-venture partnerships. It may be necessary to settle for the more modest goal of a much smaller MNRC equity share, perhaps with further restrictions which limit the new MNRC partner's call on any profits. The incentive for the MNRC partner must then lie in the sizeable long-term benefits promised by RBI's rebound potential.

Few RBI firms adopted an appropriate product strategy. They neglected full forward integration into markets so that, as surplus RBI capacity shifted profitability along the production chain towards OECD fabricators, the new RBI enterprises could not recapture profits in that stage. A common response was to invest further domestically in order to diversify product range and increase marketing flexibility. Unfortunately, as the Malaysian Sabah experience shows, such downstream investments could sometimes rival, and occasionally surpass, the initial investment they were designed to enhance. This increases the likelihood that additional capital will secure a low or negative return as—in the absence of informal vertical integration to export markets—surplus upstream capacity is merely extended downstream.

Integration into existing downstream units is a sounder strategy under such circumstances. The Venezuelan state oil corporation, PDVSA, provided one of the few examples of such a move in the eight countries and was sensibly copied by CVG for aluminium in 1987. Between 1983 and 1987 PDVSA secured refinery outlets in major markets for more than two-thirds of its crude exports at relatively modest cost. SABIC had already secured such outlets informally for a significant fraction of its output through its use of joint-ventures in most of its operations. However, careful choice of partners is required. For example, there is reason to believe that far from providing the benefits of a link to fabrication units, the partnership between the Cameroon government and Pechiney permitted the latter to use transfer pricing to make Cameroon a lucrative market for its surplus alumina.

Appropriate joint-venture partners may be no more easily secured for a restructured enterprise than for one before the investment has been made. In the latter case governments should not proceed if private equity partners are not forthcoming. Such a rule would have improved the market-sensitivity of past RBI investments, notably in steel, had it been followed. For restructured ventures, the experience of Trinidad and Tobago indicates that willing partners may take several years to secure. Nevertheless, the single most appropriate policy for rescuing ailing RBI ventures appears to be the acquisition of experienced private equity partners who can provide the catalyst for financial restructuring, reinforce barriers against political corrosion of commercial criteria, improve operational efficiency, and integrate projects to markets.

CONCLUSION

In developing countries, high construction costs and remoteness from markets make large greenfield RBI plants relatively uneconomic. Under such conditions, 'cheap' suppliers' credits may appear to ease the capital barrier, but they do so at the expense of reduced flexibility in the face of low prices and competition *vis-à-vis* established amortized producers. Heavily front-loaded RBI plants in developing countries are likely to experience technical as well as capital service problems. After an initial construction-related boost, the economic stimulus from RBI is muted. Productive and final demand linkages are strongly lagged as the debt-burdened plants' uncertain viability discourages investment in linked activities. They are also volatile because of the market rigidity which arises from the lumpiness of RBI capacity expansion.

However, reformed RBI projects have considerable rebound potential as depressed prices ease and debt is amortized. Moreover, linkage proliferation may be triggered a decade after start-up when full debt retirement permits capture of agglomeration benefits (including brown-field expansion), provided commercial criteria prevail and expanding non-resource activities boost domestic revenue retention.

There is some evidence, albeit weak, from the pre-shock generation of RBI projects that such a trajectory for the RBI economic stimulus is inherent to RBI—rather than uniquely a product of the post-1960s period. However, the heightened uncertainty of the post-1960s global economy did greatly intensify RBI entry problems: the sharp accelera-tion in inflation simultaneously increased rents to amortized producers while encouraging premature entry. Markets were then depressed by unexpected falls in the energy and materials intensity of GDP while a marked decline in producer homogeneity impeded exit.

A prudent RBI strategy is one which is large enough to capture the advantages of RBI project diversity without dominating development policy. Implementation risks are reduced by careful project sequencing of prudently-levered MNRC joint-ventures. Marketing risks are also lowered by participation with vertically integrated MNRCs and (where domestic markets permit) a product strategy of backward integration. Providing nationalistic objections can be overcome, failing state-owned RBI projects can be strengthened by securing an MNRC partner with sufficient equity to ensure economic criteria prevail over socio-political ones.

The ease with which the large oil-exporting countries squandered their size advantage underlines the importance of efficiency criteria to successful RBI. Sound macro-economic policy requires commitments to fiscal prudence and a competitive exchange rate. It helps insulate RBI, with its long lead-times from cost inflation and provides sustained growth in domestic markets and/or competitive access to export markets. Even so, RBI on its own is not an effective vehicle for accelerating economic growth, promoting healthy structural change and speeding geographical dispersal. It must be part of a broader development strategy which promotes the non-resource tradeables sectors. RBI is a minimal diversification away from hydrocarbon dependence with the further disadvantage arising from its muted and lagged economic stimulus.

13
Conclusion: RBI Risk

CONTEXT

Tropical primary products such as crops and minerals, especially the latter, have been particularly disappointing as engines of economic growth. Historically, the large capital investment required by mining created economic enclaves, i.e. enterprises which transferred their economic benefits out of the mining region (and often out of the developing country) to stimulate economic growth far away in the industrial countries. Even after post-war developing-country gains in political and economic power, tropical mining still triggered little direct economic growth (downstream resource processing remained largely absent, for example) though the domestic spending of mineral taxes did become more important.

Ironically, the successful capture by governments of mineral taxes (as from the oil windfalls) raised new problems of public sector management. Most developing countries found it difficult to resist domestic political pressures for rapid spending and/or buying political favours and this often led to poor investment decisions and unsustainable patterns of subsidized consumption.

RBI proved a popular use of the oil windfalls triggered by the 1973–4 and 1979 oil shocks. However, previous research has been equivocal about RBI's merits and silent about implementation constraints. Three important, but neglected, constraints are: inadequate country size, poor macro-economic management, and the absence of efficient enterprises with which to establish and run RBI.

THE POTENTIAL ECONOMIC STIMULUS FROM RIB

The potential economic stimulus from RBI can be measured under 'base case' assumptions, defined as a large (Brazil-sized) developing country with an efficient government and competitive enterprises in which appropriately scaled RBI projects can be effectively implemented. Among the four natural resources examined (iron ore, bauxite, oil, and gas), the downstream processing of iron ore opens more investment options than bauxite, but the processing of hydrocarbons, notably gas, yields more options still.

Assuming normal profits and long-term prices, the direct potential economic stimulus from RBI (measured in terms of added value) is modest so that RBI's attraction rests heavily on capturing resource rents and the indirect effects (i.e. the linked activities for the supply of manufactured inputs and also for further, more labour-intensive downstream processing).

However, resource rents (which have historically been higher for oil than gas and for hydrocarbons than for metals) may not be enhanced by resource processing. Moreover, since low-rent RBI exports may displace high-rent crude resource exports, RBI production may actually diminish total resource rents. Furthermore, the indirect economic stimulus from RBI, while potentially large under highly specific circumstances (where many projects do capture sizeable rents and are concentrated in nucleations within large, low-wage countries), is invariably lagged. As a result of the operation of all three key RBI characteristics (low added value, the displacement of high-rent crude resource exports and the delayed indirect stimulus) the initial economic impact from RBI investments may be disappointing.

All else being equal, small countries are disadvantaged in the pursuit of RBI. The economies of scale are substantial in most RBI projects, they increase moving upstream from fabrication through RBI to resource extraction and they are reinforced by agglomeration economies (i.e. efficiency gains from the clustering of such economic activity) as well as—in the cases of aluminium, ethylene, and LNG—by vertical integration (the execution of sequential processing stages by a single firm). Efforts to capture all the scale advantages encourage over-ambitious investment which may acquire a momentum of its own and result in the commitment of very large sums indeed to do what is under any circumstances a high-risk sector.

The oil windfalls greatly increased investment resources and so encouraged the discounting of risk. Co-operation with multinational resource corporations (MNRCs) diminished technological obstacles to RBI. Even tiny countries could contemplate investing simultaneously in several RBI projects, including a multi-billion dollar one, though the resulting domestic economic activity would be significantly below that of a larger country.

However, even the larger countries had difficulty in securing adequate markets for most RBI products, since product differentiation shrank the amount of domestic demand they could supply and forced reliance on export markets where tariffs and keen competition heightened risks. Nor were scale benefits automatically captured: they could prove elusive because they depended on so many decisions all being shrewdly taken. The result was an X-inefficiency factor whereby larger countries might squander their size advantages by the pursuit of bolder and/or less rigorously implemented RBI strategies than those of smaller countries which were more sensitive to the need for caution.

The resource rents on which RBI projects in both large and small countries were heavily dependent were not forthcoming and RBI performed far worse than expected. The RBI feasibility studies projected sizeable resource rents which encouraged the oil-exporting countries to discount risk. Many RBI projects were highly levered (i.e. used loans for over three-quarters of their finance), a step reinforced by the steady availablility of cheap loans. This resulted in high fixed capital service charges which impeded flexibility of response to depressed RBI prices.

The feasibility studies were based on a forecasting consensus which overestimated the benefits of cheap natural resources and undervalued market access. The consensus erroneously assumed rising real energy prices and rapid global economic growth. The feasibility study sensitivity tests focused on changes in single parameters whose impact on returns was minor, while the actual outcome was that a combination of market-related parameters fell well below expectations. Actual mid-1980s' prices were between two-thirds and half the levels projected. The reasons why RBI product markets fell so far short of the universally overoptimistic feasibility projections remain controversial. Whatever its cause, price depression severely tested the resilience of the highly levered RBI projects so that much depended on the efficiency with which they had been executed.

THE MACRO-ECONOMIC EFFICIENCY CONSTRAINT ON RBI

The oil windfalls created major opportunities to accelerate economic growth and diversify away from oil dependence, as well as potential pitfalls. RBI is a large, complex, and long-term investment which calls for sound macro-economic management if its potential benefits are to be realized. It required the avoidance of overrapid absorption of the oil windfalls. This in turn called for the prudent division of the windfall between overseas savings, domestic investment (including allocations to RBI), and domestic consumption so as not to overstretch domestic implementation capacity and trigger destabilizing inflation. Revenue sources also required broadening to ensure that patterns of public expenditure were sustainable.

Effective RBI implementation called for macro-economic policies that stressed fiscal prudence and a competitive exchange rate. In particular, minimization of cost inflation during the long RBI plant construction period required the removal of social and economic infrastructure bottlenecks. Adequate market access called for sustained economic growth to ensure satisfactory domestic demand and/or a competitive exchange rate for exports. Such macro-economic policies also furnished an appropriate framework within which to nurture a robust non-hydrocarbon tradeables sector (agriculture and non-RBI manufacturing) as a complement to RBI and a buffer against overreliance on oil.

The more successful governments like those of the Arabian countries, had sufficient autonomy to insulate policy-makers from domestic political pressures for overrapid domestic spending. Saudi Arabia, which experienced windfalls equivalent to almost twice its non-oil output, successfully launched a bold, well-synchronized economic diversification strategy with RBI as the catalyst. However, the abrupt mid-1980s' oil price downturn proved harder to manage than the upswings. It exposed the Arabian countries to RBI's two principal weaknesses. First, RBI represents a minimal diversification from hydrocarbon dependence since product prices (and rents) tend to rise and fall with oil prices. Second, RBI has a very lengthy gestation period before its benefits emerge.

Those oil-exporters which received more modest windfalls than the Arabian countries tended to be less successful in containing inflation, sustaining domestic non-oil growth, and maintaining a competitive exchange rate. Only Indonesia (helped by fortuitously curbed spending plans) and Trinidad and Tobago (which experienced a relatively large windfall) accumulated significant overseas savings to offset unexpected windfall decline. Saving efforts by Cameroon failed as did those of Nigeria and Venezuela which both accumulated burdensome debts. Public investment received sizeable fractions of the oil windfall in all six 'high-absorbing' countries, but its quality was poor—especially in Nigeria, Venezuela, and Cameroon. Domestic consumption reached unsustainable levels, notably in Nigeria and Trinidad and Tobago, due to subsidies and exchange-rate overvaluation (which encouraged heavy import dependence).

Summarizing, among the 'high-absorbing' oil-exporting countries Indonesia's paternalistic autocracy, cushioned by a large dynamic agricultural sector, pursued the most successful deployment strategy. The weaker Venezuelan and Nigerian regimes performed least well.

Trinidad and Tobago was deflected from its initially prudent strategy while there is little evidence that the late-starters, Malaysia and Cameroon, learned by observing the mistakes of others. Given Saudi Arabia's downswing problems, the conclusion emerges that (Bahrain apart) no regime successfully withstood the pressures for overrapid domestic absorption of the windfall over the entire cycle (boom to bust). In consequence, the macro-economic conditions under which many RBI projects were launched were not propitious being inflationary, prone to wide swings in demand and subject to lags in adjustment—especially exchange-rate adjustment.

THE ENTERPRISE EFFICIENCY CONSTRAINT ON RBI

State enterprises played a prominent role in RBI project launch because nationalistic objectives frequently overrode caution and so discouraged heavy reliance on MNRC partnerships. The state enterprises differed considerably in their size, product strategy, organizational structure, autonomy, and degree of commercial orientation. Ten groups of state enterprise may be recognized based on high and low autonomy subclasses of five product strategies. They are:

- single product firms with horizontal integration;
- single product firms without horizontal integration;
- vertically integrated dominant product firms;
- related diversified firms;
- conglomerates (i.e. unrelated diversified firms).

Few RBI state enterprises adopted an appropriate product strategy and the organization of many failed to secure sufficient managerial autonomy to ensure commercial operation.

The wholly state-owned firms dependent on a single product aimed at (shrinking) national markets experienced the most severe adjustment problems when demand fell below the universally overoptimistic projections. Fewest problems were encountered by joint-venture firms (in which MNRC partners held over 25 per cent of the equity and thereby ensured adequate commercial autonomy) that had diversified into related product lines orientated towards export markets. The state enterprises tended to reflect, and therefore amplify, macro-economic efficiency—though not inevitably so. Efficiently launched RBI projects complemented the solid macro-economic achievements of the Middle East, where high MNRC equity participation was widespread. The macro-economic woes of Nigeria and Venezuela were compounded by their strongly nationalistic RBI strategies.

Depressed prices eliminated or sharply reduced the expected resource rents of the RBI projects and tested their resilience. The typically debt-heavy finance imposed onerous fixed capital service charges, albeit ones which some projects found easier to meet than others. Large projects, when undertaken by wholly state-owned enterprises, experienced more implementation and operating problems than small ones. Metals projects proved more marginal than petrochemicals, with steel especially so. LNG and fertilizer projects were most viable. The dominance of large state-owned metals projects (especially steel) in the RBI strategies of Nigeria and Venezuela therefore compounded the poor macro-economic management of those countries. Such projects experienced cost overruns well in excess of 50 per cent, encountered severe technical and logistical problems, were grossly overmanned, and incurred heavy losses. Projects implemented as joint-ventures in soundly managed economies, notably those in the Middle East countries, encountered fewest implementation problems. Yet the unexpectedly low prices threatened to eliminate even their viability.

THE ACTUAL ECONOMIC IMPACT OF RBI

The added value from the RBI projects was disappointingly small and the immediate contribution of RBI to economic growth and viable economic diversification was therefore minimal. The performance of the oil-exporters' non-oil economy therefore depended on how effectively they managed their non-resource tradeables sectors (i.e. agriculture and non-RBI manufacturing). Yet the large RBI investments bred complacency towards the non-oil tradeables sectors.

Although the growth rate of the non-oil economy did accelerate through the two oil booms in the Arabian countries and Cameroon, it was little changed in the South-east Asian and South American countries and declined significantly in Nigeria. Only Cameroon escaped a post-boom slowdown in non-oil growth while the South American countries and Nigeria experienced sharply negative growth and faced the most painful adjustments after the 1986 oil slump.

The poor RBI performance reflected universally weak industrial policies and overly slow expansion (and even overrapid contraction) of the non-oil tradeables sectors. The Gulf countries started with the least developed non-oil sectors, but whereas Bahrain progressed significantly, Saudi Arabia placed more reliance on RBI and remained heavily oil-dependent in the mid-1980s. The South American countries slowed the decline in their initially shrunken agricultural sectors—but this required protection and subsidies (as, more ominously, did their manufacturing). Indonesia also failed to promote competitive industry but did retain a healthy agricultural cushion against the post-boom downturn. The two late-starters, Malaysia and Cameroon, were well-cushioned by dynamic rural sectors; but became uncomfortably dependent on oil revenues. Nigeria's severe 'Dutch disease' effects (i.e. the undermining of the competitiveness of the non-oil tradeables sector) left it most vulnerable.

A third objective of RBI, along with accelerated economic growth and faster structural change, was geographical decentralization. The location of hydrocarbon resources *vis-à-vis* core and peripheral regions in the larger countries gave RBI the potential to intensify spatial concentration in Nigeria and Cameroon and to offset it in Indonesia, Malaysia, Saudi Arabia, and Venezuela. However, RBI had little immediate spatial impact since both the direct (value added) and indirect (linkage) effects were disappointingly small, the construction phase apart, so that its significance is more long-term. Implementation problems aside, the RBI regional stimulus was less effective the less geographically clustered the plants, the further (and smaller) the market, and the later the start.

Nigeria dispersed its RBI plants and thereby markedly reduced investment efficiency, as would Cameroon's similar (but more structured) plans have done had they not been aborted. Indonesia and Malaysia vainly clustered small numbers of RBI plants at remote locations to reinforce existing regional policies (transmigration and industrial estates respectively), though each had more success with such clusters close to their major market. The large remote industrial complexes of Saudi Arabia and Venezuela achieved greater spatial changes, especially the longer-established Venezuelan one, but at very high cost. Although also costly, Nigeria's administrative growth pole (the new federal capital, Abuja) promises to be far less effective.

POLICY IMPLICATIONS

The disappointing performance of RBI may reflect problems peculiar to the heightened uncertainty of the post-1960s international economy. However, there is evidence of more fundamental factors at work that are rooted in the rigidity imposed by RBI's high fixed investment and suggest a simple model of RBI. In developing countries, high infrastructure costs (for communication systems, utilities, and social services) compound the cost penalty imposed by high plant construction costs and distance from markets. Recource to cheap finance places an initial debt burden on new RBI projects which diminishes their flexibility *vis-à-vis* established amortized producers.

This imparts a characteristic trajectory through time for the direct and indirect RBI economic stimulus. After an initial construction-related boost, the economic stimulus from RBI is muted. The debt-burdened plants' uncertain viability depresses direct returns and discourages investment in linked activities which are therefore strongly lagged. Linkage proliferation may be triggered a decade after start-up when full debt retirement enhances RBI viability and permits capture of the dynamic economies of scale arising from increasingly clustered activities (including cheaper RBI capacity expansion)—provided commercial criteria prevail and expanding non-resource based economic activities help to reduce the economic stimulus leaking abroad on imported goods and services.

The heightened uncertainty of the post-1960s global economy intensified RBI entry problems. The sharp acceleration in inflation simultaneously increased rents to established amortized producers while encouraging new producers to make rash investments. RBI markets were depressed by unexpected falls in the amount of energy and materials used to generate global GDP. Worse, the proliferation of new RBI producers slowed adjustment to glutted markets and thereby prolonged low returns.

A prudent RBI policy is one which is large enough to capture the advantages of diversified RBI projects without RBI dominating development policy. Start-up and operational risks are reduced by MNRC joint-ventures and careful project sequencing, while marketing risks are lowered by MNRC participation and (where domestic markets permit) full operational integration from resource to final demand. Failing state-owned RBI projects can be strengthened by financial restructuring and securing an MNRC partner with sufficient equity to ensure commercial criteria prevail over socio-political ones.

RBI demonstrates the weakness of public sector management in most oil-exporting countries. The severe oil price downswing tested even the most cautious regimes while few could provide the protection from political corrosion that large commercial state enterprises need. The proliferation of so many new enterprises, including large numbers of low autonomy state ventures, increased the rigidity arising from RBI's large capital-intensive investment. Consequently, low RBI returns and their associated distortions may persist for some time. The oil-exporting countries' experience with RBI, both in the upswing and downswing stages, clearly shows the compounding nature of many of the key variables associated with the post-1960s' global economic instability.

More general lessons from the experience with RBI suggest large capital transfers may actually retard economic growth and healthy economic diversification. Certainly, the oil shocks triggered a massive misallocation of resources of which RBI was a significant part. Although the model of RBI suggests that RBI's long-term contribution may yet be substantial where the oil-exporting countries combine prudent macro-economic policies with efficient firms, the cost in terms of opportunities foregone is already very large. However, as RBI prices rebound in the late 1980s it is far from clear that the lessons from the oil-exporting countries' experience with RBI have been learned. If the lessons have not been learned, then the costs of RBI will be very high indeed.

REFERENCES

ACHARYA, S. N. (1981), 'Perspectives and problems of development in Sub-Saharan Africa', *World Development*, 9: 109–47.

ADELMAN, I. (1984), 'Beyond export-led growth', *World Development*, 12: 937–49.

ADELMAN, M. A. (1986a), Scarcity and world oil prices', *Review of Economics and Statistics*, 68: 387–97.

—— (1986b), 'The competitive floor to world oil prices', *The Energy Journal*, 7: 9–35.

ALAM, M. S. (1982), 'The basic macro-economics of the oil economies', *Journal of Development Studies*, 18: 205–16.

ALDEN, J. D. and AWANG, A. H. (1985), 'Regional development planning in Malaysia', *Regional Studies*, 19: 495–508.

ALONSO, W. (1971), 'The Economics of Urban Size', *Papers And Proceedings Of The Regional Science Association*, 26: 67–83.

Aluminum Association (1983), *Aluminum Statistical Review 1982*, Washington, DC.

ALUSUISSE (1980), *Feasibility Study on Bauxite Deposits of Los Pijiquaos*, Zurich, Mimeo.

AMSDEN, A. (1987), 'Creating competitive advantage: the South Korean steel industry', Working Paper, Harvard Business School, Boston, Mass.

AMUZEGAR, J. (1983), 'Oil exporters' economic development in an inter-dependent world', *IMF Occasional Paper 18*, International Monetary Fund, Washington, DC.

ANDERSON, P. J. and DANIELS, E. J. (1981), 'An overview of LNG operations', Paper presented on behalf of the US Institute of Gas Technology to the National Gas Symposium, Lagos, 8 Sept. Anthony Bird Associates (1983), 'Aluminium Annual Review', Mimeo, Kingston.

—— (1985), *Aluminium Production Costs*, Richmond, Mimeo.

Aramco (1982) *Indexes of Construction Activity*, Aramco Local Industrial Development Department, Altraiki Press, Dammam.

—— (1984), *Trends of the Construction Industry of the Kingdom of Saudi Arabia*, Aramco Local Industrial Development Department, Altaiki Press, Dammam.

AUTY, R. M. (1975), 'Small factories and the measurement of internal economies of scale', *Professional Geographer*, 27: 315–22.

—— (1980), 'Transforming mineral enclaves: Caribbean bauxite in the nineteen-seventies', *Tijdschrift voor economische en sociale geografie*, 71: 169–79.

—— (1981), 'Multinational corporate strategy, spatial diversification and nationalisation: A Guyanese comparison', *Geoforum*, 12: 349–57.

—— (1983a), 'MNCs and regional revenue retention in a vertically-integrated industry: bauxite/aluminium in the Caribbean', *Regional Studies*, 17: 3–17.

—— (1983b) 'MNC strategy and the regional growth potential of mining: Caribbean bauxite's forward linkage', in Ooi, J. B. (1983) *Natural Resources in Tropical Countries*, Singapore University Press, Singapore, 73–116.

—— (1983c), 'Multinational resource corporations, the product life-cycle and product strategy: the oil majors' response to heightened risk', *Geoforum*, 14: 1–13.

—— (1983d), 'Gas-based exports as an LDC energy strategy: Trinidad, Working Paper, Princeton, NJ.

—— (1984a), 'Resource-based diversification', in Barr, B. and Waters, N. (eds.), *Strategies For Regional Diversification and Change*, BC Geographical Series, Tantalus Press, Vancouver, 46–61.

—— (1984b), 'The energy-intensive industrial complex in developing countries: Trinidad's Point Lisas', *EIU Quarterly Review of Energy for Latin America and the Caribbean*, 1: 4–7.

—— (1984c), 'The product life-cycle and the global location of the petrochemical industry after the second oil shock', *Economic Geography*, 60: 325–38.

—— (1985a), 'Export base theory, staple flexibility and tropical regional growth', *Singapore Journal of Tropical Geography*, 6: 13–22.

—— (1985b), 'Materials intensity of GDP: research issues in the measurement and explanation of change', *Resources Policy*, 11: 275–83.

—— (1986a), 'Entry problems and investment returns in RBI: cross-country comparison', Mimeo, Development Research Department, World Bank, Washington, DC.

—— (1986b), 'Resource-based industrialisation and country size: Venezuela and Trinidad and Tobago', *Geoforum*, 17: 325–38.

—— (1986c), 'Multinational resource corporations, nationalisation and diminished viability: Caribbean plantations, mines and oilfields during the nineteen-seventies', in Drakakis-Smith, D. *et al.* (eds.) *Multinational Corporations and The Third World*, Croom Helm, London, 160–87.

—— (1987a), 'Producer homogeneity, heightened uncertainty and mineral market rigidity', *Resources Policy*, 13: 189–206.

—— (1987b), 'Backward versus forward integration in resource-based industrialisation: Indonesia and Malaysia', *Tijdschrift voor Economische en sociale geografie*, 78: 82–93.

—— (1987c), 'Large capital transfers to developing countries: the lessons of Indonesian oil windfall deployment', *Singapore Journal of Tropical Geography*, 8: 1–14.

—— (1988a), 'Internal constraints on the prudent deployment of oil windfalls for resource-based industrialisation: Nigeria and Cameroon', *Geoforum* 19: 147–60.

—— (1988b), 'Oil exporters' disappointing diversification into RBI', *Energy Policy*, 16: 230–42.

—— (1988c), 'The muted and lagged economic stimulus from RBI in developing countries: Saudi Arabia and Bahrain', *Economic Geography*, 64: 209–25.

—— and GELB, A. H. (1986), Oil windfalls in a small parliamentary democracy: their impact on Trinidad and Tobago', *World Development*, 14: 1161–75.

AYUB, M. A. and HEGSTAD, S. O. (1986), *Public Industrial Enterprises: Determinants of Performance*, Industry and Finance Series v. 17, World Bank, Washington, DC.

BAIN, J. S. (1954), 'Economies of scale, concentration and the condition of entry in twenty manufacturing industries', *American Economic Review*, 44: 15–39.

BALASSA, B. (1977), 'A "stages" approach to comparative advantage', *World Bank Staff Working Paper*, 256, World Bank, Washington, DC.

—— (1982), 'Structural adjustment policies in developing countries', *World Development*, 10: 23–38.

BALDWIN, R. E. (1956), 'Patterns of development in newly settled regions', *Manchester School of Social and Economic Studies*, 24: 161–79.

Ballantine (1985), 'Saudi Arabia', *World of Information*, London, 183–200.

Banque Indosuez (1985), 'Petrochemicals in Saudi Arabia: an attempt at dispassionate analysis', *Banque Indosuez Economic Review*, 3, (Jan.).

Barclays Bank (1987), 'Developing countries', *Barclays Review*, May, 26–34.

BARKER, P. (1982), 'Saudi Arabia: the development dilemma', *The Economist Intelligence Unit Special Report* 116, London.

BARNETT, D. F. and SCHORSCH, L. (1983), *Steel: Upheaval in a Basic Industry*, Ballinger, Cambridge, Mass.

—— and CRANDALL, R. W. (1986), *Up From The Ashes*, Brookings Institution, Washington, DC.

—— and MEUNIER, M. (1985), *Steel Strategies For the 1980s and 1990s*, World Bank, Washington, DC.

BECKFORD, G. L. (1972), *Persistent Poverty*, Oxford University Press, Oxford.

BEENSTOCK, M. (1983), *The World Economy in Transition*, Allen and Unwin, London.

BENJAMIN, N. C. and DEVARAJAN, S. (1984), 'Oil revenues and protectionism in Cameroon', Working Paper, Harvard Institute For International Development, Cambridge, Mass.

——, —— (1986) 'Oil revenues in the Cameroon economy', in Zartmann, I. W. and Schatzberg, M. G. (eds.) *The Political Economy of Cameroon*, Praeger, New York, 161–88.

BERRY, B. J. L. (1967), *Geography of Market Centers and Retail Distribution*, Prentice-Hall, Engelwood Cliffs, NJ.

BEYER, H. (1985), 'Petrochemical industry in Malaysia', Paper presented to Tenega 85 Seminar on Energy and Industrialization, Kuala Lumpur.

BIENEN, H. (1983), 'Oil revenue and policy choice in Nigeria', *World Bank Staff Working Paper*, 592, Washington, DC.

BINA, C. (1985), *Economics of the Oil Crisis*, Merlin Press, London.

BLANCO, A. and GANZ, A. (1969), 'Economic diagnosis and plans', in Rodwin,

L. (1969), *Planning Urban Growth and Regional Development: The Experience of the Guayana Program in Venezuela*, MIT, Cambridge, Mass., 60–90.

BLUESTEIN, H. (1977), *Area Handbook of Venezuela*, American University Foreign Area Studies, Washington, DC.

BOURGUINON, F. (1983), 'A decade of oil bonus in Venezuela: 1973–82', Draft for Development Research Department, World Bank.

BOVENTER, E. G. VON, (1970), 'Optimal spatial structure and regional development', *Kyklos*, 23: 903–24.

BREWSTER, H. (1972), 'The growth of employment under export-based underdevelopment', *Social and Economic Studies*, 21: 153–69.

BROADMAN, H. G. (1981), 'Intraindustry structure, integration strategies and petroleum industry performance', unpublished Ph.D., University of Michigan, Mich.

BRODSKY, D. A. and SAMPSON, C. P. (1980), 'Retained value and export performance of developing countries', *Journal of Development Economics*, 17: 32–47.

BROWN, M. *et al.* (1983), 'Worldwide investment analysis: the case of aluminium', *World Bank Staff Working Paper 603*, World Bank, Washington, DC.

BROWNING, J. (1984), 'Oil and the Gulf: a survey', *The Economist*, 28 Apr. centre supplement.

BRUNO, M. (1984), 'Raw materials, profits and the productivity slowdown', *Quarterly Journal of Economics*, 99: 1–29.

BUNGE, F. M. (1983), *Indonesia: A Country Study*, American University, Washington, DC.

—— (1984), *Malaysia: A Country Study*, American University, Washington, DC.

CASSON, M. (1986), *Multinationals and World Trade: Vertical Integration and the Division of Labour in World Industries*, Allen and Unwin, London.

CARTER, C. P. (1982), 'How much cracking do we need?' *Chase Energy*, Chase Manhattan, New York, NY.

CHANDLER, A. D. (1962), *Strategy and Structure*, MIT Press, Cambridge, Mass.

CHAPMAN, K. (1982), 'Petrochemicals and economic development: the implications of the Puerto Rican experience', *Professional Geographer*, 34: 405–16.

CHENERY, H. B. and SYRQUIN, M. (1975), *Patterns of Development 1950–70*, Oxford University Press, Oxford.

——, —— (1986), 'Patterns of development 1950–83', Mimeo, Harvard Institute for International Development, Cambridge, Mass.

——, ROBINSON, S. and SYRQUIN, M. (1986), *Industrialization and Growth*, Oxford University Press, New York.

CHINITZ, B. (1961), 'Contrasts in agglomeration: New York and Pittsburg', *American Economic Review: Papers and Proceedings*, 279–89.

CLINE, W. R. (1982), 'Can the East Asian model of development be generalised?', *World Development*, 10: 81–90.

CONWAY, P. J. and GELB, A. H. (1988), 'Oil rents in a controlled economy: a case study of Algeria', *Journal of Development Economics*, 28: 63–82.

CORDEN, W. M. (1982), Booming sector and Dutch disease economics: a survey, Working Paper 78, Australian National University, Canberra.

—— and NEARY, J. P. (1982), 'Booming sector and de-industrialisation in a small open economy', *Economic Journal*, 92: 826–44.

CORPORACIÓN VENEZOLANA DE GUAYANA (1984), *Informe 1980–83*, CVG, Ciudad Guayana.

—— (1985), *Principales proyectos del grupo de empresas de la CVG*, CVG, Caracas.

—— (1986), *Estadísticas de la región Guayana 1985*, Gerencia de Investigación y Planificación Regional, Ciudad Guayana.

CROWSON, P. C. F. (1985), 'The changing scene in the world metal markets', Paper presented to *M. K. Wong and Associates Clients' Seminar*, Feb. Vancouver.

Daily Sketch (1984), 'Delta Steel', *Daily Sketch*, 18 July.

Debell and Richardson, Inc. (1974), *Impact of Energy Costs, Environmentalism and Technological Change: Aluminium*, Mimeo, Enfield.

DEVARAJAN, S., JAKOBEIT, C., and DE MELO, J. (1986), 'Growth and adjustment in an African monetary union: the CFA Franc Zone', Mimeo, World Bank, Washington, DC.

DINAPOLI, R. N. (1984), 'Economics of LNG Projects', *Oil and Gas Journal*, 20 Feb., 47–51.

DUNCAN, E. (1986), 'Growing pains: a survey of the Gulf Cooperation Council', *The Economist*, 8 Feb. Centre Supplement.

DUNNING, J. H. (1980), 'Toward an eclectic theory of international production: some empirical tests', *Journal of International Business Studies*, 11: 9–31.

Economist, The (1979), 'Indonesia after Pertamina', *The Economist*, 11 Oct., 80–1.

—— (1982), 'Slaking the Saudis thirst', *The Economist*, 6 Feb., 70–1.

—— (1984a) 'Spoiling the works', *The Economist*, 3 Nov., 68.

—— (1984b), 'Indonesian transmigration', *The Economist*, 4 Aug., 63–4.

—— (1986), 'Oil: Arabian daze', *The Economist*, 8 Nov., 78–9.

Economist Intelligence Unit (1986), *Venezuela: Country Survey*, London.

—— (1987), *Saudi Arabia: Country Survey*, Number 1.

EMMERSON, C. (1980), 'Taxing natural resource projects', *Natural Resources Forum*, 4: 127–45.

EMMERSON, D. K. (1983), 'Understanding the new order: bureaucratic pluralism in Indonesia', *Asian Survey*, 23: 1220–41.

ENDERS, T. O. and MATTIONE, R. P. (1984), *Latin America: The Crisis of Debt and Growth*, Brookings Institution, Washington, DC.

ESCOBAR, J. K. (1982), 'Comparing state enterprises across international boundaries: The Corporación Venezolana de Guayana and the Companhia Vale do Rio Doce', in Jones, L. P. (ed.), *Public Enterprise in Less Developed Countries*, Cambridge University Press, Cambridge, 103–27.

Far Eastern Economic Review (1982a), 'The aluminium equation', *Far Eastern Economic Review*, 15 Feb., 76–85.

—— (1982b), 'LNG: the chill digs in', *Far Eastern Economic Review*, 15 Oct., 69–84.

—— (1983a), 'Steel: a costly status symbol', *Far Eastern Economic Review*, 23 June 60–72.

—— (1983b), 'Indonesia: shaking the industrial cocktail', *Far Eastern Economic Review*, 18 Aug., 39–58.

—— (1983c), 'Sabah: A fragile prosperity', 14 Apr., 54–70.

—— (1985a), 'Energy: Open to change', *Far Eastern Economic Review*, 28 Mar. 77–84.

—— (1985b), 'Focus Indonesia 1985', *Far Eastern Economic Review*, 7 Feb., 43–62.

—— (1986a), 'Slippery oil slope', *Far Eastern Economic Review*, 21 Aug., 52–4.

—— (1986b), 'The boom is over: Gulf/Mid East', *Far Eastern Economic Review*, 13 Nov., 71–102.

FESHARAKI, F. and ISAAK, D. T. (1985), 'Impact of OPEC oil refineries on the world refining industry', Paper presented to the National Petroleum Refiners Association Meeting, March, San Antonio, Texas.

Financial Times (1985a), 'Saudis tighten belts as oil revenues remain low', *Financial Times*, 29 Mar.

—— (1985b), 'Saudi Arabia: A Survey', *Financial Times*, 22 Apr.

—— (1985c), 'Trinidad and Tobago: a survey', *Financial Times*, 8 July.

—— (1986a), 'Saudi Arabia: a survey', *Financial Times*, 21 Apr.

—— (1986b), 'Cameroon state to sell 62 holdings', *Financial Times*, 3 June.

—— (1986c), 'SABIC lifts output and profits', *Financial Times*, 16 Sept.

—— (1986d), 'Survey of Indonesia', *Financial Times*, 10 Mar.

—— (1987), 'Survey of Nigeria', 2 Mar.

FISHLOW, A. (1984), 'Summary comments on Adelman, Balassa and Streeten', *World Development*, 12: 979–82.

FLATTERS, F. and JENKINS, G. (1986), 'Trade policy in Indonesia', Mimeo, Harvard Institute For International Development, Cambridge, Mass.

FONTIVEROS, D. and PALMA, P. A. (1987), 'External debt and the recessive impact of devaluation: the Venezuelan case', Paper presented to the Edward S. Mason Program on Public Policy and Management, John F. Kennedy School, Cambridge, Mass., March.

FRANCIS, A. A. (1981), *Taxing the Transnationals in the Struggle for Bauxite*, Institute of Social Studies Research Paper Series No. 9, The Hague.

FRANZ, J. et al. (1985), 'Iron ore: global industry prospects 1985–95, *World Bank Technical Paper*, World Bank, Washington, DC.

FRIEDMANN, J. (1966), *Regional Development Policy: A Case Study of Venezuela*, MIT Press, Cambridge, Mass.

FURTADO, C. (1976), *Economic Development of Latin America*, Cambridge University Press, Cambridge.

GALE, B. (1981), 'Petronas; Malaysia's national oil corporation', *Asian Survey*, 21: 1129–44.

GELB, A. H. (1986a), 'Adjustment to windfall gains: a comparative analysis of oil exporting countries', in Neary, J. P. and Van Wijnbergen, S. (eds.), *Natural Resources and the Macroeconomy*, Centre For Economic Policy Research, MIT Press, Cambridge, Mass. 54–93.

—— (1986b), 'From boom to bust—oil exporting countries over the cycle 1970–84', *Institute of Development Studies Bulletin*, 17, no. 4: 22–9.

—— (1988), *Windfall Gains: Blessing Or Curse?*, Oxford University Press, New York.

—— KNIGHT, J. B. and SABOT, R. H. (1986), 'Lewis through the looking-glass: public sector employment, rent-seeking and economic growth', Mimeo, Employment and Enterprise Policy Analysis Project, Harvard Institute For International Development, Cambridge, Mass.

GILLIS, M. (1984), 'Episodes in Indonesian economic growth', in Harberger, A. C. (ed.), *World Economic Growth*, San Francisco, Calif. 231–64.

GILMOUR, J. M. (1964), *The Spatial Evolution of Manufacturing Industry*, University of Toronto Press, Toronto.

GIRVAN, N. (1971), *Foreign Capital and Economic Underdevelopment in Jamaica*, Allen and Unwin, London.

GLASSBURNER, B. (1983), 'Oil, public policy and economic performance: Indonesia in the 1970s', Draft for Development Research Department, World Bank.

GLENTON, D. (1985), 'Optimising the economics and finance of petrochemical projects', Paper presented to the *Pertamina Seminar on Project Economics: Petrochemical and Related Hydrocarbon Projects*, Jakarta, 28 Feb.–1 Mar.

GOULD, P. (1963), 'Transport expansion in underdeveloped countries: a comparative analysis', *Geographical Review*, 53: 503–29.

—— (1970), 'Tanzania 1920–63: the spatial impact of the modernisation process', *World Politics*, 22: 149–70.

GRAHAM, E. and FLOERING, I. (1984), *The Modern Plantation in the Third World*, Croom Helm, London.

GRINDLE, M. (1986), 'The question of political feasibility: approaches to the study of policy space', *Employment and Enterprise Policy Analysis Discussion Papers*, no. 3, USAID, Washington, DC.

HABLUTZEL, R. (1981), *Development Prospects of the Capital-Surplus Oil Exporting Countries*, World Bank Staff Working Paper 483, Washington, DC.

HAGGARD, S. (1986), 'Explaining development strategies', Mimeo, Department of Sociology, Harvard University, Cambridge, Mass.

HALLWOOD, P. and SINCLAIR, S. (1980), *Oil, Debt and Development: OPEC in the Third World*, Wiley, London.

HAMER, A. M., STEER, A. D. and WILLIAMS, D. G. (1986), 'Indonesia: the challenge of urbanization', *World Bank Staff Working Paper 787*, World Bank, Washington, DC.

HARMAN, N. (1986), 'After the ball: a survey of Nigeria', *The Economist*, 3 May, Centre Supplement.

HARVEY, J. (1982), 'Filling the void: a survey of Saudi Arabia', *The Economist*, 13 Feb., Centre Supplement.

HASAN, P. (1984), 'Adjustment to external shocks', *Finance and Development*, 21 no. 4: 14–17.

HASHIMOTO, H. (1983), 'Bauxite processing in developing countries', in World Bank (1983), *Case Studies in the Industrial Processing of Primary Products*, World Bank, Washington, DC, 1–102.

HICOM (1985), *Annual Report and Accounts 1984*, Kuala Lumpur.

HIRSCHMAN, A. O. (1958), *The Strategy of Economic Development*, Yale University Press, New Haven, Conn.

—— (1977), 'A generalised linkage approach to economic development with special reference to staples', in Nash, M. (1977), *Essays in Economic Development and Cultural Change in Honor of Bert F. Hoselitz*, University of Chicago Press, Chicago, Ill. 67–88.

HOUGH, G. V. (1984), 'LNG market: sales increase as price weakens', *Petroleum Economist*, Dec. 439–41.

Institute for International Finance (1986), *Cameroon*, Report CAM (86) 1R.

International Iron and Steel Institute (1984), *Steel Statistical Yearbook*, IISI, Brussels.

International Monetary Fund (1984), *World Economic Survey*, Washington, DC.

JOHANY, A. D., BERNE, M. and MIXON, J. W. (1986), *The Saudi Arabian Economy*, Croom Helm, London.

JOHNSTON, B. F. and MELLOR, J. W. (1961), 'The role of agriculture in economic growth', *American Economic Review*, 51: 566–93.

JOHNSON, E. A. J. (1970), *The Organisation of Space in the Developing Countries*, Harvard University Press, Cambridge, Mass.

JONES, L. P. (1982), *Public Enterprise in Less Developed Countries*, Cambridge University Press, Cambridge.

KANOVSKY, E. (1986), 'Saudi Arabia's dismal economic future: regional and global implications', *Occasional Paper*, Dayan Centre For Middle Eastern and African Studies, Tel Aviv University, Tel Aviv.

KATZMAN, M. J. (1977), *Cities and Frontiers in Brazil*, Harvard University Press, Cambridge, Mass.

KESSEL, N. (1977), 'Financial aspects of the mining industry in Zambia', in Newlyn, W. T. (1977), *The Financing of Economic Development*, Clarendon Press, Oxford.

KIRK-GREENE, A. and RIMMER, D. (1981), *Nigeria Since 1970*, Hodder and Stoughton, London.

KRUGMAN, P. (1979), 'A model of innovation diffusion and technology transfer and the world distribution of income', *Journal of Political Economy*, 87: 253–66.

—— (1988), 'The narrow moving band, the Dutch disease, and the competitive consequences of Mrs Thatcher', *Journal of Development Economics*, 27: 41–55.

KUBURSI, A. (1984), *The Economies of the Arabian Gulf: A Statistical Source Book*, Croom Helm, London.

LAL, D. (1983), *The Poverty of 'Development Economics'*, Hobart Paperback 16, Institute of Economic Affairs, London.

LAWRENCE, R. Z. (1984), *Can America Compete?* Brookings Institution, Washington, DC.

LE GUERN, L. (1986), *Groupe Petrochimie-Chimie*, Mimeo, UNIDO, Yaounde.

LEVY, B. (1982) 'World oil marketing in transition', *International Organization*, 36: 113–33.

LEWIS, S. R. (1982), 'Development problems of the mineral-rich countries', Williams College Centre for Development Economics, Research Memo 74, Williamstown, Mass.

LEWIS, W. A. (1978), *Growth and Fluctuations 1870–1913*, Allen and Unwin, London.

LIPTON, M. (1977), *Why Poor People Stay Poor*, Temple Press, London.

MABOGUNJE, A. (1972), 'Spatial structure and process in tropical West Africa', *Economic Geography*, 48: 229–55.

MALLON, R. D. (1982), 'Public enterprise versus other methods of state intervention as instruments of redistribution policy: the Malaysian experience', in Jones, L. P. (1982), *Public Enterprise in Less-Developed Countries*, Cambridge University Press, Cambridge, 313–26.

MANDEVILLE, T. D. and JENSEN, R. G. (1979), *The Economic Impacts of Industrial Developments in the Gladstone District of Central Queensland*, Department of Economics, University of Queensland, St Lucia.

——, —— (1980), *The Impact of the Weipa Bauxite Mine on the Queensland Economy*, Comalco, Queensland.

MARTZ, J. D. (1984), 'Venezuela: Democratic Politics of Petroleum', in Wesson, R. (1984), *Politics, Policies and Economic Development in Latin America*, Hoover Institution Press, Stanford, Calif. 161–87.

MEADOWS, D. et al. (1972), *Limits to Growth*, Potomac, Washington, DC.

MELLOR, J. (1976), *The New Economics of Growth*, Cornell, Ithaca, NY.

MILLER, J. (1976), 'The direct reduction of iron ore, *Scientific American*, 238, no. 1: 68–80.

MENDOZA, C. A. (1987), *Sidor: Past, Present and Future*, Mimeo, CVG, Matanzas.

MIKESELL, R. F. (1979), *New Patterns of World Mineral Development*, British North America Committee, London.

—— (1986), 'New taxation formulas in mine investments: sharing the risks and the rents', Paper Presented to the Conference of the Institute for Foreign and International Trade Law, Frankfurt.

Ministry of Finance (1986), *Economic report 1986–87*, National Printing Department, Kuala Lumpur.

Ministry of Planning (1986), *Achievements of the Development Plans 1970–1985: Facts and Figures*, Ministry of Planning Press, Riyadh.

MITRA, P. (1983), 'World Bank research on adjustment to external shocks', *World Bank Research Newsletter*, 3: 3–14.

Mobil Chemical Company (1985), Presentation to the Indonesian Seminar, *Project Economics and Financing of Petrochemicals and Related Hydrocarbon Projects*, Mimeo, Jakarta.

MOSCOVITCH, E. (1969), 'Evaluating the allocation of resources to urban development', in: Rodwin, L. (ed.) *Planning Urban Growth and Regional Development: The Experience of the Guayana Program of Venezuela*, MIT Press, Cambridge, Mass. 378–99.

MURPHY, K. J. (1983), *Macroproject Development in the Third World: An Analysis of Transnational Partnerships*, Westview Press, Boulder, Colo.

MYINT, H. (1964), *The Economics of the Developing Countries*, Hutchinson, London.

NANKANI, G. (1979), 'Development problems of mineral exporting countries', *World Bank Staff Working Paper*, no. 354, Washington, DC.

NELLIS, J. (1986), 'Public enterprises in sub-Saharan Africa', Mimeo, Public Sector Management Unit, World Bank, Washington, DC.

NELSON, H. D. (1982), *Nigeria: A Country Study*, American University Foreign Studies, US Government Printer, Washington, DC.

NYROP, R. F. (1977a), *Area Handbook For Saudi Arabia*, American University, US Government Printing Office, Washington, DC.

—— (1977b), *Area Handbook For Persian Gulf States*, American University, US Government printer, Washington, DC.

ODELL, P. (1978), 'Geography and economy development with special reference to Latin America', *Geography*, 59: 208–22.

Office of Technology Assessment (1980), *Alternative Energy Futures: Future of Liquified Natural Gas Imports*, Washington, DC.

ONOH, J. K. (1984), *The Nigerian Oil Economy: From Prosperity to Glut*, Croom Helm, London.

ONYEMELUKE, J. O. C. (1984), *Industrialisation in West Africa*, Croom Helm, London.

OWEN, W. (1968), *Distance and Development*, Brookings Institution, Washington, DC.

PEARSON, S. R. and COWNIE, J. (1974), *Commodity Exports and African Economic Development*, Lexington Books, Lexington, Mass. 1–10.

PERKINS, D. and SYRQUIN, M. (1987), 'The development of large countries: the influence of size', Mimeo, Harvard Institute For International Development, Cambridge, Mass.

PDVSA (1985), *Informe Annual 1984*, Caracas.

PERROUX, F. (1950), 'Economic space: theory and application, *Quarterly Journal of Economics*, 64: 89–104.

Petroleum Economist (1983), 'Less downstream profit for the Mid East, *Petroleum Economist*, Nov. 410–12.

—— (1985), 'Viewpoint: Petronas Managing Director', *Petroleum Economist*, Jan. 23–4.

—— (1986), 'Internal problems impede progress', *Petroleum Economist*, May, 177–9.

Petromin (1984), *Annual Report and Accounts*, General Petroleum and Mineral Organization, Riyadh.

Petronas (1984), *Petronas: A Decade of Growth*, Kuala Lumpur.

PINTO, B. (1987), 'Nigeria during and after the oil boom: a policy comparison with Indonesia', *World Bank Economic Review*, 1: 419–45.

PLATTNER, S. (1975), 'Rural market networks', *Scientific American*, 235, no. 1: 154–63.

PRAIN, R. (1975), *Copper: The Anatomy of an Industry*, Mining Journal Books, London.

QUINTERO, E. *et al.* (1985), 'In search of an economic strategy', Mimeo, Dividendo Voluntario para la Communidad, Caracas.

RADETZKI, M. (1977), 'Where should developing countries' minerals be processed?', *World Development*, 5: 325–34.

—— (1985), *State Mineral Enterprises: An Investigation into their Impact on International Mineral Markets*, Resources For The Future, Washington, DC.

—— and VAN DUYNE, C. (1983), 'The response of mining investment to a decline in economic growth: the case of copper in the 1970s', *Research Memorandum 86*, Centre for Development Economics, Williams College, Williamstown, Mass.

RAMESH, J. (1982), 'The market for petrochemical products in India', Mimeo, Fertilizer, Refining, and Other Chemical Industries Division, World Bank, Washington, DC.

RANIS, G. and STEWART, F. (1987), 'Rural linkages in the Philippines and Taiwan', Mimeo, Yale, New Haven Conn.

RAPID (1985), *Nigeria: The Effects of Population Factors on Social and Economic Development*, National Population Bureau, Lagos.

RAZAVI, H. and FESHARAKI, F. (1983), 'OPEC's push into refining: Dilemma of interactions between crude and product market', Working Paper WP–83–8, Resource Systems Institute, East–West Centre, Honolulu, Hawaii.

Resources Systems Institute (1985), *The Changing Structure of the World Refining Industry: Implications for the United States and Other Consuming*

Country Regions, Contract DE-FGO1–82PE70040, Office of Economic Analysis, US Department of Energy, Washington, DC.

RICHARDSON, H. W. (1987), 'The costs of urbanisation: a four-country comparison', *Economic Development and Cultural Change*, 35: 561–80.

—— and RICHARDSON, M. (1975), 'The relevance of growth centre strategies to Latin America', *Economic Geography*, 51: 135–49.

RISCHARD, J. F. (1982), *Emerging Energy and Chemical Applications For Methanol in Developing Countries*, World Bank, Washington, DC.

RODWIN, L. (1969), *Planning Urban Growth and Regional Development: The Experience of the Guayana Program in Venezuela*, MIT Press, Cambridge, Mass.

ROEMER, M. (1979), 'Resource-based industrialisation in the developing countries', *Journal of Development Economics*, 6: 162–202.

—— (1985), 'Dutch disease in developing countries: swallowing bitter medicine', in Lundahl, M. (1985), *The Primary Sector in Economic Development*, Croom Helm, London, 234–52.

ROPSTORFF, T. M. (1985), 'Industrial development in Indonesia: performance and prospects', *Bulletin of Indonesian Economic Studies*, 21: 32–62.

ROSENSTEIN-RODAN, P. N. (1943), 'Problems of industrialisation in eastern and southeastern Europe', repr. in Agarwala, A. N. and Singh, S. P. (1963), *The Economics of Underdevelopment*, Oxford University Press, Oxford.

RUGMAN, A. M. (1978), *International Diversification and the Multinational Enterprise*, Lexington Books, Lexington, Mass.

RUMELT, R. P. (1974), *Strategy, Structure and Economic Performance*, Harvard University Press, Cambridge, Mass.

SABIC (1985), *SABIC: Eighth Annual Report and Accounts*, Obekan, Riyadh.

SACHS, J. D. (1985), 'External debt and macroeconomic performance in Latin America and East Asia', *Brookings Papers on Economic Activity*, 2: 523–73.

SANSUI, B. (1985), 'Developing from a hydrocarbon economy base', *Pertambangen dan Energi*, 3: 41–6.

SCHATZ, S. P. (1984), 'Pirate capitalism and the inert economy of Nigeria', *Journal of Modern African Studies*, 22: 45–57.

SCOTT, B. R. (1986), 'Venezuela 1986', Mimeo, Harvard Business School, Cambridge, Mass.

SHAFER, M. (1983), 'Capturing the multinationals: advantage or disadvantage?', *International Organization*, 37: 93–119.

SHELDRICK, W. F. (1985a), 'Investment and production costs for fertilizer', FAO Commission of Fertilizers, 19–20 Feb. Rome, NY.

—— (1985b), 'The economics and outlook for fertilizer', Paper presented to the the World Food Production Conference, Beijing. Shell (1985), *Refining Under Review*, Shell Brief Number 1, London.

SHIRLEY, M. M. (1983), 'Managing state-owned enterprises', *World Bank Staff Working Paper*, 577, Washington, DC.

SIGMUND, P. E. (1980), *Multinationals in Latin America: The Politics of Nationalization*, University of Wisconsin Press, Madison, Wis.

SINGER, H. (1950), 'The distribution of gains between investing and borrowing countries', *American Economic Review: Papers and Proceedings*, May.

—— (1962), 'The mechanism of an open petroleum economy', *Social and Economic Studies*, 13: 233–42.

SINGH, S. P. (1963), *The Economics of Underdevelopment*, Oxford University Press, Oxford.

SNI (1985), *SNI: Rapport d'Activité de l'exercise 1983–4*, Edition Cape, Yaounde.

STAUFFER, T. (1975), 'The prospects of energy-intensive industry in the Persian/Arabian Gulf', Mimeo, Centre For Middle Eastern Studies, Harvard University, Cambridge, Mass.

—— (1983), 'Oil-exporting counties need nuclear power', *OPEC Review*, 7: 357–80.

—— (1985), 'Accounting for wasting assets: measurements of income and dependency in oil-rentier states', *Journal of Energy and Development*, 11: 69–93.

STEVENS, C. (1984), *The Political Economy of Nigeria*, The Economist, London.

STERMAN, J. D. (1985), 'An integrated theory of the economic long wave, *Futures*, 17: 104–31.

STOBART, C. (1984), 'The effects of government investment in the economics of the base metals industry', *Natural Resources Forum*, 8: 259–66.

STREETEN, P. (1981), 'A cool look at "outward-oriented" strategies for development, *The World Economy*, 5: 159–69.

STUCKEY, R. (1983), *Vertical Integration and Joint Ventures in the Aluminium Industry*, Harvard University Press, Cambridge, Mass.

SVEJNAR, J. and HARIGU, M. (1987), 'Public versus private ownership, export orientation and enterprise productivity in a developing economy: evidence from Tunisia', Paper presented to the North-east Universities Development Colloquium, Boston University.

TANAKA, H. (1985), 'An analysis of elements affecting project profitability related to contract market and contracting'. Paper presented to the *Pertamina Symposium*, Feb. Jakarta.

TEECE, D. J. (1982), 'Toward an economic theory of the multi-product firm', *Journal of Economic Behaviour and Organization*, 3: 39–63.

TEITEL, S. and THOUMI, F. (1986), 'From import substitution to exports: the recent experience of Argentina and Brazil', *Economic Development and Cultural Change*, 24: 455–90.

THOBURN, J. T. (1973), 'Exports and economic growth in West Malaysia', *Oxford Economic Papers*, 25: 88–111.

—— (1977), *Primary Commodity Exports and Economic Development*, Wiley, London.

TILTON, J. E. (1985), 'Atrophy in metals demand', *Earth and Mineral Science*, 54, no. 2: 13–18.

Transcentury (1982), *Aceh Planning Assessment Team: Preliminary Report*, Mimeo, Washington, DC.

TREBAT, T. J. (1983), *Brazil's State-Owned Enterprises: A Case Study of the State as Entrepreneur*, Cambridge University Press, Cambridge.

TRICHEM (1983), *Hydrocarbon Product Exports from the Middle East and North Africa*, Trichem, London.

TURNER, L. and BEDARE, J. M. (1979), *Middle East Industrialisation*, Saxon House, London.

UN (1984), *Mineral Processing in Developing Countries*, Graham and Trotman, London.

UNICO (1974), *Republic of Indonesia Survey Report on Petrochemical Industry Development*, vol. 1–6, UNICO International Corporation, Tokyo.

UNIDO (1981), *Second Worldwide Study of the Petrochemical Industry*, UNIDO, Vienna.

—— (1983), *The Public Sector and the Industrialization of Venezuela*, UNIDO IS/391, Mimeo, Regional and Country Studies Branch, Vienna.

US EMBASSY (1985), *The Petroleum Report: Indonesia*, US Embassy, Jarkarta.

USITC (1983), *Probable Impact on the US Petrochemical Industry of the Expanding Petrochemical Industries in the Conventional Energy-Rich Nations*, USITC, Washington, DC.

VANCE, J. E. (1970), *The Merchant's World: The Changing Geography of Wholesaling*, Prentice-Hall, Engelwood Cliffs, NJ.

VERNON, R. (1982), 'Uncertainty in the resource industries: the special role of state-owned enterprises', Draft Working Paper, Cambridge, Mass.

—— (1983a), 'Ten years after the oil embargo: can Humpty Dumpty be put back together again?', Cambridge Energy Associates, Cambridge, Mass.

—— (1983b), *Two Hungry Giants*, Harvard University Press, Cambridge, Mass.

VREELAND, N. (1977), *Area Handbook For Malaysia*, American University, Washington, DC.

WADSTED, O. G. (1984), 'Industrialization Programs, Factor Proportions and Employment: Brazil's Northeast and Venezuelan Guayana', *Harvard Institute For International Development Discussion Paper 177*, HIID, Cambridge, Mass.

WALL, D. (1980), Industrial processing of natural resources, *World Development*, 8: 303–16.

WELLS, D. A. (1986), 'The effects of Saudi industrialization on employment', *Journal of Energy and Development Studies*, 11: 273–84.

WHEELER, D. (1984), 'Sources of stagnation in sub-Saharan Africa', *World Development*, 12: 1–23.

WIJETILLEKE, L. and ODY, A. J. (1984), *World Refinery Industry: Need For Restructuring*, World Bank, Washington, DC.

WILLAME, J.-C. (1985), 'The practices of a liberal political economy: import and export substitution in Cameroon 1975–83', in Zartmann, I. W. and Schartzberg, M. G. (1985), *The Political Economy of Cameroon*, Praegar, New York, 111–32.

WILLIAMS, M. L. (1975), 'The extent and significance of the nationalisation of foreign-owned assets in the developing countries', *Oxford Economic Papers*, 27: 260–73.

WILSON, G. D. (1985), 'Assessment of projects in the petrochemical sphere: an operating company's view', Paper Presented to the *Pertamina Seminar on Project Economics: Petrochemical and Related Hydrocarbon Projects*, Jakarta, 28 Feb.–1 Mar.

World Bank (1974) *Nigeria: Options For Long-Term Development*, Washington, DC.

—— (1980), *Prospects For Primary Commodities*, Washington, DC.

—— (1982), *World Development Report 1982*, Washington, DC.

—— (1983a), *World Development Report 1983*, Washington, DC.

—— (1983b), *The Energy Transition in Developing Countries*, Washington, DC.

—— (1985), *Commodity Trade and Price Trends*, Washington, DC.

—— (1986a), *Korea: Managing the Industrial Transition*, Washington, DC.

—— (1986b), *World Development Report 1986*, Washington, DC.

—— (1986c), 'Sustainability of projects: review of experience in the fertilizer subsector', Report 6023, Operations Evaluation Department, Washington, DC.

YOTOPOULOS, P. A. and NUGENT, J. (1973), 'A balance-growth version of the linkage hypothesis: a test', *Quarterly Journal of Economics*, 87: 151–71.

YOUNG, K. et al. (1980), *Growth and Equity in a Multiracial State*, Oxford University Press, Kuala Lumpur.

INDEX